How do I get a *free driving lesson?*

It's easy. Just pre-pay for 12 hours of driving tuition and we'll give you an additional hour free, plus we will discount your first 12 hours by £24*.

Best of all, we're the only national driving school exclusively using fully qualified instructors. And you'll be learning in a Ford Focus with air conditioning and power steering.

Great value. A great instructor. And a great car. You get it all.

*Terms and Conditions apply.

Just AAsk.

AA driving school
0800 60 70 80
www.theAA.com

Free hour when you pre-pay for 12 hours

Complete this voucher and hand it to your instructor at the start of your first lesson.

Name _____

Pupil Number (given on calling 0800 60 70 80) _____

I apply for my one hour of free driving tuition having pre-paid for 12 hours and confirm I am not an existing pupil of AA driving school.

Signed _____

For Instructor Use Only:

Instructor Name _____ Instructor Number _____

All-in-One ext.

AA ALL-IN-ONE

DRIVING TEST
THEORY & PRACTICAL
The *OFFICIAL* Questions & Answers

AA Publishing

Produced by AA Publishing.
© Automobile Association Developments Limited 2004

Crown copyright material reproduced under licence from the Controller
of HMSO and the Driving Standards Agency.

ISBN 0 7495 4145 8

Published by AA Publishing (a trading name of Automobile Association
Developments Limited, whose registered office is Millstream,
Maidenhead Road, Windsor, SL4 5GD; registered number 1878835).
A2024

The AA's web site address is **www.theAA.com/bookshop**

The contents of this book are believed correct at the time of printing.
Nevertheless, the publishers cannot be held responsible for any errors
or omissions or for changes in the details given in this book or for the
consequences of any reliance on the information provided by the
same. This does not affect your statutory rights.

Colour separation by Keene Group, Andover
Printed by Graficas Estella

While every effort has been made to include the
widest possible range of questions available at the
time of printing, the Government may from time to
time change, add or remove questions, and the
publisher cannot be held responsible for questions
that may appear on a question paper which were
not available for inclusion in this book.

Contents

Introduction and How to Use this Book

Introduction

You want to pass the driving test and take advantage of the freedom and mobility that driving a car can give you. Do the following three things and you will achieve your goal – passing the driving test.

Acquire **knowledge** of the rules through your instructor and by studying the Highway Code. A key element is to test and reinforce your knowledge.

Take the right **attitude**. Be careful, courteous and considerate to all other road users.

Learn and understand the **skills** of driving by taking lessons from a trained and fully qualified driving instructor.

We're here to help you become a careful and safe driver and we've designed this book to help you take the first steps towards achieving your goal – preparing for your **Theory Test**.

SIX ESSENTIAL STEPS TO GETTING YOUR LICENCE

1. GET YOUR PROVISIONAL LICENCE

Use form D1, available from any Post Office, to apply for your provisional licence. The driving licence is issued in the form of a two-part document: a photo card and paper counterpart. So that you can legally begin learning to drive, at the appropriate date, you must be in possession of the correct licence documents. Take care when completing all the forms. Many licences cannot be issued for the required date because of errors or omissions on the application forms. You will have to provide proof of identity such as a current UK passport; make sure you have all the documents needed.

2. LEARN THE HIGHWAY CODE

The Highway Code is essential reading for all drivers not just those learning to drive. It sets out all the rules for good driving, as well as the rules for other road users such as pedestrians and motorcycle riders. When you have learned the rules you will be able to answer most of the questions in the Theory Test and be ready to start learning the driving skills you will need to pass your Practical Test.

3. APPLY FOR AND TAKE THE THEORY TEST

The driving test is in two parts, the Theory Test and the Practical Test.

Once you have a valid provisional licence you may take the Theory Test at any time, but you must pass it before you are allowed to apply for the Practical Test. However, it is important that you should not take your Theory Test too early in your course of practical lessons. This is because you need the experience of meeting real hazards while you are learning to drive, to help you pass the Hazard Perception element of the Theory Test.

You can book your Theory Test by post, by calling or online. MasterCard, Visa, Switch, Delta, Solo and Electron are accepted. Application forms are available from test centres, Approved Driving Instructors or by calling the booking number below. Forms need to be sent with a cheque, postal order or credit or debit card details. The Theory Test currently costs £18.

By Post DSA (Driving Standards Agency), PO Box 148, Salford, M5 3SY

By Phone 0870 010 1372

Online www.dsa.gov.uk

For more information on the Theory Test see pages 115–46.

4. START TO LEARN TO DRIVE

We recommended that you learn with an Approved Driving Instructor (ADI). Only an ADI may legally charge for providing tuition.

Choose an instructor or driving school by asking friends or relatives who they recommend. Price is important, so find out whether the school offers any discounts for blocks or courses of lessons paid in advance; if you decide to pay in advance, make sure the driving school is reputable. If lesson prices are very low, ask yourself 'why?' Check how long the lesson will last. And don't forget to ask about the car you'll be learning to drive in. Is it modern and reliable? Is it insured? Does it have dual controls?

The most efficient and cost-effective way to learn to drive is to accept that there is no short-cut approach to learning the necessary skills. Agree with your instructor on a planned course of tuition suited to your needs, take regular lessons, and don't skip weeks and expect to pick up where you left off. Ensure the full official syllabus is covered and, as your skills develop, get as much practice as possible with a relative or friend – but make sure they are legally able to supervise your practice. They must be over 21 years of age and have held a full driving licence for at least three years.

5. APPLY FOR AND TAKE THE PRACTICAL TEST

Once you have passed the Theory Test, and with your instructor's guidance based on your progress, you can plan ahead for a suitable test date for the Practical Test.

You can book your Practical Test by calling 0870 010 1372 at any time between 8am and 6pm Monday to Friday. The tests costs £39 and you can pay using a credit or debit card. The person who books the test must be the cardholder.

Make sure you have the following details to hand when booking your Practical Test.

- Theory Test pass certificate number
- driver number shown on your licence
- driving school code number (if known)
- your preferred date
- unacceptable days or periods
- if you can accept a test at short notice
- disability or any special circumstances
- your credit/debit card details

Saturday and weekday evening tests are available at some driving test centres. The fee is higher than for a driving test during normal working hours on weekdays. Evening tests are available during the summer months only.

Telephone bookings and enquiries
0870 010 1372

Facsimile
0870 010 2372

Welsh speakers
0870 010 0372

Minicom
0870 010 7372

6. APPLY FOR YOUR FULL DRIVER'S LICENCE

To obtain a full licence you need to send your Pass Certificate, your provisional licence and a cheque for £12 to the DVLA, Swansea, within two years of passing your Practical Test.

AFTER THE PRACTICAL TEST

The Driving Standards Agency and the insurance industry recognise and seek to reward those drivers who enhance their basic skills and widen their experience by taking further training in the form of a Pass Plus scheme.

This is a six-module syllabus which covers town and rural driving, night driving, driving in adverse weather conditions, and on dual carriageways and motorways. It offers you the opportunity to gain more driving experience with the help of an instructor to hand. An increasing number of insurance companies are prepared to offer discounts to new drivers who have completed the course. There is no test to take at the end of the course.

MORE INFORMATION

For more practical information on learning to drive including the Theory Test, Hazard Perception and the Practical Test visit
www.theAA.com
and
www.dsa.gov.uk.
For information on the Pass Plus scheme visit
www.passplus.org.uk

Note: Prices are correct at the time of going to press.

How to Use this Book

This book is arranged in 6 sections.

Part 1 explains what to expect and how to prepare for each part of the Test: **Theory, Hazard Perception** and **Practical**.

This section explains how to take the **Theory Test** using a touch-screen computer and gives details of the video clips used in the **Hazard Perception** part of the test. In the **Practical** section we have included information about the **Driver Record** which your instructor will complete after each lesson.

We tell you what to expect on the day you take your test, details of the documents you must have with you, and tell you what the examiner will be looking for in your general driving. We

have also included information on the new **Vehicle Safety Check** questions which now form part of the Practical Test.

Part 2 contains questions and answers for learner drivers set by the experts at the AA driving school as an aid to help you pass your Practical Test. They are designed to test your knowledge of what is required before you even sit in the driver's seat. Topics include **parallel parking, reversing** and **motorway driving.**

Part 3 is designed to hep you understand each of the 14 topics in the **Theory Test**. This section will tell you what type of questions you can expect in each section and we've included lots of helpful tips. Each topic is colour coded to its relevant section in Part 4 of this book, which

Talk to your driving instructor and learn about good driving practice on the road

contains all the official Theory Questions. Experience has taught us that learner drivers find particular questions difficult and are often confused when they see questions which are similar. Reading through the background to each topic, before looking at the questions, will help you to avoid the pitfalls and help you to group questions together as you will often find several questions are asking the same thing but in a slightly different way.

Part 4 contains all the official Theory Test questions for car drivers which appear in the question bank of the DSA. You could be tested on any of these questions when you take your touch-screen Theory Test.

The questions are arranged in topics, such as **Safety Margins** and **Rules of the Road**. Each theme has its own colour band to help you find your way around. However, as you start to work through the questions you will soon discover that similar question on the same topic may appear in different sections. Don't be put off by this, but read each question and the choice of answers very carefully. Similar questions may be asked in a slightly different way to test your knowledge.

Most of the Theory Test questions can be answered if you learn *The Highway Code*. However, you will only find the answers to some questions by talking to your driving instructor and learning about good driving practice on the road.

You'll find all the correct answers to the Theory Test questions in Part 6 at the back of the book, that way, you can easily test yourself to see what you are getting right and what you need to work on.

Part 5 is a short **glossary**, which explains some of the more difficult words and terms used in the theory questions and *The Highway Code*. It's in alphabetical order and you can use this to check if you're not sure what a **chicane** is, for example, or what **brake fade** means.

Part 6 has all the answers to the 893 official Theory Test questions.

Part 1

The Tests: What to Expect

You now have to pass two driving tests before you can apply for a full driving licence – the Theory Test, including Hazard Perception, and the Practical Test. The Theory Test was introduced in 1996 to check that drivers know more than just how to operate a car, and the Hazard Perception element was introduced in 2001 to test learner drivers on their hazard awareness skills.

You are strongly recommended to prepare for the Theory Test and Hazard Perception at the same time as you develop your skills behind the wheel for the Practical Test. Obviously, there are many similarities between the two tests and you need the experience of meeting real hazards in order to pass the Hazard Perception element of the Theory Test.

It is all about making you a safer driver on today's busy roads. By preparing for both tests at the same time, you will reinforce your knowledge and understanding of all aspects of driving and you will improve your chances of passing both tests first time.

The Practical Test was extended in September 2003 to include Safety Vehicle Check questions that test the driver's ability to carry out basic procedures to ensure that the vehicle is safe to drive. Checks include the tyre tread and oil level.

WHAT TO EXPECT IN THE THEORY TEST

You will have 40 minutes to complete the questions in the test, using a touch-screen to select your answers. The test is a set of 35 questions drawn from a bank of almost a 1,000, all of which have multiple-choice answers. In order to pass the test you must answer a minimum of 30 questions correctly within the given time. The Government may change the pass mark from time to time. Your driving school or the DSA will be able to tell you if there has been a change. The questions appear on the screen one at a time and you can return to any of the questions within the 40 minutes to re-check or alter your answers. The system will prompt you to return to any questions you have not answered fully.

Preparing for the Theory Test

Read and get to know *The Highway Code*. you'll find that many of the theory questions relate directly to it. Look at the list of topics on page 115, then read through the topic summary. Now turn to the section containing the questions. Read through the questions and tick your choice of answer(s). Now check your answer(s) against the answer section at the back of the book. If you don't understand the answer(s), look up the subject in your copy *The Highway Code* or take a note of the question and discuss it with your driving instructor.

Questions marked with an **NI** symbol are those **not** found in Theory Test papers in Northern Ireland.

Remember
- Don't try too many questions at once.
- Don't try to learn the answers by heart.
- The order of the questions in this book may be different from how they are arranged in the test – so don't try to memorise the order.

How to answer the questions

Each question has four, five or six possible answers. You must mark the boxes with the correct answer(s). Each question tells you how many answers to mark.

Study each question carefully, making sure you understand what it is asking you. Look carefully at any diagram, drawing or photograph. Before you look at the answer(s) given, decide what you think the correct answer(s) might be. You can then select the answer(s) that matches the one you had decided on. If you follow this system, you will avoid being confused by answers that appear to be similar.

WHAT TO EXPECT IN THE HAZARD PERCEPTION TEST

After a break of up to three minutes you will begin the Hazard Perception part of the test. The Hazard Perception test lasts for about 20 minutes. Before you start you will be given some instructions explaining how the test works; you'll also get a chance to practise with the computer and mouse before you start.

Real road scenes feature in the video clips in the Hazard Perception test

Next you will see 14 film or video clips of real street scenes with traffic such as cars, pedestrians, cyclists etc. The scenes are shot from the point of view of a driver in a car. You have to notice potential hazards that are developing on the road ahead – that is, problems that could lead to an accident. As soon as you notice a hazard developing, click the mouse. You will have plenty of time to see the hazard – but the sooner you notice it, the more marks you score.

Click the mouse when you spot potential hazards – the pedestrian crossing the side road and the cyclist approaching a parked vehicle (ringed in yellow). Click again as the hazard develops when the cyclist (ringed in red) moves out to overtake the parked vehicle

Each clip has at least one hazard in it – some clips may have more than one hazard. You have to score a minimum of 44 out of 75 to pass, but the pass mark may change so check

with your instructor or the DSA before sitting your test. (Note that the computer has checks built in to show anyone trying to cheat – for example someone who keeps clicking the mouse all the time.) Be aware that, unlike the Theory Test questions, you will not have an opportunity to go back to an earlier clip and change your response, so you need to concentrate throughout the test.

Preparing for the Hazard Perception test

Who do you think have the most accidents – new or experienced drivers? New drivers have just had lessons, so they should remember how to drive safely, but in fact new drivers have the most accidents.

Learner drivers need training in how to spot hazards because they are often so busy thinking about the car's controls that they forget to watch the road and traffic – and losing concentration for even a second could prove fatal to you or another road user.

> You have to pass both the Hazard Perception test and the Theory Test questions. At the end of the test they will tell you your scores for both parts. Even if you only failed on one part of the Theory Test, you still have to take both parts again next time.

Proper training can help you to recognise more of the hazards that you will meet when driving and to spot those hazards earlier. So you are less likely to have an accident.

Your driving instructor has been trained to help you learn hazard perception skills and can give you plenty of practice in what to look out for when driving, how to anticipate hazards, and what action to take to deal with hazards of all kinds.

You won't be able to practise with the real video clips used in the test, of course, but training books and practice videos are available.

For more help with HAZARD PERCEPTION see pages 123–7.

WHAT TO EXPECT IN THE PRACTICAL TEST

Once you have passed both parts of your Theory Test, you can apply for the Practical Test. The Practical Test is all about making sure that those who pass are competent and safe in the basic skills of driving.

> The requirements for passing your test are a combination of practical skills and mental understanding. The open road can be a risky environment, and your test result will show whether you're ready to go out there alone or whether you need a little more practice first.

> You'll be asked to sign a declaration that the insurance of your car is in order. Without this, the test can't proceed.

The paperwork

You'll need to have with you:
- your signed provisional driving licence (both parts if you've got a photo licence)
- your Theory Test pass certificate
- additional photographic identity (ID), if your licence doesn't have a photo.
- your completed Driver's Record (if you have one) signed by your instructor

If you have to provide additional photographic ID, this can be a current signed passport, a railcard, credit card or other official signed card (e.g. student's union membership card).

Eyesight test

Your driving test begins with an eyesight test. You have to be able to read a normal number plate at a minimum distance of 20.5 metres (about 67½ feet). If you fail the eyesight test your driving test will stop at that point and you will have failed.

Vehicle safety checks

You will have to answer two vehicle safety check questions. The questions fall into three categories:
- identify
- tell me how you would check…
- show me how you would check…

These questions are designed to make sure that you know how to check that your vehicle is safe to drive.

> If you turn up for your test in an unsuitable vehicle, you will forfeit your test fee.

Although some checks may require you to identify where fluid levels should be checked you will not be asked to touch a hot engine or physically check fluid levels. You may refer to vehicle information systems (if fitted) when answering questions on fluid levels and tyre pressures.

All vehicles differ slightly so it is important that you get to know all the safety systems and engine layout in the vehicle in which you plan to take your practical test.

Don't worry about making a few mistakes. You can still pass your test as long as they are only minor driving faults.

The Driving Test

During the test you will be expected to drive for about 40 minutes along normal roads following the directions of the examiner. The roads are selected so as to provide a range of different conditions and road situations and a varied density of traffic.

Your examiner will select suitable areas for you to carry out the set exercises. He or she will tell you to pull up and stop, then he will explain the exercise to you before you do it:

* you *may* or *may not* be asked to perform an emergency stop
* you *will* be asked to perform two reversing exercises selected by the examiner from: reversing round a corner; reverse parking (behind a parked car, or into a marked bay); turning in the road

Driving test standards are monitored so that whatever examiner you get, or whatever test centre you go to, you should get the same result. You might find a senior officer in the car as well as the examiner; he or she is not watching you, but checking that the examiner is doing his or her job properly.

Throughout the test, the examiner will be assessing:

* whether you are competent at controlling the car
* whether you are making normal progress for the roads you are on
* how you react to any hazards that occur in the course of the test
* whether you are noticing all traffic signs and signals and road markings, and reacting to them in the correct manner.

In order to pass the driving test, you must drive

* without committing any serious fault or...
* without committing more than 15 driving errors of a less serious nature.

If, during the test, you do not understand what the examiner says to you, ask him or her to repeat the instruction.

If you are faced with an unusually difficult or hazardous situation in the course of your test, that results in you making a driving fault, the examiner will take the circumstances into account when marking you for that part of the test.

How to prepare for the Practical Test

Be sure that you are ready to take the test. This is where choosing a reliable qualified driving instructor is vital (see page 9).

You should feel:

* confident about driving in all conditions
* confident that you know your *Highway Code*

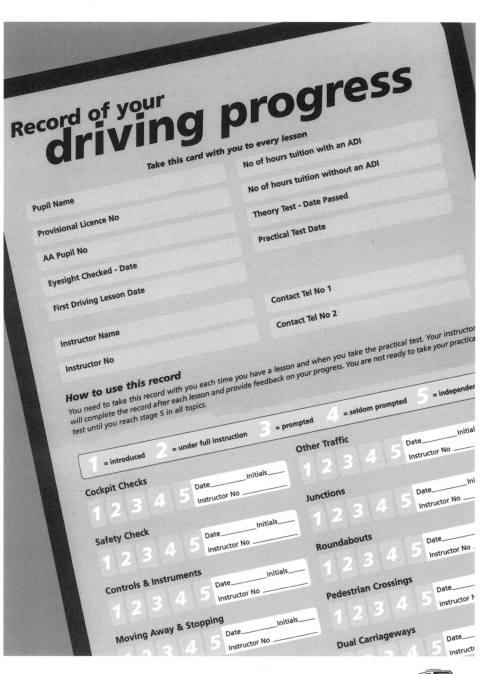

Record of your driving progress

Take this card with you to every lesson

Pupil Name

Provisional Licence No

AA Pupil No

Eyesight Checked - Date

First Driving Lesson Date

Instructor Name

Instructor No

No of hours tuition with an ADI

No of hours tuition without an ADI

Theory Test - Date Passed

Practical Test Date

Contact Tel No 1

Contact Tel No 2

How to use this record

You need to take this record with you each time you have a lesson and when you take the practical test. Your instructor will complete the record after each lesson and provide feedback on your progress. You are not ready to take your practical test until you reach stage 5 in all topics.

1 = introduced   **2** = under full instruction   **3** = prompted   **4** = seldom prompted   **5** = independent

Cockpit Checks
1 2 3 4 5   Date_____ Initials_____ Instructor No _____

Safety Check
1 2 3 4 5   Date_____ Initials_____ Instructor No _____

Controls & Instruments
1 2 3 4 5   Date_____ Initials_____ Instructor No _____

Moving Away & Stopping
3 4 5   Date_____ Initials_____ Instructor No _____

Other Traffic
1 2 3 4 5   Date_____ Initial_____ Instructor No _____

Junctions
1 2 3 4 5   Date_____ Ini_____ Instructor No _____

Roundabouts
1 2 3 4 5   Date_____ Instructor No _____

Pedestrian Crossings
3 4 5   Date_____ Instructor N_____

Dual Carriageways
3 4 5   Date_____ Instruct_____

- confident that you can make decisions on your own about how to cope with hazards, without having to wait for your instructor to tell you what to do.

Driver's Record

Completing a Driver's Record (see page 19) with your instructor should help you feel confident that you're ready to take your driving test.

The Driver's Records comes in two parts – one part for you and one for your instructor. It lists all the skills you need to master to become a safe driver and charts your progress in acquiring each of these skills through the five following levels:

1 Introduced
2 Under full instruction
3 Prompted
4 Seldom prompted
5 Independent

Take your copy of the Driver's Record to each lesson for your instructor to complete. Using the Private Practice sheet you can keep a record of driving experience gained when you are out driving with a friend or relative.

When your instructor has completed all the boxes in your Driver's Record you are ready to take your test. Remember to take the completed Driver's Record along with you to the driving test centre.

AFTER THE TEST

If you passed your test you'll be given a pass certificate, and a copy of the examiner's report showing any minor faults you made during your test. You'll find it useful to know where your minor weaknesses lie, so that you can concentrate on improving those aspects of your driving in the future.

With a full driving licence you are allowed to drive vehicles weighing up to 3.5 tonnes, use motorways for the first time, drive anywhere in the European Union and in many other countries worldwide, and to tow a small trailer. You are on your own dealing with whatever circumstances arise: fog, snow, ice, other drivers' mistakes. It is a huge responsibility.

Driving on a motorway for the first time can be a daunting experience. A good driving school will offer you the option of a post-test motorway lesson with your own instructor, and it makes sense to take advantage of this.

If you failed you will naturally be disappointed, but it's not the end of the world – many people don't pass their first test, but then sail through a second or third, having built on the experience of what it's like to take a test. The examiner will give you a test report form which is a record of all the skills assessed during the test, identifying any areas of weakness. He will also provide feedback in spoken form, and will explain to you what aspects of your driving are still in need of improvement.

Part 2

The Practical Test Questions and Answers

The Practical Test

The Practical Test

Good defensive driving depends on adopting the right attitude from the start. These questions will test your knowledge of what is required before you even sit in the driver's seat.

1

What do you need before you can drive on a public road?

Fill in the missing words

P_ _ _ _ _ _ _ _ _ _ _

_ _ _ _ _ _ _

2

The best way to learn is to have regular planned tuition with an ADI (Approved Driving Instructor).

An ADI is someone who has taken and passed all three driving instructor's

e _ _ _ _ _ _ _ _ _ _ _ and is on the official r_ _ _ _ _ _ _

Complete the sentence

Answers on page 92

HINTS & TIPS

A fully qualified ADI should display a green certificate on the windscreen of their car. Ask to see it.

3

Anyone supervising a learner must be at least _ _ years old and must have held (and still hold) a full driving licence (motor car) for at least t_ _ _ _ _ years

Complete the sentence

4

Your tuition vehicle must display L-plates. Where should they be placed?

Answer_____

_____

_____

5

Young and inexperienced drivers are more vulnerable. Is this true or false?

Tick the correct box **True** ☐ **False** ☐

6

Showing responsibility to yourself and others is the key to being a safe driver. Ask yourself, would you ...

Tick the correct box

1 Want to drive with someone who has been drinking? **YES** ☐ **NO** ☐

2 Want to drive with someone who takes risks and puts other lives at risk? **YES** ☐ **NO** ☐

3 Want to drive with someone who does not concentrate? **YES** ☐ **NO** ☐

4 Want to drive with someone who drives too fast? **YES** ☐ **NO** ☐

7

Do you want to be a safe and responsible driver?

Tick the correct box   **YES** ☐ **NO** ☐

8

You must pass a theory test before you can take the practical test. When would be the best time to sit this test?

Mark two answers

1 Before applying for a provisional licence ☐

2 Just before taking the practical test ☐

3 Some time during the early weeks of your driving lessons ☐

4 After full study of available training materials ☐

9

To use the controls safely you need to adopt a suitable driving position. There are a number of checks you should make.

Fill in the missing words

1 Check the h _ _ _ _ _ _ _ _ _ is on.

2 Check the d _ _ _ _ are shut.

3 Check your s _ _ _ is in the correct position.

4 Check the h _ _ _
r _ _ _ _ _ _ _ _ is adjusted to give maximum protection.

5 Check the driving m _ _ _ _ _ _ are adjusted to give maximum rear view.

6 Check your s _ _ _ b _ _ _ is securely fastened.

10

Here is a list of functions and a list of controls.

Match each function to its control by placing the appropriate letter in the box

THE FUNCTIONS	THE CONTROLS
A To control the direction in which you want to travel	☐ The handbrake
B To slow or stop the vehicle	☐ The driving mirrors
C To increase or decrease the engine's speed	☐ The gear lever
D To give you a clear view behind	☐ The clutch
E To hold the vehicle still when it is stationary	☐ The steering wheel
F To enable you to change gear	☐ The foot-brake
G To enable you to make or break contact between the engine and the wheels	☐ The accelerator

Fill in the missing word

The accelerator can also be called the
g _ _ pedal

Answers on page 92

11

Which foot should you use for each of these controls (in cars with a manual gearbox)?

R = Right foot   **L** = Left foot

The foot-brake ☐
The clutch ☐
The accelerator ☐

12

Are the following statements about steering true or false?

Tick the appropriate boxes   **True False**

1 I must keep both hands on ☐ ☐
the wheel at all times.

2 To keep good control ☐ ☐
I should feed the wheel
through my hands.

3 I can place my hands at ☐ ☐
any position as long as I am
comfortable.

4 When going round corners, ☐ ☐
it is best to cross my hands
(hand over hand).

5 I should never take both ☐ ☐
hands off the wheel when
the vehicle is moving.

6 To straighten up I should ☐ ☐
feed the wheel back through
my hands.

13

Match each of the following functions to its control.

THE FUNCTIONS   **THE CONTROLS**

A To enable you to see   ☐ The direction
the road ahead and   indicators
other road users to
see you without
causing dazzle

B To show other road   ☐ Dipped beam
users which way you
intend to turn

C To use only when   ☐ Main beam
visibility is 100 metres/
yards or less

D To enable you to see   ☐ Rear fog lamp
further, but not to be
used when there is
oncoming traffic

E To warn other road   ☐ Horn
users of your presence

F To warn other road   ☐ Hazard lights
users when you are
temporarily obstructing
traffic

Answers on page 92

1

The following is a list of actions involved in moving off from rest. Number the boxes 1 to 9 to show the correct sequence

The first box has been filled in to give you a start

| 1 | **A** Press the clutch down fully

| | **B** Check your mirrors

| | **C** Set the accelerator pedal

| | **D** Move the gear lever into 1st gear

| | **E** Decide whether you need to give a signal

| | **F** Let the clutch come to biting point and hold it steady

| | **G** Check your blind spot

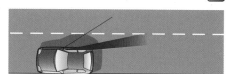

| | **H** If safe, release the handbrake and let the clutch up a little more

| | **I** Press the accelerator pedal a little more and let the clutch up fully

Answers on page 93

2

The following is a list of actions required for stopping normally.
Number the boxes 1 to 9 to show the correct sequence.

The first box has been filled in to give you a start

| 1 | **A** Check your mirrors |

☐ **B** Take your foot off the accelerator pedal

☐ **C** Decide whether you need to signal and, if necessary, do so

☐ **D** Press the brake pedal, lightly at first and then more firmly

☐ **E** As the car stops, ease the pressure off the foot-brake
(except when you are on a slope)

☐ **F** Just before the car stops, press the clutch pedal right down

☐ **G** Put the gear lever into neutral

☐ **H** Apply the handbrake fully

☐ **I** Take both feet off the pedals

Answers on page 93

Gears enable you to select the power you need from the engine to perform a particular task.

3

Which gear gives you the most power?

Answer ☐

4

If you were travelling at 60mph on a clear road, which gear would you most likely select?

Answer ☐

5

When approaching and turning a corner, as shown in the diagram, which gear would you most likely use?

Answer ☐

6

You need to change gear to match your e_ _ _ _ _ speed to the speed at which your v_ _ _ _ _ _ is travelling. The s_ _ _ _ _ the engine is making will help you know w_ _ _ to change gear.

Complete the sentences

7

Number the boxes to show the correct sequence of actions required when changing up.

The first box has been filled in for you

☐1 **A** Place your left hand on the gear lever

☐ **B** Move the gear lever to the next highest position

☐ **C** Press the clutch pedal down fully and ease off the accelerator pedal

☐ **D** Let the clutch pedal come up fully and, at the same time, press the accelerator pedal

☐ **E** Put your left hand back on the steering wheel

Answers on page 93

8

Are the following statements about changing down true or false?

Tick the appropriate boxes   **True False**

1 I would stay in the highest ☐ ☐
gear as long as possible, even
if my engine started to labour

2 I would change down early ☐ ☐
so that the engine helps to
slow the car down

3 I would avoid using the ☐ ☐
foot-brake as much as possible

4 I would usually slow the car ☐ ☐
down by using the foot-brake
first. Then, when I am at the
required speed, I would change
down to the appropriate gear

5 I would always change down ☐ ☐
through the gears so that I
do not miss out any
intermediate gears

Answers on page 94

HINTS ✔ & TIPS

In your driving test, you
will be expected to show
that you can control the
car smoothly.
If you should stall, put
the gears in neutral and
the handbrake on, and
start again.

9

When changing gear, I should look ...

1 Ahead ☐
2 At the gear lever ☐
3 At my feet ☐

Which is correct?

10

Do's and don'ts

Tick the appropriate boxes   **Do Don't**

1 Force the gear lever if there ☐ ☐
is any resistance

2 Rush the gear changes ☐ ☐

3 Match your speed with the ☐ ☐
correct gear

4 Use the brakes, where ☐ ☐
necessary, to reduce speed
before changing down

5 Listen to the sound of ☐ ☐
the engine

6 Take your eyes off the road ☐ ☐
when changing gear

7 Hold the gear lever longer ☐ ☐
than necessary

8 Coast with the clutch down ☐ ☐
or the gear lever in neutral

11

Which wheels turn when you turn the steering wheel?

A The front wheels

B The back wheels

Answer ☐

12

When you turn your steering wheel to the right, which way do your wheels turn?

A To the right

B To the left

Answer ☐

13

The steering lock is ...

A The locking mechanism that stops the steering wheel from moving when the ignition key is removed

B The angle through which the wheels turn when the steering wheel is turned

Answer ☐

14

Which wheels follow the shorter pathway?

A The front wheels

B The back wheels

Answer ☐

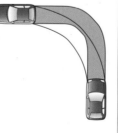

15

Which is the correct position for normal driving?

Put letter A, B or C in the box

Answer ☐

A  B  C

16

Which diagram shows the correct pathway when driving normally?

Put a letter A or B in the box

Answer ☐

A  B

Answers on page 94

17

Pushing the clutch pedal down ...

A Releases the engine from the wheels

B Engages the engine with the wheels

Answer ☐

18

The point where the clutch plates meet is called the b_ _ _ _ _ point.

Fill in the missing word

19

By controlling the amount of contact between the clutch plates, it is possible to control the speed of the car.

Would you use this control ...

Tick the appropriate boxes

	True	False
1 When moving away from rest?	☐	☐
2 When manoeuvring the car in reverse gear?	☐	☐
3 When slowing down to turn a corner?	☐	☐
4 In very slow moving traffic?	☐	☐
5 To slow the car down?	☐	☐

HINTS ✔ & TIPS

Remember:
MSM stands for Mirror, Signal, Manoeuvre. Always use this routine when moving off, turning or overtaking.

Answers on page 94

1

A junction is a point where t __ __
o__ m__ __ __ r__ __ __ __ meet.

Complete the sentence

2

**Here are five types of junction.
Name them**

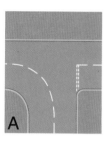

A

_____

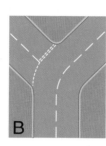

B

_____

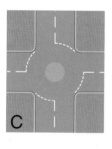

C

_____

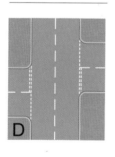

D

_____

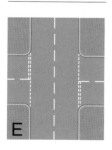

E

_____

3

**Match these road signs to the junctions
shown opposite.**

Put letters A, B, C, D and E in the boxes

 1 ☐

 2 ☐

 3 ☐

 4 ☐

 5 ☐

4

What do these signs mean?

1 Stop and give way

2 Slow down, look, and proceed if safe

3 Give way to traffic on the major road

Put a number in each box

**Answers on
page 95**

A ☐   B ☐

5

At every junction you should follow a safe routine.

Put the following into the correct order by numbering the boxes 1 to 5

Signal ☐   Speed ☐   Position ☐
Mirrors ☐   Look ☐

6

The diagram below shows a car turning right into a minor road. The boxes are numbered to show the correct sequence of actions.

Complete the sentence

At point 5 you should look and
a _ _ _ _ _ the situation,
d _ _ _ _ _ to go or wait,
and a _ _ accordingly.

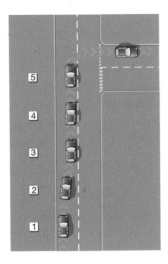

Answers on page 95

7

**Turning left into a minor road.
Which diagram below shows the best path to follow when driving a motor car A, B, C or D?**

Answer ☐

A

B

C

D

8

You turn into a side road. Pedestrians are already crossing it. Should you ...

Tick the appropriate box

A Sound your horn ☐
B Slow down and give way ☐
C Flash your lights ☐
D Wave them across ☐

9

**Turning right into a minor road.
Which diagram shows the best path to
follow: A, B, C or D?**

Answer ☐

10

**These are the golden rules for emerging
from junctions.**

Complete the sentences

1 Always use your m__ __ __ __ __ __ to
check the speed and p __ __ __ __ __ __ __
of vehicles behind.

2 Always cancel your s__ __ __ __ __ .

3 Speed up to a s__ __ __ speed after
joining the new road.

4 Keep a s__ __ __ d__ __ __ __ __ __ __
between you and the vehicle ahead.

5 Do not attempt to o__ __ __ __ __ __ __
until you can assess the new road.

Answers on page 95

11

All crossroads must be approached with caution.

Match actions 1, 2 and 3 listed below with these diagrams

Actions

1 Approach with caution, look well ahead and be prepared to stop. Remember other drivers may assume they have priority.

2 Look well ahead, slow down and be prepared to give way to traffic on the major road.

3 Look well ahead and into the side roads for approaching vehicles. Remember other drivers may not give you priority.

12

Which of the following statements describes the correct procedure when approaching a roundabout?

Put letter A, B or C in the box

A The broken white line at a roundabout means I must stop and give way to traffic already on the roundabout.

B The broken white line at a roundabout means I must give priority to traffic already on the roundabout.

C The broken white line means I should give way to any traffic approaching from my immediate right.

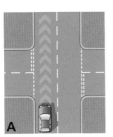

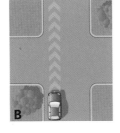

Answer ☐   Answer ☐

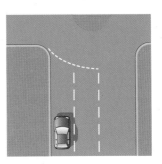

Answer ☐

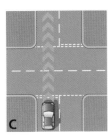

Answer ☐

HINTS ✔ & TIPS

At an unmarked crossroads, no one has priority.
Be extra-cautious at these junctions.

Answers on page 95

13

The following sentences give guidance on lane discipline on a roundabout.

Fill in the missing words

1 When turning left at a roundabout, I should stay in the _ _ _ _ hand lane and should stay in that lane throughout.

2 When going ahead at a roundabout, I should be in the _ _ _ _ hand lane, and should stay in that lane throughout, unless conditions dictate otherwise.

3 When turning right at a roundabout, I should approach in the r_ _ _ _ hand lane, or approach as if turning right at a junction, and stay in that lane throughout.

14

The letters A, B and C in the diagram mark places where you should signal.

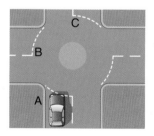

Complete the sentences

1 I would signal at **A** when turning _ _ _ _ _.

2 I would signal at **B** when g_ _ _ _ _ _ _ _ _ _ _.

3 I would signal at **A** and at **C** when turning _ _ _ _ _ _.

15

At a roundabout you should always use a safe routine.

Fill in the missing words

M_ _ _ _ _ _, s _ _ _ _ _,
p_ _ _ _ _ _ _ _, s_ _ _ _,
l_ _ _.

16

What does this sign mean?

Write 1, 2 or 3 in the box

1 Roundabout

2 Mini-roundabout

3 Vehicles may pass either side.

Answer ☐

> **HINTS** ✔ **& TIPS**
> Be careful at roundabouts where destinations are marked for each lane. Make sure you are in the correct lane for your destination.

Answers on page 95

1

It is safest to park off the road or in a car park whenever possible. If you have to park on the road, think ...

Fill in the missing words

1 Is it s_ _ _ ?

2 Is it c_ _ _ _ _ _ _ _ _ _ _?

3 Is it l_ _ _ _ ?

2

In this diagram four of the cars are parked illegally or without consideration of others.

Put the numbers of these cars in the boxes

☐ ☐ ☐ ☐

For reverse parallel parking manoeuvres, see pages 52–4.

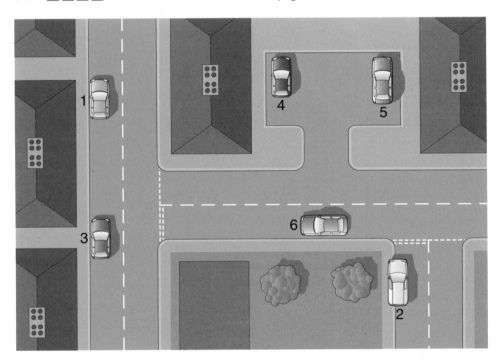

Answers on page 96

3

Check how well you know the rules about where you may and may not park. Are the following statements true or false?

Tick the correct boxes

	True	False
1 In a narrow street, I should park with two wheels up on the pavement to leave more room for other traffic.	☐	☐
2 I am allowed to park in a 'Disabled' space if all other spaces are full.	☐	☐
3 I should not park on the zig-zag lines near a zebra crossing.	☐	☐
4 Red lines painted on the road mean 'No Stopping'.	☐	☐

4

List three places not mentioned in Question 3 where you should *not* park.

1 _____
_____
_____
_____
_____
_____

2 _____
_____
_____
_____
_____
_____

3 _____
_____
_____
_____
_____
_____

HINTS ✔ & TIPS
Use your *Highway Code* to find out more about parking regulations

Answers on page 96

1

The diagram shows a stationary vehicle on the left-hand side of the road.
Which should have priority, vehicle 1 or vehicle 2?

Answer ☐

2

This diagram shows a steep downward hill with an obstruction on the right-hand side of the road.
Which vehicle should be given priority, vehicle 1 or vehicle 2?

Answer ☐

Answers on page 96

3

The diagram shows two vehicles, travelling in opposite directions, turning right at a crossroads.

Are these statements true or false?

Tick the appropriate boxes **True False**

1 The safest route is to pass ☐ ☐
each other offside to offside.

2 If the approaching vehicle ☐ ☐
flashes its headlamps, I should
turn as quickly as possible.

3 I should always try to get ☐ ☐
eye-to-eye contact with the
driver of the other vehicle to
determine which course to take.

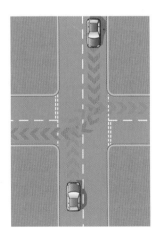

4

Which of the following factors, illustrated in the diagram, should be taken into consideration when turning right into a side road?

Tick the appropriate boxes **YES NO**

1 The speed of the ☐ ☐
approaching vehicle (**A**)

2 The roadworks ☐ ☐

3 The speed of vehicle **B** ☐ ☐

4 The cyclist ☐ ☐

5 Your speed (vehicle **C**) ☐ ☐

6 The pedestrians ☐ ☐

7 The car waiting to turn ☐ ☐
right (**D**)

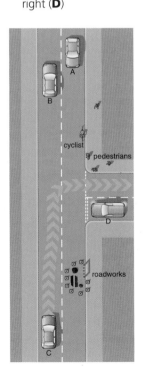

*Answers on
page 96*

1

Are the following statements true or false when stopping in an emergency?

Tick the correct boxes   **True False**

1 Stopping in an emergency ☐ ☐
increases the risk of skidding.

2 I should push the brake pedal ☐ ☐
down harder as I slow down.

3 It is important to react quickly. ☐ ☐

4 I should always remember ☐ ☐
to look in my mirrors as I
slow down.

5 I should signal left to tell ☐ ☐
other road users what I
am doing.

6 I should keep both hands ☐ ☐
on the wheel.

7 I should always check my ☐ ☐
mirrors and look round
before moving off.

2

Is the following statement true or false? An emergency stop will be carried out on every driving test

Tick the correct box **True** ☐ **False** ☐

3

Cadence braking is a technique which can be used in very slippery conditions in an emergency.

Fill in the missing words

The technique requires you to p_ _ _ _ the brake pedal.

The procedure to follow is:

1 Apply m_ _ _ _ _ _ pressure.

2 Release the brake pedal just as the wheels are about to l_ _ _.

3 Then q_ _ _ _ _ _ apply the brakes again. Apply and release the brakes until the vehicle has stopped. This technique should only be used in emergency situations.

4

Anti-lock braking systems (ABS)* work in a similar way to cadence braking.

Fill in the missing words

When braking in an emergency, ABS brakes allow you to s_ _ _ _ and b_ _ _ _ _ at the same time. You do not have to p_ _ _ the brakes as you would in cadence braking. When using ABS you keep the p_ _ _ _ _ _ _ applied.

HINTS ✔ & TIPS

If a vehicle is travelling too close behind you, then increase the gap you have ahead. Always think for the driver behind.

Answers on page 97

Are these statements about ABS braking true or false?

Tick the correct boxes   **True**   **False**

1 Cars fitted with ABS braking ☐ ☐
cannot skid.

2 I do not need to leave as ☐ ☐
much room between me and
the car in front if I have ABS
brakes because I know I can
stop in a shorter distance.

**ABS is a registered trade mark of Bosch
(Germany). ABS stands for Anti-Blockiersystem*

The distance taken for a car to reach
stopping point divides into thinking
distance and braking distance.

5

Could these factors affect thinking distance?

Tick the appropriate boxes   **YES**   **NO**

1 The condition of your tyres ☐ ☐
2 Feeling tired or unwell ☐ ☐
3 Speed of reaction ☐ ☐
4 Going downhill ☐ ☐

6

Most drivers' reaction time is well over ...

Tick the appropriate box

½ second ☐
1 second ☐
5 seconds ☐

7

Stopping distance depends partly on the speed at which the car is travelling.

Complete the sentences

1 At 30mph your overall stopping distance
will be __ __ metres or __ __ feet.

2 At 50mph your thinking distance will
be __ __ metres or __ __ feet.

3 At 70mph your overall stopping distance
will be __ __ metres or __ __ __feet.

8

Stopping distance also varies according to road conditions.

Complete the sentences

In wet weather your vehicle will take
l __ __ __ __ __ to stop. You should
therefore allow m __ __ __ time.

9

**Too many accidents are caused by drivers
driving too close to the vehicle in front. A
safe gap between you and the vehicle in
front can be measured by noting a
stationary object and counting in seconds
the time that lapses between the vehicle
in front passing that object and your own
vehicle passing that object.**

Complete the sentence

Only a fool b __ __ __ __ __ the t __ __
s __ __ __ __ __ rule.

Answers on page 97

1

Are these statements about moving off at an angle true or false?

Tick the correct boxes **True False**

1 I should check my mirrors as I am pulling out. ☐ ☐

2 I should check my mirrors and blindspot before I pull out. ☐ ☐

3 I should move out as quickly as possible. ☐ ☐

4 The amount of steering required will depend on how close I am to the vehicle in front. ☐ ☐

5 I should look for oncoming traffic. ☐ ☐

6 As long as I am signalling, people will know what I am doing. I will be able to pull out because somebody will let me in. ☐ ☐

2

Are these statements about moving off uphill true or false?

Tick the correct boxes **True False**

1 On an uphill gradient the car will tend to roll back. ☐ ☐

2 To stop the car rolling back I need to use more acceleration. ☐ ☐

3 I do not need to use the handbrake. ☐ ☐

4 The biting point may be slightly higher. ☐ ☐

5 I need to press the accelerator pedal further down than when moving off on the level. ☐ ☐

6 I need to allow more time to pull away. ☐ ☐

7 The main controls I use will be the clutch pedal, the accelerator pedal and the handbrake. ☐ ☐

Answers on page 98

3

Are these statements about moving off downhill true or false?

Tick the correct boxes

	True	False
1 The car will tend to roll forwards.	☐	☐
2 The main controls I use will be the handbrake, the clutch pedal and the accelerator pedal.	☐	☐
3 The only gear I can move off in is 1st gear.	☐	☐

	True	False
4 I should release the handbrake while keeping the foot-brake applied.	☐	☐
5 I should look round just before moving off.	☐	☐
6 I must not have my foot on the foot-brake as I start to release the clutch.	☐	☐

Answers on page 98

4

The following statements are about approaching a junction when going uphill or downhill. With which do you agree?

When going downhill ... | **YES** | **NO**

1 It is more difficult to slow down

2 Putting the clutch down will help slow the car down

3 The higher the gear, the greater the control

4 When changing gear you may need to use the foot-brake at the same time as the clutch

When going uphill ... | **YES** | **NO**

5 Early use of mirrors, signals, brakes, gears and steering will help to position the car correctly

6 You may need to use your handbrake more often

7 When you change gear, the car tends to slow down

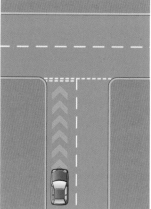

Answers on page 98

1

Before reversing there are three things to consider.

Fill in the missing words

1 Is it s__ __ __?

2 Is it c__ __ __ __ __ __ __ __ __?

3 Is it within the l__ __?

2

Are the following statements about reversing true or false?

Tick the appropriate boxes   **True   False**

1 Other road users should see ☐ ☐
what I am doing and wait
for me.

2 I should wave pedestrians ☐ ☐
on, so that I can get on with
the manoeuvre more quickly.

3 I should avoid being too ☐ ☐
hesitant.

4 I should avoid making other ☐ ☐
road users slow down or
change course.

3

How should you hold the steering wheel when reversing left?

Which is correct?   Answer ☐

A   B   C

4

These statements are all about reversing.

Tick those which you think are correct

                                             True   False

1 My car will respond ☐ ☐
differently in reverse gear.

2 My car will feel no different. ☐ ☐

3 Steering is not affected. ☐ ☐
The car responds the same
as when going forward.

4 The steering will feel ☐ ☐
different. I will have to wait
for the steering to take effect.

5

Which way will the rear of the car go when it is reversed? Left or right?

A   B

Answer _____   Answer_____

Answers on page 99

6

It is important to move the vehicle slowly when reversing.

Complete the sentence

Moving the vehicle slowly is safer because I have control and it allows me to carry out good o_ _ _ _ _ _ _ _ _ _ checks.

7

When reversing, good observation is vital. Where should you look?

Tick the correct answer

1 At the kerb ☐
2 Ahead ☐
3 Where your car is going ☐
4 Out of the back window ☐

8

Are these statements about reversing round a corner true or false?

Tick the correct boxes   **True**   **False**

1 If the corner is sharp, I need ☐ ☐
to be further away from
the kerb.

2 The distance from the kerb ☐ ☐
makes no difference.

3 I should try to stay ☐ ☐
reasonably close to the kerb
all the way round.

9

Before reversing I should check ...

Tick the correct box

1 Behind me ☐
2 Ahead and to the rear ☐
3 My door mirrors ☐
4 All round ☐

10

Which position is the correct one in which to start steering?

A, B, C or D? Answer ☐

11

Which way should you steer?

Answer_____

12

What will happen to the front of the car?

Answer_____

Answers on page 99

13

Are these statements about steering when reversing round a corner true or false?

Tick the correct boxes

	True	False
1 The more gradual the corner, the less I have to steer.	☐	☐
2 I need to steer the same for every corner.	☐	☐
3 The sharper the corner, the more I have to steer.	☐	☐

14

As I enter the new road, I should continue to keep a look-out for

p_ _ _ _ _ _ _ _ _ _ _ **and other**

r_ _ _ _ u_ _ _ _ _.

I should s_ _ _ if necessary.

Complete the sentences

15

True or false? When reversing from a major road into a side road on the right, I have to move to the wrong side of the road.

Tick the correct box **True** ☐ **False** ☐

16

Which diagram shows the correct path to follow when moving to the right-hand side of the road? A or B?

Answer ☐

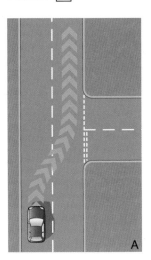

A

B

Answers on page 99

17

Which of the following correctly describes your sitting position for reversing to the right?

1 I will need to sit so that I can see over my right shoulder.

2 I will need to sit so that I can see over my right shoulder, ahead and to the left.

3 My position is the same as when reversing to the left.

Which statement is correct? 1, 2 or 3

Answer ☐

18

True or false? I may need to change my hand position on the wheel.

Tick the correct box **True** ☐ **False** ☐

19

True or false? It is easier to judge my position from the kerb when reversing to the right than when reversing to the left.

Tick the correct box **True** ☐ **False** ☐

20

Reversing to the right is more dangerous than reversing to the left because ...

1 I cannot see as well

2 I am on the wrong side of the road

3 I might get in the way of vehicles emerging from the side road

Which statement is correct – 1, 2 or 3?

Answer ☐

21

How far down the side road would you reverse before moving over to the left-hand side?

Which diagram is correct? A or B?

Answer ☐

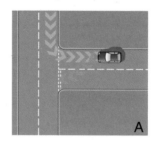

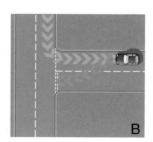

Answers on page 99

22

Look at the diagrams and decide which is safer.

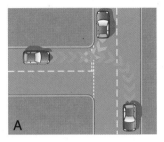

A Reversing into a side road

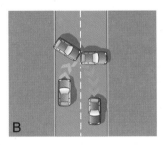

B Turning round in the road

Answer ☐

23

The secret of turning in the road is to move the vehicle s_ _ _ _ _ and steer b_ _ _ _ _ _.

Complete the sentence

24

I must be able to complete the manoeuvre in three moves: 1 forward, 2 reverse, 3 forward. True or false?

Tick the correct box **True** ☐ **False** ☐

25

Before manoeuvring what should you take into consideration?

Tick the correct boxes

1 The size of your engine ☐
2 The width of the road ☐
3 The road camber ☐
4 The steering circle of your vehicle ☐
5 Parking restrictions ☐

26

Before moving forward, it is important to check a_ _ r_ _ _ _ for other road users.

Complete the sentence

> **HINTS ✔ & TIPS**
>
> When taking your test, you will be assessed on how well you can control the car; so don't rush your manoeuvres.

Answers on page 100

27

Turning in the road requires proper use of the steering wheel.

Answer the following questions...

1 When going forwards, which way should you steer?

Answer _____

2 Before you reach the kerb ahead, what should you do?

Answer _____

3 When reversing, which way should you steer?

Answer _____

4 Before you reach the kerb behind you, what should you do?

Answer _____

5 As you move forward again, which way should you steer to straighten up?

Answer _____

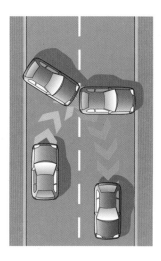

28

Reversing is a potentially dangerous manoeuvre. Good observation is essential.

Answer the following questions

1 If you are steering left when reversing, which shoulder should you look over?

Answer _____

2 As you begin to steer to the right, where should you look?

Answer _____

29

When parking between two cars ...

1 The car is more manoeuvrable when driving forwards

2 The car is more manoeuvrable when reversing

3 There is no difference between going into the space forwards or reversing into it

Which statement is correct? 1, 2 or 3?

Answer ☐

HINTS ✔ & TIPS

In your driving test you may be asked to reverse into a parking bay at the test centre, or to park behind another car, using reverse gear. So make sure you practise these manoeuvres.

Answers on page 100

30

The diagram shows a car preparing to reverse into a parking space. Which position is the correct one in which to start steering left, A, B, C or D?

Answer ☐

31

With practice you should be able to park in a gap ...

1 Your own car length
2 1½ times your own car length
3 2 times your own car length
4 2½ times your own car length

Answer ☐

32

Use the diagram to help you answer the following questions.

1 Which way would you steer?

Answer _____

2 At this point what would you try to line up with the offside (right-hand side) of your vehicle?

Answer _____

3 As you straighten up what do you have to be careful of?

Answer _____

4 What do you need to do to straighten up?

Answer _____

5 What would you need to do in order to position the vehicle parallel to the kerb?

Answer _____

Answers on page 100

33

True or false? During my driving test ...

Tick the correct boxes

	True	False
1 I will certainly be asked to perform the manoeuvre in Question 32	☐	☐
2 I have to be able to park in a tight space between two cars	☐	☐
3 It may be that only the lead car is present	☐	☐

34

When carrying out this manoeuvre, where is it important to look?

Answer _____

35

Look at the diagram and answer the following question.

Which bay should you use and why?

Answer _____

_____

_____

36

Why, wherever possible, should you choose to reverse into a parking bay?

Answer _____

_____

_____

_____

37

As well as being very aware of how c_ _ _ _ I am to the parked cars on either side, I should also be alert for cars moving near me from all d_ _ _ _ _ _ _ _ _ _, as well as the possibility of p_ _ _ _ _ _ _ _ _ _ walking around my car.

Complete the sentence

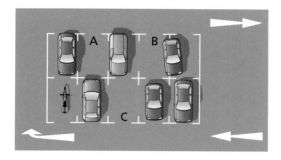

Answers on page 100

1

Traffic lights have three lights, red, amber, and green, which change from one to the other in a set order. Number the boxes 1 to 5 to show the correct order. The first answer has been filled in to give you a start.

☐ Amber ☐1☐ Red ☐ Red and amber
☐ Red ☐ Green

2

What do the colours mean?

Fill in the correct colour for each of the following

1 Go ahead if the way is clear.

Colour _____

2 Stop and wait.

Colour _____

3 Stop unless you have crossed the stop line or you are so close to it that stopping might cause an accident.

Colour _____

4 Stop and wait at the stop line.

Colour _____

3

Which of the following statements are true?

On approach to traffic lights you should ...

Tick the appropriate boxes

1 Speed up to get through before they change ☐

2 Be ready to stop ☐
3 Look for pedestrians ☐
4 Sound your horn to urge pedestrians to cross quickly ☐

4

Some traffic lights have green filters. Do they mean ...

1 You can filter in the direction of the arrow only when the main light is showing green?

2 You can filter even when the main light is not showing green?

Answer ☐

5

The diagram shows the three lanes at a set of traffic lights.

Which lane would you use for ...

1 Going ahead Answer _____
2 Turning right Answer _____
3 Turning left Answer _____

Answers on page 101

6

At some traffic lights and junctions you will see yellow criss-cross lines (box junctions). Can you ...

Tick the correct boxes

	YES	NO
1 Wait within them when going ahead if your exit is not clear?	☐	☐
2 Wait within them when going right if your exit is not clear?	☐	☐
3 Wait within them if there is oncoming traffic stopping you turning right but your exit is clear?	☐	☐

Pedestrians have certain rights of way at pedestrian crossings.

7

On approaching a zebra crossing, drivers will notice four features. Name them

1 _____

_____

2 _____

_____

3 _____

_____

4 _____

_____

8

Are these statements about pedestrian crossings true or false?

Tick the correct boxes

	True	False
1 I cannot park or wait on the zig-zag lines on the approach to a zebra crossing.	☐	☐
2 I cannot park or wait on the zig-zag lines on either side of the crossing.	☐	☐
3 I can overtake on the zig-zag lines on the approach to a crossing as long as the other vehicle is travelling slowly.	☐	☐
4 I must give way to a pedestrian once he/she has stepped on to the crossing.	☐	☐

Answers on page 101

5 If, on approach to a crossing, ☐ ☐
I intend to slow down or
stop, I should use a
slowing-down arm signal.

9

On approaching a pelican crossing, drivers will notice three key features. Name them

1 _____

_____

_____

_____

2 _____

_____

_____

_____

3 _____

_____

_____

_____

10

If you see a pedestrian at a zebra crossing or pelican crossing carrying a white stick, do you think ...

Tick the correct box

1 He/she has difficulty walking? ☐

2 He/she is visually handicapped? ☐

11

The traffic lights at a pelican crossing have the same meaning as ordinary traffic lights, but they do not have a red and amber phase.

1 What do they show instead of the red and amber phase?

Answer_____

_____

2 What does the light mean?

Answer_____

_____

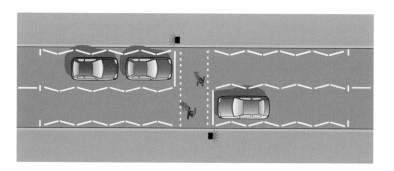

**Answers on pages 101–2**

12

What sound is usually heard at a pelican crossing when the green man is shown to pedestrians?

Answer_____

_____

_____

_____

13

Toucan and puffin crossings are similar to pelican crossings but with one main difference. Name it.

Answer_____

_____

_____

_____

14

As well as pedestrians, what other type of road users should you watch for at a toucan crossing?

Answer_____

_____

_____

_____

Answers on page 102

A level crossing is where the road crosses at a railway line. It is potentially dangerous and should be approached with caution.

15

Match each traffic sign below with its correct meaning.

1 Level crossing without gates or barriers ☐
2 Level crossing with lights ☐
3 Level crossing with gates or barriers ☐
4 Level crossing without lights ☐

A   B   C   D

16

If you break down on a level crossing, should you ...

Tick the appropriate boxes

1 Tell your passengers to wait in the vehicle while you go to get help? ☐

2 Get everybody out and clear of the crossing? ☐

3 Telephone the police? ☐

4 Telephone the signal operator? ☐

5 If there is still time, push your car clear of the crossing? ☐

One-way systems are where all traffic flows in the same direction.

1

Which of these signs means one-way traffic?

A   B

Answer ☐

2

Are these statements about one-way systems true or false?

Tick the correct boxes

	True	False
1 In one-way streets traffic can pass me on both sides.	☐	☐
2 Roundabouts are one-way systems.	☐	☐
3 For normal driving I should stay on the left.	☐	☐
4 I should look out for road markings and get in lane early.	☐	☐

As a rule, the more paint on the road, the more important the message.

3

Road markings are divided into three categories.

Fill in the missing words

1 Those which give

i _ _ _ _ _ _ _ _ _ _.

2 Those which give w _ _ _ _ _ _ _.

3 Those which give o _ _ _ _ _.

4

There are two main advantages which road markings have over other traffic signs. Name them.

1 _____

_____

2 _____

_____

Answers on page 102

5

What do these lines across the road mean?

A

1 Stop and give way

2 Give priority to traffic coming from the immediate right.

3 Give way to traffic coming from the right.

Answer ☐

B

1 Give way to traffic on the major road.

2 Stop at the line and give way to traffic on the major road.

Answer ☐

6

Where you see double solid white lines painted along the centre of the road, what does this mean?

Tick any boxes you think are appropriate.

More than one answer may be correct.

1 I must not park or wait on the carriageway. ☐

2 I can park between 7pm and 7am. ☐

3 I must not overtake. ☐

4 I must not cross the white line except to turn right or in circumstances beyond my control. ☐

7

What is the purpose of these hatched markings (chevrons)?

Answer_____

_____

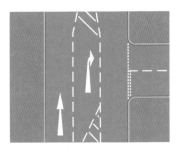

Answers on page 102

8

What does it mean if the chevrons are edged with a solid white line?

Answer_____

_____

The shape and colour of a sign will help you understand what it means.

9

Look at the sign shapes below and say whether each gives an order, a warning or information.

1

2

Answer_____   Answer_____

3

Answer_____

10

Complete the sentences

1 A circular sign with a blue background tells you what you m__ __ __ do.

2 A circular sign with a red border tells you what you m__ __ __ n__ __ do.

Answers on pages 102–3

11

What do these signs mean?

GIVE WAY

Answer_____

_____

_____

_____

STOP

Answer_____

_____

_____

12

Some junctions have a stop sign, others have a give way sign. *Complete the sentence*

A stop sign is usually placed at a junction where v__ __ __ __ __ is l__ __ __ __ __ __.

13

Information signs are colour-coded.

Match each of the following signs to its colouring.

A White letters on a brown background

B Black letters on a white background

C Black letters on a white background with a blue border

D White letters on a blue background with a white border

E White letters on a green background, yellow route numbers with a white border

☐ Motorway signs

☐ Primary routes

☐ Other routes

☐ Local places

☐ Tourist signs

1

Good observation is vital in today's busy traffic.

Complete the sentence

When using my mirrors I should try to make a mental note of the s_ _ _ _ _,
b_ _ _ _ _ _ _ _ and
i_ _ _ _ _ _ _ _ _ of the driver behind.

2

Driving in built-up areas is potentially dangerous.

Look at the diagram opposite

1 What action should the driver of car **A** take?

List four options

A _____

B _____

C _____

D _____

2 What action should the driver of car **B** take?

List four options

A _____

B _____

C _____

D _____

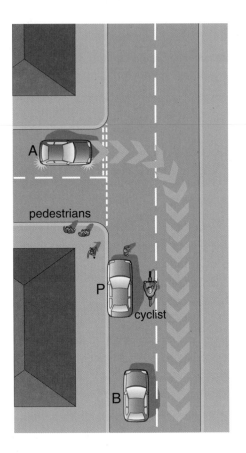

pedestrians

P

cyclist

B

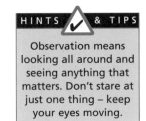

HINTS ✔ & TIPS

Observation means looking all around and seeing anything that matters. Don't stare at just one thing – keep your eyes moving.

Answers on pages 102–4

3

Motorcyclists are often less visible than other road users.

Complete this well-known phrase

Think once, think twice, think b__ __ __.

4

When you observe traffic following too close behind you, would you

Tick the correct box

1 Speed up to create a bigger gap? ☐

2 Touch your brake lights to warn the following driver? ☐

3 Keep to a safe speed, and keep checking the behaviour and intentions of the following driver? ☐

5

Some hazards are potential, others are actual and there all the time, such as a bend in the road.

A Name five more actual hazards

1 _____

_____

2 _____

_____

3 _____

_____

4 _____

_____

5 _____

_____

B Name five potential hazards, such as a dog off its lead

1 _____

_____

2 _____

_____

3 _____

_____

4 _____

_____

5 _____

_____

6

Modern driving requires full concentration. Are the following statements true or false?

Tick the correct boxes   **True False**

1 Carrying a mobile phone can reduce the stress of a long journey.   ☐   ☐

2 I must not use a hand-held phone while driving.   ☐   ☐

3 Conversation on a hands-free phone can still distract my attention.   ☐   ☐

4 I should pull up in a safe place to make or receive calls.   ☐   ☐

Answers on page 104

7

When driving, all the following actions have something in common.

What is it?

Reading a map

Eating

Changing a cassette

Listening to loud music

Answer_____

_____

_____

_____

One of the features of driving on the open road is taking bends properly.

8

As a rule you should be travelling at the correct s_ _ _ _, using the correct g_ _ _, and be in the correct p_ _ _ _ _ _ _.

9

Should you brake ...

Tick the appropriate box

1 Before you enter the bend? ☐

2 As you enter the bend? ☐

3 While negotiating the bend? ☐

Answers on page 104

10

Which way does force push a car on a bend?

A Inwards or **B** Outwards

Answer ☐

11

What happens to the weight of the car when you use the brakes?

A It is thrown forwards

B It remains even

C It is thrown back

Answer ☐

12

When you approach a bend, what position should you be in?

Complete the sentences

A On a right-hand bend I should keep to the _____

_____

B On a left-hand bend I should keep to the _____

_____

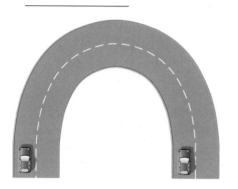

Overtaking is a potentially dangerous manoeuvre.

13

Before overtaking, consider whether it is really n__ __ __ __ __ __ __ __.

Fill in the missing word

Always use the safety routine when overtaking.

Put these actions into their correct sequence by putting numbers 1 to 7, as seen in the diagram, in the boxes

☐ Signal ☐ Mirrors ☐ Look
☐ Position ☐ Mirrors ☐ Speed
☐ Manoeuvre

14

What is the minimum amount of clearance you should give a cyclist or motor cyclist?

Answer _____

_____

Answers on pages 104–5

15

There are four situations in which you may, with caution, overtake on the left-hand side of the car in front.

Name them

1 _____
_____
_____

2 _____
_____
_____

3 _____
_____
_____

4 _____
_____
_____

16

List four places where it would be dangerous to overtake.

1 _____
_____
_____

2 _____
_____
_____

3 _____
_____
_____

4 _____
_____
_____

17

Dual carriageways can appear similar to motorways, but there are important differences. Which of the following statements apply to dual carriageways?

Tick the relevant boxes

1 Reflective studs are not used ☐.

2 Cyclists are allowed. ☐

3 The speed limit is always 60mph. ☐

4 You cannot turn right to enter or leave a dual carriageway. ☐

5 Milk floats and slow moving farm vehicles are prohibited. ☐

18

When turning right from a minor road on to a dual carriageway, where would you wait ...

A When there is a wide central reserve?

Answer_____
_____
_____

B When the central reserve is too narrow for your car?

Answer_____
_____
_____

19

When travelling at 70mph on a dual carriageway, which lane would you use?

Answer_____

Answers on pages 105–6

20

What do these signs mean?

A

Answer_____

B

Answer_____

C

Answer_____

21

Which of the signs in Question 20 (see opposite) would you expect to see on a dual carriageway?

Answer_____
_____
_____
_____

22

Why is it important to plan your movements especially early when leaving a dual carriageway to the right (see diagram below)?

Answer_____
_____
_____
_____
_____

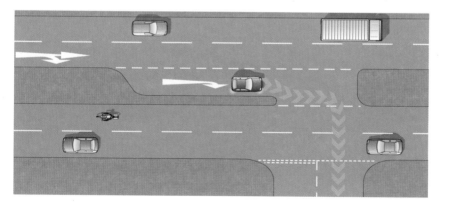

Answers on page 106

1

Cars fitted with automatic transmission select the gear depending on the road speed and the load on the engine. They therefore have no c_ _ _ _ _ **pedal.**

Fill in the missing word

2

The advantages of an automatic car are ...

1 _____

_____

2 _____

_____

3

The gear selector has the same function as a manual selector, but what function do each of the following have?

P	Park	_____
R	Reverse	_____
N	Neutral	_____
D	Drive	_____
3	3rd	_____
2	2nd	_____
1	1st	_____

4

Automatic cars have a device called a kickdown. Is its function ...

Tick the correct box

1 To select a higher gear? ☐

2 To select a lower gear manually? ☐

3 To provide quick accelerations when needed? ☐

5

When driving an automatic car, would you select a lower gear ...

Tick the correct boxes

	True	False
1 To control speed when going down a steep hill?	☐	☐
2 To slow the car down in normal driving?	☐	☐
3 When going uphill?	☐	☐
4 To overtake, in certain circumstances?	☐	☐
5 When manoeuvring?	☐	☐
6 Before stopping?	☐	☐

6

An automatic car has two foot pedals, the foot-brake and the accelerator.

For normal driving, which foot would you use ...

1 For the brake?

Answer_____

2 For the accelerator?

Answer_____

Answers on pages 106–7

7

When you are driving an automatic car, using one foot to control both pedals is preferable to using both the left and the right foot. Why?

Answer_____

_____

_____

8

Some cars with automatic transmission have a tendency to 'creep'.

Which gears allow the car to creep?

Answer_____

_____

_____

9

When driving an automatic car, would you use the handbrake ...

Tick the correct box

1 More than in a manual car? ☐

2 The same? ☐

3 Less? ☐

10

In which position should the gear selector be when you are starting the engine?

Answer_____

or _____

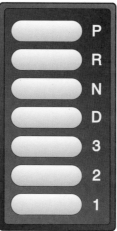

11

As you approach a bend, an automatic car will sometimes change up because there is less pressure on the accelerator. What should you do to prevent this happening?

Tick the correct box

1 Slow down before the bend and accelerate gently as you turn. ☐

2 Brake as you go round the bend. ☐

3 Brake and accelerate at the same time. ☐

Answers on page 107

The Driving Test – **Section 13**

1

There are many myths and misunderstandings surrounding the driving test.
Are the following true or false?

Tick the correct boxes **True False**

1 The driving test is designed ☐ ☐
to see whether I can drive
around a test route without
making any mistakes.

2 The driving test is designed ☐ ☐
to see whether I can drive
safely under various traffic
conditions.

3 I do not need to know any ☐ ☐
of *The Highway Code*.

4 The examiner has a set ☐ ☐
allocation of passes
each week.

5 I may be expected to drive ☐ ☐
up to the maximum national
speed limit, where appropriate.

2

The length of the normal driving test is approximately ...

Tick the correct box

1 60 minutes ☐
2 90 minutes ☐
3 40 minutes ☐

3

If, during the test, you do not understand what the examiner says to you, you would take a guess because you must not talk to him or her.

Is this statement true or false?

Tick the correct box **True** ☐ **False** ☐

4

You may have heard people say that it is easier to pass the driving test in certain parts of the country.

Tick the correct box **YES NO**
Do you agree with this ☐ ☐
statement?

5

If you fail your test, you can take it again. Which of the following statements is correct?

Tick the correct box(es)

1 If you fail the test, you can apply straight
away for another appointment. ☐

2 If you fail the test you have to wait a
month before you can apply for another
appointment. ☐

3 You can re-take your test, subject to
appointment availability, any time. ☐

4 You have to wait 10 working days before
you can re-take the test. ☐

Answers on page 107

6

Before the practical part of your test, the examiner will test your eyesight. This is done by asking you to read a number plate at a distance of ...

Tick the correct box

1 30.5 metres (100 feet) ☐
2 20.5 metres (67 feet) ☐
3 40.5 metres (133 feet) ☐

7

What will happen if you fail your eyesight test?

Answer_____

_____

8

It is essential that you take both sections of your p_ _ _ _ _ _ _ _ _ _ _ l_ _ _ _ _ _ to the test centre. This document must be s_ _ _ _ _ in ink.

Complete the sentence

9

You will also be required to produce another form of identification; this could be a p_ _ _ _ _ _ _ _ , or a photograph signed and authorised by your i_ _ _ _ _ _ _ _ _ _.

Complete the sentence

10

The examiner will expect you to drive without making any mistakes. Do you think this statement is true or false?

Tick the correct box **True** ☐ **False** ☐

11

Is this statement about what you will be asked to do during the test true or false? I will be asked to perform four set exercises:

Tick the correct boxes

	True	False
1 The emergency stop	☐	☐
2 The turn in the road	☐	☐
3 Reversing into a side road on the right or left	☐	☐
4 Reverse parallel parking or reversing into a parking bay .	☐	☐

Answers on page 108

12

When reversing, are you allowed to undo your seat belt?

Tick the correct box **Yes** ☐ **No** ☐

13

If you fail your test, what will the examiner do?

1 _____

_____

2 _____

_____

14

When you have passed your driving test, what are you entitled to do?

1 _____

_____

2 _____

_____

3 _____

_____

15

I have within the last month passed my test.

Can I supervise a learner driver?

Tick the correct box **YES** ☐ **NO** ☐

16

When you pass your test, where should you send your pass certificate?

Answer_____

_____

17

While you are waiting for your full licence to be sent to you, can you drive legally?

Tick the correct box **YES** ☐ **NO** ☐

18

It is recommended that you take further tuition once you have passed your test, especially on motorway driving.

Complete the sentence

As a learner driver you will not have experienced the special r__ __ __ __ that apply on the motorway and the h__ __ __ s__ __ __ __ of the other traffic.

19

While taking your driving test, you should drive ...

Tick the correct box

1 Especially carefully, keeping about 5mph below the speed limit ☐

2 As you would normally drive with your instructor ☐

3 With confidence, keeping at or just over the speed limit, to show that you can really drive ☐

20

Can you take a driving test if you are deaf?

Tick the correct box **YES** ☐ **NO** ☐

Answers on page 108

The driving test ensures that all drivers reach a minimum standard.

1

Do you think that learning to drive ends with passing the test?

Tick the correct box **YES** ☐ **NO** ☐

2

What knowledge and skills are not necessarily assessed in the present driving test?

List three

1 _____

_____

2 _____

_____

3 _____

_____

3

Which of these statements do you think best describes advanced driving?

Tick the correct box

1 Advanced driving is learning to handle your car to its maximum performance. ☐

2 Advanced driving is learning to drive defensively with courtesy and consideration to others. ☐

3 Advanced driving is learning to drive fast. ☐

4

Some people have difficulty in driving at night.
Which age group would you expect, in general, to experience most difficulties?

Tick the correct box

1 Older people ☐
2 Younger people ☐

5

Once you have passed your driving test, your licence is usually valid until you reach __ __ years of age.

Complete the sentence

6

There are particular circumstances under which you are required to take a driving test again. Name them

Answer_____

_____

_____

HINTS ✔ & TIPS

Driving is a skill you can improve for the rest of your life; consider further training after the test.

Answers on page 109

7

Motorways are designed to enable traffic to travel faster in greater safety. Compared to other roads, are they statistically ...

Tick the correct box

1 Safer? ☐
2 Less safe? ☐
3 No different? ☐

8

Are the following groups allowed on the motorway?

Tick the correct boxes

1 Provisional licence holders ☐
2 Motor cycles over 50cc ☐
3 Pedestrians ☐
4 HGV learner drivers ☐
5 Newly qualified drivers with less than three months' experience ☐
6 Motor cycles under 125cc ☐
7 Cyclists ☐

9

There are some routine checks you should carry out on your car before driving on the motorway.
Name four of them

1 _____
_____

2 _____
_____

3 _____
_____

4 _____
_____

10

On the motorway, if something falls from either your own or another vehicle, should you ...

Tick the correct box

1 Flash your headlights to inform other drivers? ☐
2 Pull over, put your hazard warning lights on and quickly run on to the motorway to collect the object? ☐
3 Pull over on to the hard shoulder, use the emergency telephone to call the police? ☐
4 Flag another motorist down to get help? ☐

Answers on page 109

11

Which colour do you associate with motorway signs?

Tick the correct box

1 Black lettering on a white background ☐

2 White lettering on a green background ☐

3 White lettering on a blue background ☐

12

At night or in poor weather conditions, your headlights will pick out reflective studs. Match the colour of the studs to their function by placing the appropriate letter in the box.

A Amber   Marks the edge of the hard shoulder ☐

B Red   Marks the edge of the central reservation ☐

C Green   Marks the lane lines ☐

D White   Marks exits and entrances ☐

13

Do the broken lines at the end of the acceleration lane mean ...

Tick the correct box

1 The edge of the carriageway? ☐

2 Other traffic should let you in? ☐

3 Give way to traffic already on the carriageway? ☐

14

If you see congestion ahead, is it legal to use your hazard warning lights to warn drivers behind you?

Tick the correct box **YES** ☐ **NO** ☐

15

What is the most common cause of accidents on motorways?

Tick the correct box

1 Vehicles breaking down ☐

2 Drivers falling asleep ☐

3 Drivers travelling too fast, too close to the vehicle in front ☐

4 Fog ☐

16

Are the following statements true or false?

I can use the hard shoulder ...

Tick the correct boxes

	True	False
1 To take a short break	☐	☐
2 To stop and read a map	☐	☐
3 To allow the children to stretch their legs	☐	☐
4 To pull over in an emergency	☐	☐
5 To answer a phone call	☐	☐

Answers on pages 109–10

17

In normal driving on the motorway, you should overtake ...

Tick the correct box

1 On the right ☐
2 On the left ☐
3 On either side ☐

Driving at night can cause problems.

18

Which of these statements do you think is correct?

Tick the correct box

1 Street lighting and my car's headlights mean that I can see just as well as in the daylight. Therefore driving at night is just like driving in the daylight. ☐

2 At night I have to rely on my car's headlights and any additional lighting. Therefore I cannot see as far or drive as fast as in the daylight. ☐

19

At dusk and dawn what action should you take to compensate for driving a dark coloured car?

Answer_____

_____

20

When driving after dark in a built-up area, should you use ...

Tick the correct box

1 Dipped headlights? ☐
2 Side or dim-dipped lights? ☐

21

***The Highway Code* says you should not use your horn in a built-up area between 11.30pm and 7am.**

What is the exception to that rule?

Answer_____

_____

22

The diagram below illustrates two vehicles parked at night on a two-way road.

Which one is parked correctly?

Tick the correct box

A ☐   B ☐

Answers on page 110

23

Certain groups of road users are particularly vulnerable at night. Name two of them

1 _____

2 _____

24

Under what circumstances would you use dipped headlights during the day?

Answer_____

_____

and then complete the sentence

S__ __ and b__ s__ __ __.

25

When you are waiting at a junction after dark, your brake lights might d__ __ __ __ __ the driver behind. It is better to use your h__ __ __ __ __ __ __ __.

Complete the sentences

Certain weather conditions can create hazardous driving conditions in the summer as well as in the winter.

26

Which of the following causes greatest danger to drivers?

Tick the correct box

1 Snow ☐

2 Ice ☐

3 Heavy rain ☐

4 Not being able to see properly ☐

27

In wet weather conditions your tyres can lose their grip. You should allow at least d__ __ __ __ __ the distance between you and the car in front that you allow on a dry road.

Fill in the missing word

28

In very wet conditions there is a danger of a build-up of water between your tyres and the road. This is called a__ __ __ __ __ __ __ __ __ __.

Fill in the missing word

Answers on page 110

29

How can you prevent a build-up of water occurring?

S__ __ __ d__ __ __ .

30

How should you deal with floods?

Tick the correct box

1 Drive through as fast as possible to avoid stopping ☐

2 Drive through slowly in 1st gear, slipping the clutch to keep the engine speed high ☐

3 Drive through in the highest gear possible, slipping the clutch to keep the engine speed high ☐

31

Will less tread on your tyres ...

Tick the correct box

1 Increase your braking distance? ☐

2 Decrease your braking distance? ☐

32

When the tyres lose contact with the road, the steering will feel v__ __ __ l__ __ __ __.

Complete the sentence

33

After you have driven through a flood, should you check ...

Tick the correct box

1 Your speedometer? ☐

2 Your brakes? ☐

3 Your oil? ☐

34

There are certain key precautions you should take when driving in fog.

Complete the following sentences

1 S__ __ __ d__ __ __.

2 Ensure you are able to s__ __ __ within the distance you can see to be clear.

3 Use your w__ __ __ __ __ __ __ __ __ w__ __ __ __ __.

4 Use your d__ __ __ __ __ __ __ and your h__ __ __ __ __ r__ __ __ w__ __ __ __ __ __ __ __ __.

35

Under what circumstances should you use your rear fog lights?

When visibility is less than _____ metres/yards

Fill in the correct number

Answers on page 110

36

When you are following another vehicle in fog, should you ...

Tick the correct box

1 Follow closely behind because it will help you see where you are going? ☐

2 Leave plenty of room between you and the vehicle in front? ☐

37

When you are following another vehicle in fog, should you use ...

Tick the correct box

1 Main beam headlights? ☐

2 Dipped headlights? ☐

38

Extra precautions are needed when dealing with a junction in fog.

Complete the following sentences

1 Open your w_ _ _ _ _ _ and switch off your a_ _ _ _ s_ _ _ _ _ _. L_ _ _ _ _ for other vehicles.

2 Signal e_ _ _ _ _ .

3 Use your b_ _ _ _ _. The light will a_ _ _ _ following vehicles.

4 Use your h_ _ _ if you think it will w_ _ _ other road users.

39

Is the following statement about anti-lock brakes true or false?

Anti-lock brakes will stop me skidding when driving on snow or ice.

Tick the correct box **True** ☐ **False** ☐

40

When driving in snow or ice you should gently test your b_ _ _ _ _ from time to time.

Fill in the missing word

41

In order to slow down when driving on snow or ice you should ...

Fill in the missing words

1 Use your brakes g_ _ _ _ _ .

2 Get into a l_ _ _ _ g_ _ _ earlier than normal.

3 Allow your speed to d_ _ _ and use b_ _ _ _ _ gently and early.

42

On snow or ice, braking distances can increase by ...

Tick the correct box

1 10 times ☐

2 5 times ☐

3 20 times ☐

4 15 times ☐

Answers on page 111

43

When going downhill in snow, what would you do to help you slow down?

Answer_____

_____

_____

44

When cornering in snow or ice, what should you avoid doing?

Answer_____

_____

_____

45

How can you reduce the risk of wheel spin?

Answer_____

_____

_____

46

Three important factors cause a skid. Name them.

1 _____

_____

_____

2 _____

_____

_____

3 _____

_____

_____

47

Some everyday driving actions, especially in poor weather, can increase the risk of skidding.

Fill in the missing words

1 S_ _ _ _ _ _ down.

2 S_ _ _ _ _ _ _ up.

3 T_ _ _ _ _ _ corners.

4 Driving u_ _ _ _ _ and

d_ _ _ _ _ _ _.

HINTS ✔ & TIPS

If you realise that your car is starting to skid, ease off the brake and accelerator, then steer smoothly in the same direction as the skid.

Answers on page 111

All vehicles need routine attention and maintenance to keep them in good working order. Neglecting maintenance can be costly and dangerous.

1

With which of these statements do you agree?

Tick the correct box

1 Allowing the fuel gauge to drop too low is bad for the engine. ☐

2 In modern cars the fuel level makes little difference. ☐

2

What do you put into the engine to lubricate the moving parts?

Answer_____

_____

_____

3

How frequently should you check your oil level?

Tick the correct box

1 Once a month ☐

2 Once a year ☐

3 Every time you fill up with fuel ☐

4

The engine is often cooled by a mixture of w_ _ _ _ and a_ _ _ _ f_ _ _ _ _.

Some engines are a_ _ cooled.

Complete the sentence

5

How frequently should you test your brakes?

Tick the correct box

1 Daily ☐

2 Monthly ☐

3 Weekly ☐

4 When I use them ☐

6

Incorrectly adjusted headlamps can cause d_ _ _ _ _ to other road users.

Complete the sentence

7

All headlamps, indicators and brake lights should be kept in good working order. It is also important that they are kept c_ _ _ _ .

Fill in the missing word

Answers on page 111

8

Tyres should be checked for u_ _ _ _ _ wear and tyre walls for b_ _ _ _ _ and c_ _ _.

Complete the sentence

9

The legal requirement for tread depth is not less than ...

Tick the correct box

1 1.4mm ☐

2 1.6mm ☐

3 2mm ☐

10

What should you do if your brakes feel slack or spongy?

Answer_____

_____

_____

11

Vehicle breakdowns could result from ...

Fill in the missing words

1 N_ _ _ _ _ _ of the vehicle

2 Lack of r_ _ _ _ _ _ _

   c_ _ _ _ _ _

3 Little or no

   p_ _ _ _ _ _ _ _ _ _ _

   maintenance

4 A_ _ _ _ of the vehicle

Answers on page 111

12

It is advisable to carry a warning triangle.

1 On a straight road how far back should it be placed?

Tick the correct box

50 metres/yards ☐

200 metres/yards ☐

150 metres/yards ☐

2 On a dual carriageway, how far back should it be placed? At least ...

Tick the correct box

200 metres/yards ☐

150 metres/yards ☐

450 metres/yards ☐

13

If you use a warning triangle, is it worth putting your hazard lights on as well?

Tick the correct box **YES** ☐ **NO** ☐

14

If your vehicle breaks down on a motorway, should you ...

Tick the correct box

1 Gently brake, put your hazard lights on and seek assistance? ☐

2 Pull over to the central reservation as far to the right as possible? ☐

3 Pull over safely on to the hard shoulder as far away from the carriageway as possible? ☐

15

If your vehicle has broken down on the motorway, should you tell your passengers to ...

Tick the correct box

1 Stay in the vehicle while you seek assistance? ☐

2 Wait by the car on the hard shoulder but watch for other vehicles? ☐

3 Get out of the vehicle and wait on the embankment away from the hard shoulder? ☐

16

The marker posts at the side of all motorways have a picture of a telephone handset.
How can you tell which way to walk to reach the nearest telephone?
Answer_____
_____
_____

17

When you use the emergency telephone on a motorway, what will the operator ask you?

1 _____
_____
_____

2 _____
_____
_____

3 _____
_____
_____

4 _____
_____
_____

18

Disabled drivers cannot easily get to an emergency telephone. How can they summon help?

1 _____
_____
_____

2 _____
_____
_____

Answers on page 112

19

If you break down when travelling alone, there are three things you are advised NOT to do.

Complete the sentences

1 Do not ask p__ __ __ __ __ __
   m__ __ __ __ __ __ __ __ for help.
2 Do not accept help from anyone you
   d__ n__ __ k__ __ __ (except the
   emergency services or a breakdown
   service).
3 Do not l__ __ __ __ you vehicle
   l__ __ __ __ __ than necessary.

20

If I am first or one of the first to arrive at the scene of an accident, should I ...

Tick the correct boxes

	True	False
1 Always move injured people away from vehicles?	☐	☐
2 Tell the ambulance personnel or paramedics what I think is wrong with those injured?	☐	☐
3 Give casualties something warm to drink?	☐	☐
4 Switch off hazard warning lights?	☐	☐
5 Switch off vehicle engines?	☐	☐
6 Inform the police of the accident?	☐	☐

Answers on page 112

21

If you are involved in an accident, what MUST you do?

Answer_____

_____

_____

22

If you are involved in an accident and nobody is injured, do you have to call the police?

Tick the correct box **YES** ☐ **NO** ☐

23

What information do you need to exchange if you are involved in an accident?

1 _____
   _____
   _____

2 _____
   _____
   _____

3 _____
   _____
   _____

4_____
   _____

5 _____
   _____
   _____

24

If you thought you had a fire in your car's engine, what action would you take?

1 _____
  _____
  _____

2 _____
  _____
  _____

3 _____
  _____
  _____

25

There are three items of emergency equipment it is wise to carry in your car.

Fill in the missing words

1 F_ _ _ _ A_ _ kit.
2 F_ _ _
  e_ _ _ _ _ _ _ _ _ _ _ _ _.
3 W_ _ _ _ _ _ _ t_ _ _ _ _ _

26

When you rejoin a motorway from the hard shoulder, should you ...

Tick the correct box

1 Signal right and join when there is safe gap? ☐

2 Keep your hazard lights on and drive down the hard shoulder until there is a safe gap? ☐

3 Use the hard shoulder to build up speed and join the carriageway when safe? ☐

27

Fuel combustion causes waste products. One of these is a gas called

c_ _ _ _ _ d_ _ _ _ _ _.

This is a major cause of the

g_ _ _ _ _ _ _ _ _ _ **effect.**

Complete the sentences

28

How much does transport contribute to the production of carbon dioxide in the country (expressed as a percentage of the total production)?

Tick the correct box

1 10 per cent ☐
2 25 per cent ☐
3 50 per cent ☐
4 20 per cent ☐

Answers on page 113

29

The MOT test checks the roadworthiness of a vehicle.

Does it include an exhaust emission test?

Tick the correct box **YES** ☐ **NO** ☐

30

A catalytic convertor stops the emission of carbon dioxide.

Tick the correct box **True** ☐ **False** ☐

31

Which uses up more fuel?

Tick the correct box

1 A car travelling at 50mph ☐

2 A car travelling at 70mph ☐

32

There are some measures car drivers can take to help reduce damage to the environment.

List five

1 _____

_____

2 _____

_____

3 _____

_____

4 _____

_____

5 _____

_____

Before buying a used car it is best to decide what you want the car for and how much you can afford.

33

There are three main sources of supply for used vehicles. You can buy from a

d_ _ _ _ _, at an a_ _ _ _ _ _

or p_ _ _ _ _ _ _ _.

Complete the sentence

34

When reading a glowing description of a used car, what should you first consider?

Answer_____

_____

_____

Answers on page 113

35

Are these statements about buying a used car through a dealer or at an auction true or false?

Tick the correct boxes   **True False**

1 It is often cheaper to buy a ☐ ☐
car at an auction than
through a dealer.

2 I have the same legal rights ☐ ☐
when I buy at an auction as
when I buy from a dealer.

3 I should always read the ☐ ☐
terms and conditions of
trade before I buy a car
at an auction.

4 The best way to select a ☐ ☐
used car dealer is by
recommendation.

36

Cars bought through a dealer often have a warranty.
What should you check?

1 _____

_____

_____

2 _____

_____

_____

37

When you test drive a vehicle, you should make sure that it is t_ _ _ _, has a current M_ _ certificate (if applicable) and that all i_ _ _ _ _ _ _ _ requirements are complied with.

Complete the sentence

38

There are some important items that you should check on before you buy a used car.
List three

1 _____

_____

_____

2 _____

_____

_____

3 _____

_____

_____

39

Do you think the following statement is true or false?
It is advisable to have my vehicle examined by a competent and unbiased expert before I buy.

Tick the correct box **True** ☐ **False** ☐

Answers on page 113

Particular difficulties are encountered when towing a caravan or trailer. There are some very good courses which will help you master the skills required.

1

People can underestimate the length of the total combination of car and caravan or trailer.
Is the overall length usually ...
Tick the correct box
1 Twice the length of a normal car? ☐
2 Three times the length of a normal car? ☐

2

What additional fixtures should you attach to your car to help you see more clearly?
1 _____
_____
_____

Answers on page 114

3

When towing you will need more distance than normal to overtake. Is it ...
Tick the correct box
1 Twice the normal distance? ☐
2 Three times the normal distance? ☐
3 Four times the normal distance? ☐

4

A device called a s_ _ _ _ _ _ _ _ _ _ will make the combination safer to handle.
Fill in the missing word

5

The stability of the caravan will depend on how you load it. Should heavy items be loaded ...
Tick the correct box
1 At the front? ☐
2 At the rear? ☐
3 Over the axle(s)? ☐

6

There are special restrictions for vehicles which are towing.
A What is the speed limit on a dual carriageway?
Tick the correct box
1 50mph ☐
2 60mph ☐
3 70mph ☐

B What is the speed on a single carriageway?

Tick the correct box

1 40mph ☐
2 50mph ☐
3 60mph ☐

7

**There are some important checks you should make before starting off.
List four**

1 _____
_____

2 _____
_____

3 _____
_____

4 _____
_____

8

**If you decide to stop to take a break, before allowing anyone to enter the caravan you should lower the
j_ _ _ _ _ _ w_ _ _ _ _ and
c_ _ _ _ _ _ s_ _ _ _ _ _ _ _.**

Fill in the missing words

Many people now take their car abroad or hire a vehicle when on holiday.

9

**Motoring organisations, such as The Automobile Association, can help you plan and organise your trip.
The AA can provide advice on travel and v_ _ _ _ _ _ insurance.
They will also help you organise the
d_ _ _ _ _ _ _ _ that you
will need.**

Fill in the missing words

10

Before travelling to Europe, you should always ...

Complete the sentences

1 Plan the r_ _ _ _ you wish to take.
2 Know the local m_ _ _ _ _ _ _ _
  r_ _ _ _ _ _ _ _ _ _ _.

Answers on page 114

11

It is essential that your vehicle should be checked thoroughly.
List four of the routine checks you should make

1 _____
_____
_____

2 _____
_____
_____

3 _____
_____
_____

4 _____
_____
_____

12

In most European countries you are advised to carry your d__ __ __ __ __ __
l__ __ __ __ __ __ on you.
Complete the sentence

13

What do the letters IDP stand for?
Answer_____
_____
_____

14

Where might you need an IDP?
Answer_____
_____
_____

15

In most European countries what age do you have to be to drive?
Tick the correct box
1 ☐ 21 **2** ☐ 18 **3** ☐ 16

16

Some European countries can require you to carry additional emergency equipment.
List four of the items you are recommended to carry

1 _____
_____
_____

2 _____
_____
_____

3 _____
_____
_____

4 _____
_____
_____

Answers on page 114

Answers to Questions

Answers to Questions

Section 1

INTRODUCTION TO LEARNING TO DRIVE

Questions on pages 24–5

A1 A current, signed, full or provisional licence for the category of vehicle that you are driving

A2 examinations
register

A3 21 years old
three years

A4 To the front and rear. It is important not to place them in windows where they could restrict good vision.

A5 True

A6 You should have answered No to all the questions.

A7 Yes. This should be the ambition of every driver.

A8 3, 4

ADJUSTING YOUR DRIVING POSITION

Questions on page 25

A9 **1** handbrake
2 doors
3 seat
4 head restraint
5 mirrors
6 seat belt

INTRODUCTION TO VEHICLE CONTROLS

Questions on pages 25–6

A10 The handbrake E
The driving mirrors D
The gear lever F
The clutch G
The steering wheel A
The foot-brake B
The accelerator C

A11 The foot-brake R
The clutch L
The accelerator R

A12 **1** False. You will need one hand to change gear or use other controls.
2 True
3 False. The best position is quarter to three or ten to two.
4 False. It is safest to feed the wheel through your hands.
5 True
6 True

A13 The direction indicators B
Dipped beam A
Main beam D
Rear fog lamp C
Horn E
Hazard lights F

Section 2

MOVING OFF

Questions on page 27

A1
  A 1
  B 5
  C 3
  D 2
  E 6
  F 4
  G 7
  H 8
  I 9

STOPPING (NORMALLY)

Questions on page 28

A2
  A 1
  B 3
  C 2
  D 4
  E 6
  F 5
  G 8
  H 7
  I 9

GEAR CHANGING

Questions on pages 29–30

A3   1st gear

A4   5th, or 4th if the car has a 4-speed gear box

A5   Usually 2nd gear, but 1st if you need to go very slowly or 3rd if the corner is sweeping and you can take it safely at a higher speed

A6   engine
         vehicle
         sound
         when

A7
  A 1
  B 3
  C 2
  D 4
  E 5

Answers to Questions

A8   **1** False. This will cause the engine to labour.
2 False. It is good practice to use the brakes to slow the car down. Using the transmission causes wear and tear which can be very costly. Also, the brakes are more effective.
3 False
4 True
5 False. It is good practice to miss out the unwanted gears and select the gear most appropriate to your road speed.

A9   **1**
A10   **1** Don't
2 Don't
3 Do
4 Do
5 Do
6 Don't
7 Don't
8 Don't

STEERING
Questions on page 31

A11   **A**, except in a few cars fitted with four-wheel steering (in which case all four wheels will move)
A12   **A**
A13   **B**
A14   **B**

ROAD POSITIONING
Questions on page 31

A15   **C** well to the left but not too close to the kerb
A16   **B**. Avoid swerving in and out. It is unnecessary and confuses other drivers.

CLUTCH CONTROL
Questions on page 32

A17   **A**
A18   biting
A19   **1** Yes
2 Yes
3 No
4 Yes
5 No

Section 3

JUNCTIONS

Questions on pages 33–5

A1 two or more roads

A2 **A** T-junction
     B Y-junction
     C Roundabout
     D Staggered crossroads
     E Crossroads

A3 **1** E
     2 C
     3 B
     4 D
     5 A

A4 **A** 1
     B 3

A5 **1** Mirrors
     2 Signal
     3 Position
     4 Speed
     5 Look

A6 assess
     decide
     act

A7 **A**

A8 **B**

A9 **D**

A10 **1** mirrors, position
     2 signal
     3 safe
     4 safe distance
     5 overtake

CROSSROADS

Questions on page 36

A11 **A 3** Crossroads. Priority for traffic on the major road. Never assume other drivers will give you priority.
     B 1 Unmarked crossroads
     C 2 Crossroads with give way lines at the end of your road. Give way to traffic on the major road.

ROUNDABOUTS

Questions on pages 36–7

A12 **C**

A13 **1** Left
     2 Left
     3 Right. Remember to use the MSM routine before signalling left to turn off.

A14 **1** Left
     2 Going ahead
     3 Right

A15 mirrors
     signal
     position
     speed
     look

A16 **2**

Answers to Questions

Section 4

PARKING (ON THE ROAD)
Questions on pages 38–9

A1 **1** safe
      2 considerate
      3 legal
A2 Cars 1, 2, 3, 6
A3 **1** False
      2 False
      3 True
      4 True
A4 Any of the following:
      at a bus stop
      at a school entrance
      opposite a junction
      on a bend
      on the brow of a hill
      on a Clearway
      on a motorway
      at night facing oncoming traffic
      in a residents' parking zone.

Section 5

PASSING STATIONARY VEHICLES AND OBSTRUCTIONS

Questions on page 40

A1 Vehicle 2
A2 Vehicle 2, even though the obstruction is on the right. Where safe, when travelling downhill be prepared to give priority to vehicles (especially heavy vehicles) that are coming uphill.

MEETING AND CROSSING THE PATH OF OTHER VEHICLES
Questions on pages 41

A3 **1** True
      2 False. Always consider whether it is safe. Are there dangers the other driver cannot see? Remember, flashing headlamps has the same meaning as sounding the horn. It is a warning: 'I am here!' Sometimes it is taken to mean: 'I am here and I am letting you pass.'
      3 True
A4 **1** Yes
      2 Yes
      3 No
      4 Yes
      5 Yes
      6 Yes
      7 Yes

Section 6

STOPPING IN AN EMERGENCY

Questions on pages 42–3

A1 **1** True
2 True
3 True
4 False. Looking in the mirror should not be necessary. You should know what is behind you.
5 False
6 True
7 True

A2 False. An emergency stop will be conducted randomly on only some tests. You must always know how to stop safely in an emergency.

A3 pump
1 maximum
2 lock
3 quickly

A4 steer
brake
pump
pressure
1 False. Other elements beyond braking can cause skidding e.g. acceleration or going too fast into a bend.
2 False. Although you may stop in a shorter distance, you still need to leave the correct distance to allow yourself time to react and vehicles behind you time to stop.

STOPPING DISTANCES

Questions on pages 43

A5 **1** No
2 Yes
3 Yes
4 No

A6 ½ second

A7 **1** 23 metres/75 feet
2 15 metres/50 feet
3 96 metres/315 feet

A8 longer
more

A9 breaks
two-second

Answers to Questions

Section 7

MOVING OFF AT AN ANGLE

Question on page 44

A1   **1** False. You should check your mirrors and blindspot before moving out. Keep alert for other traffic as you pull out and stop if necessary.
2 True
3 False. Move out slowly and carefully.
4 True. The closer you are, the greater the angle.
5 True. As you move out, you are likely to move on to the right-hand side of the road and into conflict with oncoming vehicles.
6 False. You should signal only if it helps or warns other road users. Signalling gives you no right to pull out.

MOVING OFF UPHILL

Question on page 44

A2   **1** True
2 False. Using the accelerator pedal will not move the car forwards.

3 False. As your feet will be using the clutch pedal and the accelerator pedal you need to use the handbrake to stop the car rolling back.
4 True
5 True
6 True
7 True

MOVING OFF DOWNHILL

Question on page 45

A3   **1** True
2 False. Almost certainly you will need to use the foot-brake.
3 False. It is often better to move off in 2nd gear.
4 True. This will stop the car rolling forwards.
5 True
6 False. You will need to have your foot on the foot-brake to stop the car rolling forwards.

APPROACHING JUNCTIONS UPHILL AND DOWNHILL

Question on page 46

A4   The following statements are correct: 1, 4, 5, 6, 7

Section 8

REVERSING

Questions on pages 47–8

A1   safe
      convenient
      law

A2   **1** False
      2 False
      3 True
      4 True

A3   **A**

A4   **1, 4**

A5   Car A: to the left
      Car B: to the right

A6   observation

REVERSING INTO A SIDE ROAD ON THE LEFT

Questions on pages 48–9

A7   **3**

A8   **1** True
      2 False
      3 True

A9   **4**

A10   **C**

A11   Left

A12   The front of the car will swing out to the right

A13   **1** True
      2 False
      3 True

A14   pedestrians
      road users
      stop

REVERSING INTO A SIDE ROAD ON THE RIGHT

Questions on pages 49–50

A15   True

A16   **B**

A17   **2**

A18   True. You may need to place your left hand at 12 o'clock and lower your right hand.

A19   True

A20   **2**

A21   **B**

Answers to Questions

TURNING IN THE ROAD

Questions on pages 51–2

A22 **A**

A23 slowly
briskly

A24 False, but you should try to complete the manoeuvre in as few moves as possible.

A25 **2, 3, 4**

A26 all round

A27 **1** Right
2 Steer briskly left
3 Left
4 Steer briskly right
5 Right

A28 **1** Left
2 Over your right shoulder to where the car is going

REVERSE PARALLEL PARKING

Questions on pages 52–4

A29 **2**

A30 **C**, in line with the rear of the parked vehicle

A31 **2**

A32 **1** To the left
2 The nearside headlamp of the vehicle towards which you are reversing
3 Clipping the rear offside of the lead car
4 Take off the left lock
5 Steer to the right and then take off the right lock as you get straight

A33 **1** False
2 False
3 True. You will be expected to be able to complete the exercise within approximately two car lengths.

A34 All round, particularly for pedestrians and oncoming vehicles

A35 **C**. The other bay widths are reduced by parked vehicles. This may make opening doors a squeeze.

A36 Allows you to make best use of the area in front of the bay. Gives you a better view when driving out of the space

A37 close
directions
pedestrians

Section 9

TRAFFIC LIGHTS AND YELLOW BOX JUNCTIONS

Questions on pages 55–6

A1 **1** red
2 red and amber
3 green
4 amber
5 red

A2 **1** green
2 red and amber
3 amber
4 red

A3 **1** False
2 True
3 True
4 False. Pedestrians who are already crossing have priority.

A4 **2**

A5 **1** Lane A or B
2 Lane C
3 Lane A

A6 **1** No. If your exit is blocked you should not enter a yellow box junction.
2 No. If your exit is blocked you should not enter a yellow box junction.
3 Yes

PEDESTRIAN CROSSINGS

Questions on pages 56–8

A7 **1** Zig-zag lines
2 Flashing yellow beacons on both sides of the road
3 Black and white stripes on the crossing
4 A give way line

A8 **1** True
2 True. You must not park or wait on the zig-zag lines on either side of the crossing.
3 False. You must not overtake on the zig-zag lines on approach to the crossing.
4 True
5 True. A slowing down arm signal should be used. It helps pedestrians understand what you intend to do. They cannot see your brake lights.

A9 **1** Traffic lights
2 Zig-zag lines
3 A white stop line

A10 **2** A white stick means the pedestrian is visually handicapped. A white stick with two reflector bands means the pedestrian may be deaf as well as visually handicapped.

Answers to Questions

A11   **1** Flashing amber
2 You must give way to pedestrians on the crossing, but if it is clear you may go on.

A12   A bleeping tone. This sounds when the red light shows to drivers and helps visually handicapped pedestrians know when it is safe to cross.

A13   There is no flashing amber light sequence. The light sequence is the same as normal traffic lights.

A14   cyclists

LEVEL CROSSINGS

Questions on page 58

A15   **A** 3
         B 1
         C 2
         D 4

A16   **2**
         4
         5

ONE-WAY SYSTEMS

Questions on page 59

A1   **A** is the correct sign for a one-way street.
        B tells you 'Ahead only'.

A2   **1** True
        2 True
        3 True
        4 True

ROAD MARKINGS

Questions on pages 59–61

A3   information
        warnings
        orders

A4   **1** They can be seen when other signs may be hidden
        2 They give a continuing message

A5   **A** 2
        B 2

A6   **1, 4**

A7   They are used to separate potentially dangerous streams of traffic.

A8   You must not enter the hatched area.

Answers to Questions

TRAFFIC SIGNS

Questions on pages 61

A9   **1** Warning
     2 Order
     3 Information

A10 **1** must
      2 must not

A11 **1** You must give way to traffic on the major road. Delay your entry until it is safe to join the major road.
      2 You must stop (even if the road is clear). Wait until you can enter the new road safely.

A12 vision is limited

A13 Motorway signs D
      Primary routes E
      Other routes B
      Local places C
      Tourist signs A

Section 11

ROAD OBSERVATION

Questions on pages 62–4

A1   speed
     behaviour
     intentions

A2   **1** Observe that the view into the new road is restricted.
The driver should ...
Move forward slowly, to get a better view.
Note the pedestrian who may walk in front of or behind car **A**.
Note the pedestrian waiting to cross.
Allow the cyclist to pass.
Once in position to see car **B**, stop and give way.
2 Observe that the parked car restricts the view into and out of the side road.
The driver should ...

Slow down on approach to parked car **P**.

Take up position to gain a better view and be more visible to car A and the pedestrian.

Slow down in case the pedestrian walks out from behind the parked car **P**.

Consider signal to pass parked car **P**. Look carefully into minor road. Note the actions of car **A**. Be prepared to stop.

A3 bike

A4 **3**, but touching the brakes may encourage the driver to drop back

A5 **A**
1 Junctions
2 Hump-back bridges
3 Concealed entrances
4 Dead ground
5 Narrow lanes

B
1 Children playing
2 Horses
3 Pedestrians
4 Especially elderly and young cyclists
5 Other vehicles

A6 1 True. The ability to advise those at your destination of delays can help to reduce the worry of late arrivals
2 True
3 True
4 True

A7 All are distracting and upset concentration, and should not be carried out while driving.

DEALING WITH BENDS
Questions on pages 64–5

A8 speed
gear
position

A9 **1**

A10 **B**

A11 **A**

A12 **A** On a right-hand bend keep to the left. This will help to improve your view.
B On a left-hand bend keep to the centre of the lane. Do not move to the centre of the road to get a better view. A vehicle travelling in the opposite direction may be taking the bend wide.

OVERTAKING

Questions on pages 65–6

A13 necessary
1 Mirrors
2 Position
3 Speed
4 Look
5 Mirrors
6 Signal
7 Manoeuvre

A14 About the width of a small car, more in windy or poor weather conditions

A15 1 The vehicle in front is signalling and positioned to turn right
2 You are using the correct lane to turn left at a junction
3 Traffic is moving slowly in queues and the traffic on the right is moving more slowly than you are
4 You are in a one-way street

A16 1 On approach to a junction
2 The brow of a hill
3 The approach to a bend
4 Where there is dead ground.
NB These are examples. Be guided by *The Highway Code*.

DUAL CARRIAGEWAYS

Questions on pages 66–7

A17 2 Statements 1, 3, 4 and 5 do not apply:
1 Reflective studs are used on some dual carriageways.
3 The speed limit is subject to local conditions and may vary from 40mph up to the national speed limit.
4 You can turn right on to and off dual carriageways unlike motorways, where all traffic enters and leaves on the left.
5 You may find slow moving vehicles sometimes displaying a flashing amber light.

A18 **A** You would cross over the first carriageway then wait in the gap in the central reservation. Be careful, if you are towing or if your vehicle is long, that you do not cause other road users to change course or slow down.

Answers to Questions

B You would wait until there is a gap in the traffic long enough for you safely to clear the first carriageway and emerge into the second.

A19 The speed limit applies to all lanes. Use the first lane to travel in and the second for overtaking.

A20 **A** Dual carriageway ends
B Road narrows on both sides
C Two-way traffic straight ahead

A21 **A** and **C**

A22 Traffic is moving much faster, and one or more lanes will have to be crossed.

DRIVING AN AUTOMATIC CAR

Questions on pages 68–9

A1 Clutch

A2 **1** Driving is easier
2 There is more time to concentrate on the road

A3 Park – Locks the transmission. This should be selected only when the vehicle is stationary.
Reverse – Enables the car to go backwards, as in a manual car.
Neutral – Has the same function as in a manual car. The engine is not in contact with the driving wheels.
Drive – Is used for driving forwards. It automatically selects the most appropriate gear.
3rd – Has the same function as manual gears
2nd – Has the same function as manual gears
1st – Has the same function as manual gears

A4 **3**

A5   **1** Yes
         2 No
         3 Yes, if you needed extra control
         4 You would probably use kickdown, but possibly in certain circumstances you would manually select a lower gear
         5 Yes, maybe using 1st gear
         6 No. Use the brakes

A6   **1** The right foot
         2 The right foot

A7   It stops you trying to control the brake and accelerator at the same time. It encourages early release of the accelerator and progressive braking.

A8   Drive, reverse, all forward gears.

A9   **1** You should apply the handbrake every time you stop. Otherwise you have to keep your foot on the foot-brake.

A10 Park (P) or Neutral (N)

A11 **1**

Section 13

THE DRIVING TEST

Questions on pages 70–2

A1   **1** False
         2 True
         3 False
         4 False
         5 True

A2   **3**

A3   False. If you did not hear clearly or did not understand what the examiner said, you should ask him or her to repeat the instruction. If you have any problem with your hearing, it is advisable to tell the examiner at the start of the test.

A4   No. The standard test does not vary. The test result should be the same wherever it is taken.

A5   **1, 4**

Answers to Questions

A6 2

A7 The test will not proceed. You have failed not only the eyesight section, but the whole test. Remember, if you wear glasses or contact lenses, to wear them for the eyesight test and for the rest of the driving test.

A8 provisional licence
signed

A9 passport
instructor

A10 False. You can make some minor errors and still reach the required standard.

A11 False. Only about one third of test candidates will be asked to complete an emergency stop. You will be asked to do two out of the three reversing manoeuvres.

A12 Yes, but remember to do it up again when you have completed the exercise.

A13 **1** Give you a verbal explanation of the main reasons for failure
2 Write out a form for you to take away showing you your main errors

A14 **1** Drive unsupervised
2 Drive on a motorway
3 Drive without L-plates

A15 No. You must have had at least three years' driving experience (and be over 21 years of age).

A16 To the DVLA, Swansea

A17 Yes. It is a good idea to keep a note of your driver number and the date you passed your test.

A18 rules
high speed

A19 **2** The examiner will expect you to drive normally. You should abide by all speed limits and drive according to road and traffic conditions.

A20 Yes. The examiner will be skilled in giving instructions and directions to deaf candidates.

Section 14

BEYOND THE TEST

Questions on page 73

A1   No

A2   **1** Bad weather driving

2 Night-time driving

3 Motorway driving

4 Skid control … and more

A3   **2**

A4   **1**, although people of any age can find it difficult to drive at night

A5   70

A6   There are certain serious driving offences which carry the penalty of disqualification. In order to regain a full licence, the disqualified driver has to apply for a provisional licence and take an extended test. If, because of certain illnesses, you have been unable to drive for 10 years, you will be required to take the test again in order to gain a full licence.

For new drivers: the accumulation of six or more penalty points within two years of passing the test will mean reverting to a provisional licence and re-sitting the test.

MOTORWAY DRIVING

Questions on pages 74–6

A7   **1**

A8   **1** No

2 Yes

3 No

4 Yes

5 Yes

6 Yes

7 No

A9   **1** Oil

2 Water

3 Fuel

4 Tyre pressures

These are just some of the checks; for more information, refer to your car's manual.

A10   **3** You should never attempt to retrieve anything from the carriageway.

A11   **3**

A12   **B** Amber

A Red

D Green

C White

A13   **3**

A14   Yes

Answers to Questions

A15 3

A16 1 False
2 False
3 False
4 True
5 False

A17 1, except when traffic is moving slowly in queues and the queue on the right is travelling more slowly

SAFE NIGHT DRIVING

Questions on pages 76–7

A18 2

A19 Switch on earlier, switch off later.

A20 1. It helps others to see you.

A21 If you are stationary, to avoid danger from a moving vehicle.

A22 A. Always park with the flow of traffic. You will show red reflectors to vehicles travelling in your direction.

A23 1 Pedestrians
2 Cyclists } two of these
3 Motor cyclists

A24 In poor weather conditions – see and be seen

A25 dazzle
handbrake

ALL-WEATHER DRIVING

Questions on pages 77–80

A26 4

A27 double

A28 aquaplaning

A29 Slow down
Allow time for the tread patterns to disperse the water.

A30 2

A31 1

A32 very light

A33 2

A34 1 Slow down
2 stop
3 windscreen wipers
4 demister, heated rear windscreen

A35 100 metres/yards

A36 2

A37 2

A38 **1** windows, audio system.
Listen
2 early
3 brakes, alert
4 horn, warn

A39 False, because your tyres are not in contact with the road

A40 brakes

A41 **1** gently
2 lower gear
3 drop, brakes

A42 1

A43 If possible, control your speed before reaching the hill. Select a low gear early.

A44 Using your brakes

A45 Avoid harsh acceleration

A46 **1** The driver
2 The vehicle
3 The road conditions

A47 **1** Slowing
2 Speeding
3 Turning
4 uphill, downhill

Section 15

VEHICLE CARE
Questions on pages 81–2

A1 **1**

A2 Oil

A3 **3**

A4 Water, anti-freeze, air

A5 **1**

A6 dazzle

A7 clean

A8 uneven, bulges, cuts

A9 **2**

A10 Get them checked as quickly as possible

BREAKDOWNS, ACCIDENTS AND EMERGENCIES
Questions on pages 82–5

A11 **1** Neglect
2 routine checks
3 preventative
4 abuse

A12 **1** 50 metres/yards
2 At least 150 metres/yards

A13 Yes. Try to give as much warning as possible.

A14 **3**

Answers to Questions

A15 3

A16 Under the drawing of the handset is an arrow which points to the nearest telephone.

A17 **1** The emergency number (painted on the box)
2 Vehicle details (make, registration mark, colour)
3 Membership details of your motoring organisation
4 Details of the fault

A18 **1** By displaying a Help pennant
2 By using a mobile telephone

A19 **1** passing motorists
2 do not know
3 leave, longer

A20 **1** False. Do not move injured people unless they are in danger.
2 False. Tell them the facts, not what you think is wrong.
3 False. Do not give those injured anything to eat or drink. Keep them warm and reassure them.
4 False. Keep hazard lights on to warn other drivers.
5 True. Switch off engines. Put out cigarettes.
6 True, in the case of injury.

A21 Stop

A22 No

A23 **1** The other driver's name, address and contact number
2 The registration numbers of all vehicles involved
3 The make of the other car
4 The other driver's insurance details
5 If the driver is not the owner, the owner's details.

A24 **1** Pull up quickly

       2 Get all passengers out

       3 Call assistance

A25 **1** First aid

       2 Fire extinguisher

       3 Warning triangle

A26 **3**

THE MOTOR CAR AND THE ENVIRONMENT

Questions on pages 85–6

A27 carbon dioxide, greenhouse

A28 **4**

A29 Yes

A30 False. A catalytic convertor reduces the level of carbon monoxide, nitrogen oxide and hydrocarbons by up to 90 per cent. Carbon dioxide is still produced.

A31 **2**

A32 Nine measures are listed here:

       1 Make sure your vehicle is in good condition and regularly serviced.

       2 Make sure tyres are correctly inflated. Under-inflated tyres waste fuel.

       3 Push the choke in as soon as possible when starting from cold.

       4 Avoid harsh braking.

       5 Buy a fuel-efficient vehicle.

       6 Use the most appropriate gear.

       7 Use your accelerator sensibly and avoid harsh acceleration.

       8 Use unleaded fuel.

       9 Dispose of waste oil, old batteries and used tyres sensibly.

BUYING A USED CAR

Questions on pages 86–7

A33 dealer, auction, privately

A34 Why is it being sold?

A35 **1** True

       2 False

       3 True

       4 True

A36 **1** What is covered

       2 The length of the agreement

A37 taxed, MOT, insurance

A38 Four items to check are listed here:

       1 Mileage

       2 Has it been involved in any accidents?

       3 Number of owners

       4 Is there any hire purchase or finance agreement outstanding?

A39 True. The AA offer a national inspection scheme.

Answers to Questions

Section 16

TOWING A CARAVAN OR TRAILER
Questions on pages 88–9

A1 1

A2 Exterior towing mirrors, to give you a good view

A3 2

A4 stabilizer

A5 3

A6 **A** 2

B 2

A7 Seven checks are listed here:

1 Is the caravan or trailer loaded correctly?

2 Is it correctly hitched up to your vehicle?

3 Are the lights and indicators working properly?

4 Is the braking system working correctly?

5 Is the jockey wheel assembly fully retracted?

6 Are tyre pressures correct?

7 Are all windows, doors and roof lights closed?

A8 jockey wheel, corner steadies

DRIVING IN EUROPE
Questions on pages 89–90

A9 vehicle, documents

A10 **1** route

2 motoring regulations

A11 Here are five routine checks:

1 Tyres, including spare. Always carry a spare tyre.

2 Tool kit and jack.

3 Lamps and brake lights.

4 Fit deflectors to your headlamps to prevent dazzle to other drivers approaching on the left.

5 Check you have an extra exterior mirror on the left.

A12 driving licence

A13 International Driving Permit

A14 Some non-EU countries

A15 2

A16 Five items are listed here:

1 Spare lamps and bulbs

2 Warning triangle

3 First aid kit

4 Fire extinguisher

5 Emergency windscreen

Part 3

Contents

Understanding the Theory Behind the Test

Alertness

Section 1
Alertness

The first section in the Theory Test questions is headed ALERTNESS. Alertness is a short section and is a good place to start.

- Alertness means being wide awake and concentrating on what you are doing – driving – not being distracted by mobile phones or loud music.
- Alertness means looking out for hazards.
- Alertness means noticing all road signs and road markings, and acting on the instructions and information they give.

Are you fit to drive?
'Fit' can mean:
- Did you have any alcoholic drinks before you set out?
- Are you under the influence of illegal substances (drugs)?
- Are you feeling groggy or unwell?
- Are you taking prescription medicine which could affect your ability to control the car?
- Are you too tired to drive?

It's unwise to set out on a journey if you're not well, on the basis of 'I'll see how I go – I'll probably be all right':
- your reactions are likely to be slower
- you may be unable to judge distances properly
- your actions may be less well co-ordinated than usual and it's not legal.

If you are tired open the window for a few moments to let in some fresh air. If you drive when you are too tired, you risk falling asleep at the wheel – an all too common cause of serious accidents. Driving for long stretches on a motorway at night can be especially dangerous. If you sense that you are losing your concentration, then take a break at a motorway service station. Plan your journey ahead, giving yourself plenty of time for rest stops – at least every couple of hours.

Tackling the questions
Look at the questions in this section (pages 148–52).
You'll see that the Alertness questions are all about these:
- anticipation
- observation
- signalling
- reversing
- using your mirrors
- concentration
- getting distracted
- feeling sleepy
- using mobile phones.

> **DID YOU KNOW?**
> The main causes of distraction are:
> - Loud music in the car
> - Passengers (usually children)
> - Events happening outside (such as accidents)
> - Using a mobile phone

Now go to page 148 to test yourself on the questions about Alertness

Section 2
Attitude

The government road safety organisations believe that the ATTITUDE of learner drivers is extremely important for road safety – yours and other road users.

Attitude means
- Your frame of mind when you get in the car
- How you react when you meet hazards on the road
- How you behave towards other drivers.

Attitude is a very important part of being a good driver. Your attitude when you are driving plays a big part in ensuring your safety and that of other road users.

Do you aim to be a careful and safe driver or a fast and skilful driver? If you don't want to end up 'just another' road accident statistic then careful and safe is the way to go.

Remember
A car is not an offensive weapon, and often people don't realise what a potentially lethal machine they are in control of when they get behind the wheel. You only have to think about this to understand how important your attitude is.

You'll see that questions in this section (see pages 153–9) are concerned with encouraging you to be a careful and safe driver and cover:
- Tailgating
- Consideration for other road users, including pedestrians, buses, slow-moving vehicles and horse riders

- Driving at the right speed for the conditions
- When to flash headlights
- The right place, time and way to overtake

And remembering a few dos and don'ts will help you achieve the right attitude for driving and make passing this section of the test much easier.

Good drivers do
- Drive at the right speed and for the road and traffic conditions
- Observe speed limits
- Overtake only when it is safe to do so
- Park in correct and safe places
- Wait patiently if the driver in front is a learner or elderly or hesitant
- Look out for vulnerable road users such as cyclists, pedestrians and children
- Concentrate on their driving at all times
- Plan their journey so that they have plenty of time to get to their destination

Good drivers don't
- Allow themselves to become involved in road rage
- Break speed limits
- Drive too fast, particularly in wet, foggy or icy weather
- Accelerate or brake too harshly
- Overtake and 'cut in', forcing others to brake sharply
- Put pressure on other drivers by coming up too close behind them (this is called 'tailgating'), flashing headlights or gesturing
- Allow their attention to be distracted by passengers, mobile phones or loud music, or what is happening on the road, such as staring at an accident.

Tailgating

Driving excessively close up behind another vehicle is known as tailgating – and it's dangerous! The car in front may stop suddenly (e.g. to avoid hitting a child or animal that has dashed out into the road); when this happens the car following runs the risk of crashing into it.

You should always leave enough space between your vehicle and the one in front, so that you can stop safely if the driver in front suddenly slows down or stops.

Rear-end shunts account for a large percentage of all accidents on the road. In these situations, the driver of the car behind is almost always judged to be the guilty party.

So tailgating can be expensive as well as dangerous.

Another time when drivers are tempted to tailgate is when attempting to pass a large slow-moving vehicle. However, keeping well back will improve your view of the road ahead, so that you're better able to judge when it's safe to overtake and the driver of the large vehicle will also be able to see you.

We get asked all the time about this

If you are being followed too closely by another driver **you** should **slow down** and increase the distance between your vehicle and the one in front. If you slow down or have to stop suddenly, the driver behind may crash into you, but you will have increased your stopping distance and will not be pushed into the vehicle in front of you.

Always remember

- Expect the unexpected, and make provision for the potential errors of other drivers – everyone makes mistakes sometimes.
- Don't create unnecessary stress for other drivers by showing your frustration in an aggressive manner.

If you are driving at the right speed for the road and weather conditions and a driver behind is trying to overtake you should pull back a bit from the vehicle in front so if the driver behind insists on overtaking, there is less risk of an accident.

Do not try to stop the car behind from overtaking. Do not move into the middle of the road or move up close to the car in front. These actions could be very dangerous.

You should not give confusing signals such as indicating left or waving the other driver on.

Now go to page 153 to test yourself on the questions about Attitude

Section 3
Safety and Your Vehicle

When you go through this section (pages 160–71) you will notice that the questions are a bit of a mixture. They cover a number of topics about SAFETY, including:
- Understanding the controls of your vehicle
- What the car's warning lights tell you
- Tyres – correct inflation, pressures and tread depths
- When to use hazard warning lights
- Passenger safety
- The environment
- Security and crime prevention

Many of the questions in this section are to do with 'legal requirements' and rules regarding parking your car and using lights. Look up all the sections in *The Highway Code* that deal with parking rules. Find out the rules for red routes, white lines and zig-zag lines as well as yellow lines.

> **Seat belts**
> If any of your passengers are young people under 14, you are responsible for making sure they are wearing seat belts. You are responsible for them by law even if you are a learner driver yourself.

Tips for this section
Know your Highway Code and you will be able to answer most of the questions in this section. In particular make sure you know the rules regarding:

- Seat belts
- Tyres
- When to use your lights, including hazard warning lights

> The hazard warning system should work whether or not you have the engine switched on.

Watch out for this confusing little question
One of the most confusing questions in this section asks what kind of driving results in high fuel consumption.

The answer, of course, is **bad** driving – especially harsh braking and acceleration. This means you will use more fuel than you should and therefore cause more damage to the environment than is necessary.

BUT many people read the word 'high' as meaning 'good' – as in a level of driving skill – and so pick the wrong answer.

Don't let it be you…

Now go to page 160 to test yourself on the questions about Safety and Your Vehicle

Section 4
Safety Margins

Safety margins and learner drivers

Experienced drivers are usually better than new or learner drivers at leaving good SAFETY MARGINS. Learner drivers find it harder to keep their vehicle at a safe distance from the one in front. Therefore the questions in this section (see pages 172–9) cover:
• Safe stopping distances
and
• Safe separation distances (these are the same as safety margins).

What is a safety margin?

A safety margin is the space that you need to leave between your vehicle and the one in front so that you will not crash into it if it slows downs or stops suddenly. They are also called 'separation distances' and are an important part of anticipating road and traffic hazards.

When you are learning to drive, you can feel pressure to speed up by drivers behind you.

Don't let other drivers make you cut down on your safety margins. Stay a safe distance behind the vehicle in front. Then you will have enough time to anticipate, and react to, hazards.

The two-second rule

In traffic that's moving at normal speed, allow at least a two-second gap between you and the vehicle in front.

Stopping distances

Many people who are taking their Theory Test often get confused about this. You will notice that some of the questions ask for your overall stopping distance and others ask for you braking distance, these are different.

Overall stopping distance or stopping distance is not the same as braking distance. Stopping distance is made up of thinking distance + braking distance.

In other words, the time it takes to notice that there's a hazard ahead plus the time it takes to brake to deal with it.

Thinking distance

Thinking distance is sometimes called reaction time or reaction distance. If you are driving at 30mph, your thinking distance will be 30 feet (9 metres). That means your vehicle will travel 30 feet (9 metres) before you start braking.

What is the link between stopping distance and safety margins?

• You should always leave enough space between your vehicle and the one in front. If the other driver has to slow down suddenly or stop without warning you need to be able to stop safely.

The space is your safety margin.

Safety margins for other vehicles

• Long vehicles and motorcycles need more room to stop – in other words, you must

leave a bigger safety margin when following a long vehicle or motorbike.
- When driving behind a long vehicle, pull back to increase your separation distance and your safety margin so that you get a better view of the road ahead – there could be hazards developing and if you are too close he can't see you in his rear view mirror.
- Strong winds can blow lorries and motorbikes off course. So leave a bigger safety margin.

Thinking Distance   **Braking Distance**

6 metres + 6 metres
= 12 metres (40 feet) or 3 car lengths

9 metres + 14 metres
= 23 metres (75 feet) or 6 car lengths

12 metres + 24 metres
= 36 metres (120 feet) or 9 car lengths

15 metres + 38 metres
= 53 metres (175 feet) or 13 car lengths

18 metres + 55 metres
= 73 metres (240 feet) or 18 car lengths

21 metres + 75 metres
= 96 metres (315 feet) or 24 car lengths

The basic road safety rule here is: **don't get closer than the overall stopping distance.**

Different conditions and safety margins

One or more questions in your Theory Test might be about driving in 'different conditions'.

These questions aim to make sure you know what adjustments you should make to your driving when either:
- road conditions are different from normal, for example, when parts of the road are closed off for roadworks,

or
- weather conditions affect your driving.

Roadworks

You should always take extra care when you see a sign warning you that there are roadworks ahead. Remember, roadworks are a hazard and you have to anticipate them.

If you see the driver in front of you slowing down, take this as a sign that you should do the same – even if you can't see a hazard ahead. You still need to keep a safe distance from him.

Harassing the driver in front by 'tailgating' is both wrong and dangerous. So is overtaking to fill the gap.

Roadworks on motorways

It's especially important that you know what to do when you see a sign for roadworks ahead on a motorway.

- There may be a lower speed limit than normal – keep to it.
- Use your mirrors and indicators, and get into the correct lane in plenty of time.
- Don't overtake the queue and then force your way in at the last minute (this is an example of showing an inconsiderate attitude to other road users).
- Always keep a safe distance from the vehicle in front.

Weather conditions

In bad weather (often called 'adverse' weather) you need to increase your safety margins.

When it's raining you need to leave at least twice as much distance between you and the vehicle in front. When there's ice on the road, leave an even bigger gap because your stopping distance increases tenfold.

It's amazing how often drivers go too fast in bad weather. In adverse weather motorways have lower speed limits, but some drivers don't take any notice of them.

> When it's icy you should multiply your two-second gap by ten.

Questions that look alike

There are a number of questions about anti-lock brakes in this section. Lots of questions look the same. Some are easy and some are hard. Some of them appear to be the same but they are not.

The questions test two things:

- Your knowledge of the rules of the road and
- Your understanding of words to do with driving.

Now go to page 172 to test yourself on the questions about Safety Margins

Section 5
Hazard Awareness

How often does a motorist protest that the accident happened before they had time to realise the person they hit was there?

Some accidents will, of course, inevitably happen, but part of your instructor's job while teaching you to drive is to help you learn to anticipate problems before they happen.

What is the difference between Hazard Awareness and Hazard Perception?

- **Hazard Awareness** and **Hazard Perception** mean the same thing.
- Hazard Perception is the name for the part of the Theory Test that uses video clips. This test is about spotting developing hazards. One of the key skills of good driving, this is called **anticipation**.
- Anticipating hazards means looking out for them in advance and taking action now.
- Hazard Awareness is about being **alert** whenever you are driving.

That is why some of the questions in this HAZARD AWARENESS section (see pages 180–98) deal with things that might make you less alert – for example:
– feeling tired
– feeling ill
– taking medicines prescribed by your doctor
– drinking alcohol.

Other questions in this section cover:
- noticing road and traffic signs and road markings

- what to do at traffic lights
- when to slow down for hazards ahead.

Taking action to avoid accidents
New drivers have a greater than average chance of being involved in accidents. Statistics show that young male drivers have the most accidents.

Why are young male drivers more at risk?
- Maybe it's because when they get their licence they want to show off to other drivers.
- Some people think that driving much too fast will earn them 'respect' from their friends.
- Some people think that they are such good drivers, the rules of the road don't apply to them.

Whatever the reason – drivers who don't watch out for hazards are at risk of being involved in an accident.

The problem has a lot to do with people's **attitude** to driving; you'll find more about the part of the Theory Test that deals with attitude on pages 117–8.

We've already said that young drivers often don't learn to anticipate hazards until they are older and more experienced.

The HP test aims to 'fill the gap' in hazard perception for young drivers and other new drivers by making sure they have some proper training to make up for their lack of experience.

This should make them safer drivers when they start out on the road alone.

Hazard Awareness

Looking for clues to developing hazards

As you get more driving experience you will start to learn about the times and places where you are most likely to meet hazards.

Think about some of these examples:

Rush hour

You know that people take more risks when driving in the rush hour. Maybe they have to drop their children off at school before going to work. Maybe they are late for a business meeting. So you have to be prepared for bad driving, such as other drivers pulling out in front of you.

Dustbin day

Drivers in a hurry may get frustrated if they are held up in traffic because of a hazard such as a dustcart. They may accelerate and pull out to overtake even though they cannot see clearly ahead. You should not blindly follow the lead of another driver. Check for yourself that there are no hazards ahead.

School children

Young children are not very good at judging how far away a car is from them, and may run into the road unexpectedly. Always be on the lookout for hazards near a school entrance.

Parked cars

Imagine you are driving on a quiet one-way street with cars parked down each side. You wouldn't expect to meet any vehicles coming the other way – but what about children playing? They might run out into the road after a football. It would be difficult to see them because of the parked cars, until they were in the road in front of you.

More examples of hazards

So, what kinds of hazards are we talking about? And what should you do about them?

Road markings and road signs sometimes highlight likely hazards for you.

The list below gives some of the hazards you should look out for when driving along a busy street in town.

After each hazard there are some ideas about what you should be looking out for, and what to do next.

- You see a bus which has stopped in a lay-by ahead.
There may be some pedestrians hidden by the bus who are trying to cross the road, or the bus may signal to pull out. Be ready to slow down and stop.

- You see a white triangle painted on the road surface ahead.
This is a hazard warning sign. It tells you that there is a 'Give Way' junction just ahead. Slow down and be ready to stop.

- You see a sign for a roundabout on the road ahead.
Anticipate that other drivers may need to change lane, and be ready to leave them enough room.

• You come to some road works where the traffic is controlled by temporary traffic lights.
Watch out for drivers speeding to get through before the lights change.

Hazards may be all around you – not just in front
• You look in your rear view mirror and see an emergency vehicle with flashing lights coming up behind you.
An emergency vehicle wants to pass, so get ready to pull over when it's safe.

Not all hazards are on the road
• You see a small child standing with an adult near the edge of the pavement.
Check if the child is safely holding the adult's hand. Be ready to stop safely if the child suddenly steps into the road.

• You notice dustbins or rubbish bags put out on the pavement.
The dustcart could be around the next corner, or the bin men could be crossing the road with bags of rubbish. Be ready to slow down and stop if necessary.

Remember to listen for hazards, too.
• You hear a siren.
Look all around to find out where the emergency vehicle is. You may have to pull over to let it pass.

You will find out more about the different types of hazards you may encounter, including what to look for when driving on narrow country roads, or in bad (adverse) weather conditions, in the Vehicle Handling section, pages 132–4.

> **Always expect the unexpected**
> Don't forget: not all hazards can be anticipated. There are bound to be some you haven't expected.

> **Red flashing warning lights**
> Level crossings, ambulance stations, fire stations and swing bridges all have red lights that flash on and off to warn you when you must stop.

Observation
Another word for taking in information through our eyes is observation.

Observation is one of the three key skills needed in hazard perception:
• observation
• anticipation
• planning.

An easy way to remember this is **O A P** for

Observe
Anticipate
Plan

Talking to yourself again?
It's a good idea to 'talk to yourself' when you're learning to drive – and even after you've passed your test. Talk about all the things you see that could be potential hazards. Your driving instructor might suggest this as a way of making you concentrate and notice hazards ahead.

Hazard Awareness

Even if you don't talk out loud, you can do a 'running commentary' in your head on everything you see around you as you drive.

For example, you might say to yourself –
'I am following a cyclist and the traffic lights ahead are red. *When the lights change I shall allow him/her plenty of time and room to move off.'*
or
'The dual carriageway ahead is starting to look very busy. There is a sign showing that the right lane is closing in 800 yards. *I must get ready to check my mirrors and if safe to do so drop back, to allow other vehicles to move into the left-hand lane ahead of me.'*

Note: Don't forget the mirrors! This way, you will notice more hazards, and you will learn to make more sense of the information that your eyes are taking in.

Scanning the road

Learner drivers tend to look straight ahead of their car and may not notice all the hazards that might be building up on both sides. You will spot more hazards when driving if you train yourself to scan the road.

- Practice looking up and ahead as far as possible.
- Use all your mirrors to look out for hazards too.
- Don't forget that you have 'blind spots' when driving – work out where they are and find safe ways of checking all round for hazards.
- Ask your driving instructor to help you with all of this.

Learn your road signs!
Look in your copy of *The Highway Code* at the information on the bottom of the first page of traffic signs. It explains that you won't find every road sign shown here.

You can buy a copy of *Know Your Traffic Signs* from a bookshop to see some of the extra signs that are not in *The Highway Code*.

Note: In Wales, some signs have the Welsh spelling as well as the English; and in Scotland, some signs have Gaelic spelling. You'll also see some 'old-style' road signs around, which are slightly different too.

How is learning to scan the road going to help me pass my Theory Test?

- As we have said before, the idea of the Hazard Perception element of the test is to encourage you to get some real experience of driving before you take the Theory Test.
- If you meet real hazards on the road and learn how to anticipate them, you'll learn how to pass the Hazard Perception element of the test.
- In the video test you may not be able to look all around you as you would when driving a car; but the clips will be as realistic as possible in giving you a wide 'view' of the road ahead.

Observation questions

Study some of the pictures in the Hazard Awareness section on pages 180–98.

They include photographs of scenes such as:

• a cyclist at traffic lights, seen from the viewpoint of a driver in a car behind the cyclist

• what you see as a driver when you are approaching a level crossing

• what you see when coming up to a 'blind bend'

• a view of the road ahead with traffic building up where one lane is closing.

Look out for situations like these when you are out driving with your instructor, and use the practice to improve your hazard awareness.

As well as photographs, there are pictures of road and traffic signs.

What do these signs mean?

What actions should you take when you see these signs?

• If you are not sure, look them up in your copy of *The Highway Code*.

• Think about why the square yellow sign with the two children is in the Vehicle Markings section and not with the rest of the road signs.

Now go to page 180 to test yourself on the questions about Hazard Awareness

Section 6
Vulnerable Road Users

Today's vehicles are getting safer all the time for the driver inside the car – but not always for the pedestrian, cyclist etc outside. Many road users who are not driving cars have nothing to protect them if they are in an accident with a motor vehicle.

The questions in the VULNERABLE ROAD USERS section (see pages 199–212) deal with the following:
- why different types of road users are vulnerable
- what you as a driver must do to keep them safe.

Vulnerable road users include:
- pedestrians
- children
- elderly people
- people with disabilities
- cyclists
- motorcycle riders
- horse riders
- learner drivers and new drivers
- animals being herded along the road.

You must drive with extra care when you are near vulnerable road users.

Cyclists
Give cyclists plenty of room. Remember to **keep well back** from cyclists when you are coming up to a **junction** or a **roundabout** because you cannot be sure what they are going to do. On the roundabout they may go in any direction – left, right, or straight ahead.

They are allowed to stay in the left lane and signal right if they are going to continue round. Leave them enough room to cross in front of you if they need to. Turn to the section headed Vulnerable Road Users in the Theory Test questions (pages 199–212) to see some pictures of this. You must also give way to cyclists at toucan crossings and in cycle lanes (see the rules for cyclists in your copy of *The Highway Code*).

Look out for cyclists!
- It can be hard to see cyclists in busy town traffic.
- It can also be hard to see them coming when you are waiting to turn out at a junction. They can be hidden by other vehicles (see below).

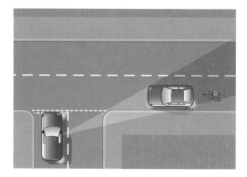

Always be on the lookout for cyclists. Especially, **check your mirror** to make sure you do not trap a cyclist on your left when you are turning left into a side road. Check your **blind spots** for cyclists, too.

Controlling your vehicle near cyclists
When you are following a cyclist, you must be able to drive **as slowly as they do**, and keep

your vehicle under control. Only overtake when you can allow them plenty of room, and it is safe to do so.

Cycle lanes

Cycle lanes are for cyclists. Car drivers should not use them.

A cycle lane is marked by a white line on the road.

A solid white line means you must not drive or park in the cycle lane during the hours it is in use.

A broken white line means you should drive or park in it only if there is no alternative. You should not park there at any time when there are waiting restrictions.

When you overtake a cyclist, a motorcyclist or a horse rider, **give them at least as much room as you would a car.**

Cyclists and motorcycle riders

Cyclists and motorcycle riders are more at risk than car drivers because:

- they are more affected by strong winds, or by turbulence caused by other vehicles
- they are more affected by an uneven road surface, and they may have to move out suddenly to avoid a pot-hole
- car drivers often cannot see them.

Pedestrians

Pedestrians most at risk include **elderly people** and **children**. Elderly people and others who cannot move easily may be slower to cross roads – you must give them plenty of time. Children don't have a sense of danger on the road; they can't tell how close a car is, or how fast it is going. They may run out into the road without looking. Or they may step out behind you when you are reversing – you may not see them because they are small.

People who are unable to see and/or hear

A blind person will usually carry a white stick to alert you to their presence.

If the stick has a red band, this means that the person is also deaf, so will have no warning of an approaching car either visually or from engine noise.

When to give way to pedestrians

At any pedestrian crossing, if a pedestrian has started to cross, wait until they have reached the other side. Do not harass them by revving your engine or edging forward.

- **On a light-controlled pedestrian crossing**

At a crossing with lights (pelican, toucan or puffin crossings), pedestrians have priority once they have started to cross even if, when on a pelican crossing, the amber lights start flashing.

- **On a zebra crossing**

Once the pedestrian has stepped on to the crossing you must stop and wait for them to cross.

Note: It is courteous to stop at a zebra crossing if a pedestrian is waiting to cross.

Vulnerable Road Users

When you take your Practical Driving Test, you must stop for any pedestrians who are waiting on the pavement at a zebra crossing – even if they haven't stepped on to the crossing yet. However, you must not wave to them to cross.

- **When they have started to cross a road that you want to turn into**

If you want to turn left into a side road and people are crossing the side road on foot, wait for them to finish crossing – people on foot have priority over car drivers.

DID YOU KNOW?

If a car hits a pedestrian at **40mph**, the pedestrian will probably be killed.
Even at **30mph**, 50% of pedestrians hit by cars will be killed.
At **20mph**, pedestrians have a better chance of surviving. This is why you will find 20mph limits and other things to slow traffic in some residential streets and near school entrances.

Signs that alert you to road users at risk

Look up the Traffic Signs and Vehicle Markings sections in your copy of *The Highway Code* and find the following signs:

- Pedestrians walking in the road ahead (no pavement).
- Cycle lane and pedestrian route.
- Advance warning of school crossing patrol ahead.
- School crossing patrol.
- Elderly or disabled people crossing.
- Sign on back of school bus or coach.

Other types of vulnerable road users

Be prepared to slow down for **animals, learner drivers,** and other more unusual hazards such as people walking along the road in **organised groups** (for example, on a demonstration, or a sponsored walk). There are rules in *The Highway Code* that walkers must follow. But even if they break the rules, make sure you keep to them.

Animals

Drive slowly past horses or other animals. Allow them plenty of space on the road. Don't frighten them by sounding your horn or revving your engine.

If you see a flock of **sheep** or a herd of **cattle** blocking the road, you must:
- stop
- switch off your engine
- and wait until they have left the road.

People riding **horses** on the road are often children, so you need to take extra care; when you see two riders abreast, it may well be that the one on the outside is shielding a less experienced rider.

Now go to page 199 to test yourself on the questions about Vulnerable Road Users

Section 7
Other Types of Vehicle

We have already come across some of the other types of vehicles that share the road with you and your car including motorbikes and bicycles. The questions in this part of the Theory Test (see pages 213–8) are mostly about long vehicles such as lorries. However, you also need to know what to do about:
– buses
– caravans
– trams
– tractors and other farm vehicles
– special vehicles for disabled drivers (powered invalid carriages)
– slow vehicles such as road gritters
– motorway repair vehicles.

Important points to remember about these types of vehicle:
• many of them can only move very slowly
• they cannot easily stop or change direction.

The driver's field of vision may be restricted – this means that car drivers have to allow them plenty of room.

Motorcycles
• Motorcycles are easily blown off course by strong winds. If you see a motorcyclist overtaking a **high-sided vehicle** such as a lorry, keep well back. The lorry may shield the motorcyclist from the wind as it is overtaking, but then a sudden gust could blow the motorcyclist off-course.
• It can be **hard to see** a motorcyclist when you are waiting at a **junction**. Always look out for them.

• If you see a motorcyclist **looking over their shoulder**, it could mean that they will **soon give a signal to turn right**. This applies to cyclists too. Keep back to give them plenty of room.
• Motorcyclists and cyclists sometimes have to **swerve to avoid hazards** such as bumps in the road, patches of ice and drain covers. As before – give them plenty of room.

Long vehicles
• Like cyclists, long vehicles coming up to roundabouts may stay in the left lane even if they intend to turn right.
This is because they need lots of room to manoeuvre. Keep well back so they have room to turn.
• Take great care when overtaking long or high-sided vehicles. Before you pull out to overtake, make sure you have a clear view of the road ahead.
• A long vehicle that needs to turn left off a major road into a minor road may prepare to do so by moving out towards the centre of the road, or by moving across to the other side.

If you're following them:
• give way, and don't try to overtake – on the right or the left
• you might need to slow down and stop while the driver of the long vehicle makes the turn.

Buses and trams
• Always give way to buses when they signal to pull out.
• Always give way to trams; they cannot steer to avoid you.

• Don't try to overtake a tram.

Trams are **quiet** vehicles – you cannot rely on engine noise to warn you that a tram is coming.

 Take extra care when you see this sign, because trams are sometimes allowed to go when car drivers are not.

Tractors and slow-moving vehicles

• Always **be patient** if you are following a slow vehicle.

Drivers of slow vehicles will usually try to find a safe place to pull in to let the traffic go past. In the meantime you should keep well back, so that you can see the road ahead. Allow a safe distance in case they slow down or stop.

Slow vehicles are not allowed on motorways because they cannot keep up with the fast-moving traffic. Vehicles not allowed on motorways include:

• motorcycles under 50cc
• bicycles
• tractors and other farm vehicles
• powered invalid carriages.

For more information on Motorway Rules, see pages 134–7 of this book.

Now go to page 213 to test yourself on the questions about Other Types of Vehicle

Section 8
Vehicle Handling

The questions in this section (see pages 219–28) test how much you know about controlling your vehicle.

Your control is affected by:

• the **road surface** – is it rough or smooth? Are there any holes or bumps? Are there any 'traffic-calming measures' such as humps or chicanes?
• the **weather conditions** – you have to drive in different ways when there is fog, snow, ice or heavy rain.

Other questions in this section cover driving on country roads – on narrow and one-way roads, humpback bridges, steep hills, fords. Other questions need practical knowledge – for example, on engine braking, brake fade, and coasting your vehicle – use the **Glossary.**

This section also has some questions on overtaking and parking.

Road surface

The condition of the road surface can affect the way your vehicle handles. Your vehicle handles better on a smooth surface than on a surface that is damaged, bumpy or full of holes. If you have to drive on an uneven surface, keep your speed down so that you have full control of your vehicle, even if your steering wheel is jolted.

Take care also where there are **tramlines** on the road. The layout of the road affects the way your vehicle handles.

You may have to adjust your driving for traffic calming measures such as **traffic humps** (sometimes called 'sleeping policemen') and **chicanes**. These are double bends that have been put into the road layout to slow the traffic down. The sign before the chicane tells you who has priority.

Traffic calming measures are often used in residential areas or near school entrances to make it safer for pedestrians.

Weather conditions
Bad weather (adverse weather) such as heavy rain, ice or snow affects the way your vehicle handles. If you drive too fast in adverse weather, your tyres may lose their grip on the road when you try to brake. This means the car may skid or 'aquaplane'.

• Aquaplaning means sliding out of control on a wet surface.

Driving in snow
In snow, the best advice is do not drive at all unless you really have to make a journey. If you have to drive in snowy conditions, leave extra time for your journey and keep to the main roads. You can fit snow chains to your tyres to increase their grip in deep snow.

Driving in fog
In fog your field of vision can be down to a few metres. Your vehicle is fitted with fog lights to help you see and be seen in fog. But you must know how and when to use them. Look up the three rules about fog lights in *The Highway Code*. You'll see that the key points to remember are:

• don't dazzle other road users with your fog lights
• and switch them off as soon as you can see better (as soon as the fog starts to clear).

> **Remember the two-second rule?**
> You should double the two-second gap to four seconds when driving in rain, and increase the gap by as much as ten times when there is ice on the road.

Country driving
If you have had most of your driving lessons in a town, you need to know how to drive on narrow country roads. Some are only wide enough for one vehicle ('single-track'), and some are on very steep hills.

Your control of the gears, clutch and brakes will be important if you have to follow a tractor very slowly up a hill. On a steep downward slope you have to make sure your vehicle does not 'run away'.

On country roads you might find **humpback bridges** and **fords**. The signs below warn you of these hazards.

• Find out what you must do **first** after you have driven through a ford.

Vehicle Handling

Technical knowledge

We have already mentioned engine braking. Understanding how engine braking works is part of good vehicle handling.

Note: If you press the footbrake constantly on a long hill, you may get brake fade. If you're not sure, check what that means in the **Glossary** at the back of this book.

Use the gears to control your vehicle on a downhill slope (or 'gradient'). If you put the vehicle in 'neutral', or drive with the clutch down (called coasting), your vehicle will increase speed beyond what is safe and will not be under proper control.

This sign warns you of a steep hill downwards.

- Coasting is wrong and dangerous – you should not be tempted to do it to save fuel.

Remember that if there is sudden heavy rain after a dry hot spell, the road surface can get very slippery.

> **Now go to page 219 to test yourself on the questions about Vehicle Handling**

Section 9
Motorway Rules

Learner drivers aren't allowed on motorways, so you can't get experience of what it's like to drive on them until you've passed your test. However, you do need to know all about MOTORWAY RULES before taking your Practical Test, and your Theory Test will most likely include a question about motorways (see pages 229–36).

As soon as you pass your driving test you will be legally allowed to drive on motorways. You need to know all the motorway rules in advance, so that you are confident and ready to cope with motorway driving when you pass your test.

There are some major roads and dual carriageways that learners can drive on which are very much like motorways. You may drive on some of these fast roads during your driving test, so that your examiner can see how well you cope with hazards at higher speeds.

When driving on these fast roads you need some of the same skills that you will need for motorway driving – for example, using lanes properly, knowing when it is safe to overtake, and controlling your vehicle at speed.

If you are learning to drive with a driving school, you will have the chance to book a motorway lesson with your instructor after you have passed your test. It makes sense to take up this offer before you drive on a motorway alone for the first time.

The differences between motorways and other roads

- On a motorway traffic is moving at high speed all the time.
- All lanes are in use.
- No stopping is allowed on a motorway – traffic only slows or comes to a stop because of accidents or other types of hold-up.
- Some road users are not allowed on motorways. These include:
- pedestrians, cyclists and learner drivers
- horses and other animals
- motorcycles under 50cc
- slow-moving vehicles, tractors and farm vehicles and invalid carriages.
- You always enter and leave a motorway on the left, via a slip road.
- To the left of the inside lane (left-hand lane) on a motorway is the hard shoulder. You can only drive on this in an emergency.
- Special signs and signals are used on motorways.

These include signs above the road on overhead gantries (see page 136), signs on the central reservation, and amber and red flashing lights.

Checks before your journey

Be extra careful about doing all your regular checks before you set out on a motorway journey; you cannot stop on the motorway to fix small problems, and no one wants to break down in the middle of fast traffic.

Always check:

- oil and coolant levels, screen wash container
- tyres and tyre pressures
- fuel gauge
- that all mirrors and windows are free of dirt and grease

- that the horn works.

Many of these checks are legally necessary, as well as important for your safety.

How to move on to the motorway

- Join the motorway by building up your speed on the slip road to match the speed of traffic in the left lane of the motorway.
- Use **MSM (Mirrors – Signal – Manoeuvre)** and move into the flow of traffic when it is safe to do so.

Changing lanes and overtaking

Driving on a motorway needs all the skills you have learned about **anticipation** and **forward planning**.

You should:

- make good use of all mirrors, and check your blind spots
- signal to move out in plenty of time
- look out for hazards ahead in the lane you want to move to
- not go ahead if it will force another vehicle to brake or swerve
- keep a safe distance from the vehicle in front.

Take a break

When you drive on motorways you will sometimes see signs that say 'Tiredness can kill – take a break!'

This is very good advice; motorways are monotonous – boring to drive, with long stretches of road that look the same for miles. A major cause of accidents is drivers falling asleep at the wheel. Plan your journey so that you have time to get out, stretch your legs and have a drink or snack.

The rules you need to know

- **Keep to the left-hand lane** unless you are overtaking and move back to the left lane as soon as it is safe to do so. Sometimes you need to stay in the centre lane for a time – for example, when a line of lorries is travelling up a hill in the left lane. Stay in the centre lane until you have passed the hazard, then signal left and return to the left lane.
- **NEVER reverse**
  park
  walk
  or **drive in the wrong direction**
on the motorway.
- Don't **exceed the speed limit**. This is normally 70mph, but lower speed limits may be signed when the road is busy, or in bad weather.
- Keep to the correct separation distance (see Safety Margins, page 121).
- Don't **overtake on the left.**
If traffic is moving slowly in all three lanes you may find that the lane on the left is moving faster than the one to its right for a short time. Or the left lane may be signed for traffic turning off at the next junction only. But these are exceptions to the rule.
- If luggage falls from your vehicle, **do not get out to pick it up**. Stop at the next **emergency phone** and tell the police. Posts on the edge of the motorway show the way to the nearest emergency phone. You should use these phones rather than your mobile, because the emergency phone connects directly to the police and tells them exactly where you are on the motorway.
- **Don't stop on the hard shoulder except**

in an emergency. The hard shoulder is an extremely dangerous place, as many as one in eight road deaths happen there.

Traffic signs and road markings on motorways
Light signals

In *The Highway Code* you'll find the light signals only seen on motorways. Signs above the roadway, or on the central reservation, are activated as needed, to warn of accidents, lane closures or weather conditions.

 Overhead gantries display arrows or red crosses showing which lanes are open or closed to traffic, and which lanes to move to when motorways merge or diverge.

They may also show temporary speed limits.

Direction signs

Direction signs on motorways are blue and those on other major roads are green – other direction signs are white with black print.

Reflective studs

It's useful to know the colours of studs on a motorway; this can help in working out which part of the road you're on if it's dark or foggy.

White studs mark lanes or the centre of the road
Red studs mark the left edge of the carriageway

Amber studs are used alongside the central reservation

Green studs mark the entry to a slip road.

Note: these markings are also found on some dual carriageways.

USING THE HARD SHOULDER

- Stop as far to the left as possible and, if you can, near an emergency phone.
- Emergency phones are situated 1 mile  apart and have blue and white marker posts (left) every 100 metres. An arrow on the posts points the direction of the nearest phone.
  - If you are using a mobile phone you can identify your location from the number on the post.
- Switch on your hazard warning lights.
- Use the left-hand door to get out of the vehicle, and make sure your passengers do too.
- Get everyone away from the road – if possible, behind the barrier or up the bank.
- Leave animals in the vehicle unless they aren't safe there.
- Phone the police with full details of where you are, then go back and wait in a safe place near your vehicle.

Now go to page 229 to test yourself on the questions about Motorway Rules

Section 10
Rules of the Road

'Rules of the Road' is a good way to describe what is in *The Highway Code*.

The questions that come under this heading in the Theory Test (see pages 237–48) include several on road signs and road markings. There are lots more road sign questions in the section on Road and Traffic Signs.

Several of the topics listed in this section have already come up.

Other questions in this section cover:
- speed limits
- overtaking
- parking
- lanes and roundabouts
- clearways
- box junctions
- crossroads
- pedestrian crossings
- towing caravans and trailers.

Speed limits
Driving too fast for the road, traffic or weather conditions causes accidents.

The right speed for the road
Make sure that you keep below the speed limit shown on the signs for the road you are on.

| **30mph** | **50mph** | or as low as |
| in a built up area | on a long, twisty country road | **20mph** in a residential area with speed humps or traffic calming measures |

> The national speed limit for cars on a dual carriageway is **70mph**.
> This is also the maximum speed for motorway driving.

National speed limit
When you leave a built up area you will usually see this sign.

- This sign tells you that the national speed limit for this type of road applies here.
- The national speed limit for cars on a normal road (single carriageway outside a built up area) is **60mph**.
- So on this road you must drive below 60mph even if it is straight and empty.

DID YOU KNOW?
Street lights usually mean that a **30mph** limit applies, unless there are signs showing other limits.

The right speed for the conditions
If it is raining or there is snow and ice on the road or if you are driving in a high wind you will have to drive more slowly than the maximum speed limit. This will keep you and other road users safe.

- Remember – you have to **double** the time you allow for stopping and braking in wet weather. Allow **even more time** in snow and ice.
- You need to be extra careful when driving in fog.

The right speed for your vehicle
Some other vehicles have lower speed limits than cars. Study the rules on speed limits in your copy of *The Highway Code*.

Parking rules
There are some general rules about parking that all drivers should know.

- Whenever you can, you should use off-street car parks, or parking bays. These are marked out with white lines on the road.
- Never park where your vehicle could be a danger to other road users.

Special rules
Look for signs that tell you

- that you cannot park there at certain times of the day
- or that only certain people can park in that place.

Examples:
- bus lanes
- cycle lanes
- residents' parking zones
- roads edged with red or yellow lines

Orange or blue badges are given to people with disabilities. Do not park in a space reserved for a disabled driver – even if that is the only place left to park. A disabled driver may need to park there. You will break the law if you park in that space.

Parking at night
- If you park at night on a road that has a speed limit higher than 30mph, you must switch on your parking lights.

You must switch on your parking lights even if you have parked in a lay-by on this type of road.
- When parking at night, always park facing in the same direction as the traffic flow.
- If your vehicle has a trailer, you must switch on parking lights, even if the road has a 30mph speed limit.

WHERE NOT TO PARK
- On the pavement
- At a bus stop
- In front of someone's drive
- Opposite a traffic island
- Near a school entrance
- On a pedestrian crossing (or inside the zig-zag lines either side of it)
- Near a junction
- On a clearway
- On a motorway

Now go to page 237 to test yourself on the questions about Rules of the Road

Section 11
Road and Traffic Signs

When you look up the chapter on ROAD AND TRAFFIC SIGNS in the Theory Test questions (see pages 249–75) you will see that it takes up a lot of pages. This is because most of the questions have a picture of a road sign or marking. You will also see that a lot of questions ask 'What does this sign mean?'

But however differently the questions are worded – it all comes down to how well you know *The Highway Code*.

You can try to learn as much of *The Highway Code* as possible, but there are other ways you can get to know the road signs.

Be aware
As you walk or drive around, look at the road signs you see in the street, and the different markings painted on the road surface.

If you are on foot:
Look at the signs and signals that all road users must obey, whether they are in a car or walking.

For example, when you use a pedestrian crossing, check what kind of crossing it is (such as a pelican, toucan or zebra crossing).

Check whether you know the following:
- What are the rules for pedestrians and drivers coming up to the crossing?
- What kinds of crossings are controlled by traffic lights?
- What is different about a zebra crossing?

Road and Traffic Signs

During your driving lessons
If you are having a driving lesson look well ahead so that you see all the signs that tell you what to do next. Obey them in good time.

During your Driving Test
When you take your Driving Test the examiner will tell you when to move off, when to make a turn and when to carry out one of the set manoeuvres. But they will expect you to **watch out for lane markings** on the road, and **signs giving directions**, and to decide how to react to these yourself.

If you see several signs all on the same post, it can be confusing. The general rule is to **start at the top** and read down the post. The sign at the top tells you about the **first hazard** you have to look out for.

If you are a passenger in a car on a **motorway,** look at the motorway signs, because you need to know them, even though you can't drive on a motorway yet yourself.

Check that you can answer the following:
What colour are the signs at the side of the motorway?
What do the light signals above the road tell you?
What signs tell you that you are coming to an exit?

Know your shapes
Road and traffic signs come in three main shapes. Get to know them. You must learn what the signs mean.

Circles
Signs in **circles** tell you **to do** (blue) or **not do** (red) something – they **give orders**.

Triangles
Signs in **triangles** tell you of a **hazard** ahead – they **give warnings.**

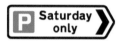

Rectangles
Signs in **rectangles** tell you about **where you are** or **where you are going** – they **give information.**

DID YOU KNOW?
There is only one sign which is **octagonal** – that is, it has eight sides. This is the sign for **STOP**. The eight-sided shape makes the sign stand out more.

Now go to page 249 to test yourself on the questions about Road and Traffic Signs

Section 12
Documents

This is quite a short section in your book of Theory Test questions (see pages 276–9). It is also different from the other sections, because it does not deal with driving skills or knowledge of *The Highway Code*.

It covers all the paperwork and the laws that you need to know about when you start learning to drive.

In this section there are questions about:
• driving licences
• insurance
• MOT certificate
• Vehicle Excise Duty (tax disc)
• Vehicle Registration Document (log book)

This section also covers:
• who can supervise a learner driver
• and changes you must tell the licensing authority about.

Driving licence
If you are learning to drive, you need a provisional licence.
• You must have a valid licence to drive legally.
• All licences now have two parts – a photo card and a paper document.
• Your signature is on both parts of the licence.
• Take good care of your provisional licence. If you lose it by mistake, you can get another one but you will have to pay a fee, and wait for the new licence to come.
• When you pass your test you can apply for a full licence.

Insurance
You must have a valid insurance certificate that covers you at least for **third party liability**. If you are learning with a driving school, you are covered by their insurance while you are in the driving school car. When you are in your own or anybody else's car, you must have insurance. Third party insurance cover usually comes as **'Third Party, Fire and Theft'. It is a basic insurance policy** that will pay for repairs to another person's car and allows you to claim on the other driver's insurance if you are in an accident that was not your fault.

If you have **comprehensive** insurance, the policy will pay for repairs to your vehicle even when the accident was your fault.

MOT certificate
Cars and motorcycles must have their first MOT test three years after they are new and first registered. After that, they must have an MOT test every year.
The MOT test checks:
• that your vehicle is roadworthy – that is, all the parts work properly and the vehicle is safe to drive
• that it keeps to the legal limits for exhaust emissions – that is, the levels of poisons in the gas that comes from the exhaust.

If your vehicle is over three years old you must not drive it without a valid MOT certificate – unless you are on your way to get an MOT and you have booked it in advance.

Vehicle Excise Duty (tax disc)

Your vehicle must have an up-to-date tax disc on the windscreen. The disc shows that you have paid Vehicle Excise Duty up to the date on the disc (you can pay for 6 or 12 months at a time). If you don't renew your tax disc within a month of the old one expiring you will be automatically fined. If you are not going to renew your tax disc (if you don't use your vehicle or keep it on a public road) you must inform the DVLA by completing a Statutory Off Road Vehicle Notification (SORN).

Vehicle Excise Duty is the tax that the government charges you to drive your vehicle on the roads. It is also sometimes called road tax. When you get your tax disc, you must show proof that your vehicle is insured, and that it has a valid MOT if required.

Vehicle Registration Document/Certificate

The Vehicle Registration Document/Certificate has all the important details about you and your vehicle, such as the make and model of the vehicle. It also has your name and address as the registered keeper of the vehicle. It is a record of the vehicle's history and is sometimes called **'the log book'**.

Changes you must tell the licensing authority about

The Driver and Vehicle Licensing Agency is known as the DVLA for short.

You must tell the DVLA

- if you are going to keep your car off road and are not renewing your tax disc
- when you buy or sell a car
- or if you change your name or address.

This is because your details go on to the **Vehicle Registration Document/Certificate** and you are legally responsible for the vehicle (car tax, parking fines etc) until you have notified the DVLA that it is off road or you have sold it.

Supervising a learner driver

As a learner driver, you cannot drive on your own. If you are not with your driving instructor, you must be supervised by a person:

- who is at least 21 years old
- and has a full licence for the kind of car you drive*
- and has had that licence for at least three years.

*Note: if a person has a licence to drive an **automatic** car only, they cannot supervise a learner in a **manual** car.

Now go to page 276 to test yourself on the questions about Documents

Section 13
Accidents

The questions in this section (see pages 280–90) are about helping anyone who is hurt in a road accident. Some people think they might do more harm than good if they try to help. But if you have some knowledge of first aid you won't panic and if you are first on the scene at accident you could even save a life.

- Look up Accidents and First Aid in your copy of *The Highway Code*.

The Theory Test questions in this section cover:
- what to do when warning lights come on in your vehicle
- what to do if you break down
- safety equipment to carry with you
- when to use hazard warning lights
- what to do – and what not to do – at the scene of an accident
- What to do in tunnels

Basic first aid
What to do at an accident scene
- Check that you are not putting yourself in danger before you go to help somebody else. You may need to warn other drivers of the accident.
- Check all vehicle engines are switched off.
- Make sure no one is smoking.
- Move people who are not injured to a safe place. If the accident has happened on a motorway, if possible get them away from the hard shoulder, behind the barrier or on to the bank.

- Call the emergency services. You will need to tell them exactly where you are, and how many vehicles are involved in the accident. On motorways, use the emergency phone which connects directly to the police and tells them exactly where you are.
- Do not move injured people – unless there is a risk of fire, or of an explosion.
- Give essential first aid to injured people (see below).
- Stay there until the emergency services arrive.

The ABC of first aid
This tells you what three things to check for when you go to help an injured person:
A is for Airway
B is for Breathing
C is for Circulation

Airway
If an injured person is breathing, but unconscious, if possible place them in the recovery position. If they are not breathing, first make sure there is nothing in their mouth that might be blocking the airway.

Breathing
If you have checked the airway and they are still not breathing, then give first aid as follows:
- lift their chin
- carefully tilt their head back to open their airway

Accidents

• pinch their nose and blow into their mouth until their chest rises.

Repeat this every 4 seconds until the person can breathe alone, or until help arrives.

Circulation

'Circulation' here means 'bleeding'. If a person is bleeding, press firmly on the wound for up to 10 minutes, until the bleeding slows or stops. You can raise an injured arm or leg to reduce the bleeding – as long as the limb is not broken. If you carry a first aid kit use a sterile dressing over the wound.

Other ways to help:

• Do speak in a calm way to the injured person.
• Do try to keep them warm and as comfortable as possible.
• Do not give them anything to drink.
• Do not give them a cigarette.
• Don't let injured people wander into the road.

The AA's advice on safety if you break down

If you are on a non-motorway road:

• Try to get your vehicle off the main road. At least, get it right to the side of the road or on to the verge.
• If the vehicle is in a place where it might be hit by another vehicle, get any passengers out and to a safer place.
• Switch on the hazard warning lights to warn other drivers.
• If you have a red warning triangle, place it at least 45 metres behind your car to warn other traffic (but don't use it on a motorway).

• If you are a member of a motoring organisation such as the AA, call them and tell them where you are and what has happened. Wait with your vehicle until the patrol arrives.

If you are on a motorway:

• If possible, leave the motorway at the next exit. If you can't get that far, drive on to the hard shoulder. Stop far over to the left, and switch on your hazard warning lights.
• Get everyone out of the vehicle, using the nearside doors (but leave pets in the vehicle). Get them to sit on the bank, well away from the traffic.
• Use the nearest orange emergency phone to call the emergency services and tell them where you are and what has happened (for your safety, face the oncoming traffic while you are on the phone).
• Go back to your vehicle and wait on the bank near by until help arrives.
• Do not cross the motorway on foot or try to do repairs yourself – even changing a wheel. This is too dangerous on a motorway.

DID YOU KNOW?
Before driving into a tunnel you should tune into a local radio station and listen to the traffic reports incase there are any accidents or problems in the tunnel.

Now go to page 280 to test yourself on the questions about Accidents

Section 14
Vehicle Loading

This last section, called VEHICLE LOADING, is the shortest of all (see pages 291–2). It covers a mixture of the following:
- how to load your vehicle safely
- using a roof rack
- towing caravans and trailers
- child restraints and safety locks.

When you have passed your test you can tow a trailer, if the combined weight of the vehicle and trailer is less than 3,500kg. So you need to know the rules about towing.

Towing
When you get your first full driving licence, check it to see how much you are allowed to tow. Do not tow any trailer that comes to more than that weight. The weight of a trailer should be no more than 85% of the weight of the car that is to pull it. But it is best to stay well below that top weight, because towing a trailer will affect the way your vehicle handles.

When you are towing, you need to allow:
- more room when overtaking
- more time to brake and stop.

When you are turning at a roundabout or junction you will need to think about where you are on the road.

Roof racks
If you put a roof rack on your car, it will make a difference to the way your vehicle handles.

- The roof rack makes your vehicle taller, so more vulnerable to strong winds.
- You will increase your fuel consumption.
- You need to change the way you drive to allow for the extra weight.

Any load that is carried on a roof rack must be tied down securely.

To find out more, look up the parts of *The Highway Code* that deal with **Loads** and **Towing**.

Loading a trailer
If the weight of the load is arranged properly, this should cut down the risk of **losing control, swerving and snaking** (see below).
- Try to **spread the weight evenly** when you load your trailer. Do not put more weight towards the front, or the back, or to one side.
- It is **against the law** to have a load that is **sticking out in a dangerous way.**
- Don't forget that if you park a vehicle with a trailer overnight, it must have **lights.**

> **DID YOU KNOW?**
> A vehicle towing a trailer:
> - must **not** go over a **maximum speed limit of 60mph** (see the rules on speed limits in *The Highway Code*)
> - must **not** use the **right (outside) lane on a motorway.**

Snaking
'Snaking' means moving from side to side. A caravan will snake if it is not properly attached or loaded, or if the car pulling it is going too fast.

Vehicle Loading

If you are towing a caravan or trailer and it starts to snake:
- slow down – stop pressing the accelerator (do not brake suddenly)
- get back in control of the steering
- then brake gently.

The driver's responsibility for the passengers

There are also questions in the Vehicle Loading section about the safety of passengers. As the driver, you are responsible for making sure your vehicle is not overloaded – and this applies to people and animals as well as to luggage.

All passengers:
- must wear a **seat belt** (unless they have a medical certificate saying they should not wear one)
- all children under 14 must wear a seat belt or be strapped into a **child seat** or other 'restraint' suitable for their age. (See the section on Child Restraints in your copy of *The Highway Code*.)

Children

Children must not sit in the space behind the back seat of a hatchback car, and no passengers should sit in a caravan while it is being towed.

Pets

Pets should be kept under careful control. You might keep them and you safe with a special harness, or behind a screen in a hatchback to stop them being thrown forward in an accident.

DID YOU KNOW?

If you are going to buy a trailer, **make sure it fits your car's tow bar**. Tow bars **must** keep to EU regulations, and must have electric sockets to connect to the lights on the trailer.

When towing a heavy load, you might need to **blow your tyres up to more than the normal pressures**. Check your vehicle's handbook for advice. Remember to change back to the normal pressures when you finish your journey.

Now go to page 291 to test yourself on the questions about Vehicle Loading

The Official Theory Test Questions

Part 4

The Official Theory Test Questions

Contents PAGE

1 Before you make a U-turn in the road, you should

Mark one answer

- [ ] **A.** give an arm signal as well as using your indicators
- [ ] **B.** signal so that other drivers can slow down for you
- [ ] **C.** look over your shoulder for a final check
- [ ] **D.** select a higher gear than normal

2 As you approach this bridge you should

Oncoming vehicles in middle of road

Mark three answers

- [ ] **A.** move into the middle of the road to get a better view
- [ ] **B.** slow down
- [ ] **C.** get over the bridge as quickly as possible
- [ ] **D.** consider using your horn
- [ ] **E.** find another route
- [ ] **F.** beware of pedestrians

3 When following a large vehicle you should keep well back because

Mark one answer

- [ ] **A.** it allows you to corner more quickly
- [ ] **B.** it helps the large vehicle to stop more easily
- [ ] **C.** it allows the driver to see you in the mirrors
- [ ] **D.** it helps you to keep out of the wind

4 In which of these situations should you avoid overtaking?

Mark one answer

- [ ] **A.** Just after a bend
- [ ] **B.** In a one-way street
- [ ] **C.** On a 30mph road
- [ ] **D.** Approaching a dip in the road

5 This road marking warns

Mark one answer

- [ ] **A.** drivers to use the hard shoulder
- [ ] **B.** overtaking drivers there is a bend to the left
- [ ] **C.** overtaking drivers to move back to the left
- [ ] **D.** drivers that it is safe to overtake

6 Your mobile phone rings while you are travelling. You should

Mark one answer

- [ ] **A.** stop immediately
- [ ] **B.** answer it immediately
- [ ] **C.** pull up in a suitable place
- [ ] **D.** pull up at the nearest kerb

> **TIP** Be aware that one in three of road accident fatalities are pedestrians or cyclists.

7 Why are these yellow lines painted across the road?

Mark one answer
- [ ] **A.** To help you choose the correct lane
- [ ] **B.** To help you keep the correct separation distance
- [ ] **C.** To make you aware of your speed
- [ ] **D.** To tell you the distance to the roundabout

8 You are approaching traffic lights that have been on green for some time. You should

Mark one answer
- [ ] **A.** accelerate hard
- [ ] **B.** maintain your speed
- [ ] **C.** be ready to stop
- [ ] **D.** brake hard

9 Which of the following should you do before stopping?

Mark one answer
- [ ] **A.** Sound the horn
- [ ] **B.** Use the mirrors
- [ ] **C.** Select a higher gear
- [ ] **D.** Flash your headlights

10 As a driver what does the term 'Blind Spot' mean?

Mark one answer
- [ ] **A.** An area covered by your right-hand mirror
- [ ] **B.** An area not covered by your headlamps
- [ ] **C.** An area covered by your left-hand mirror
- [ ] **D.** An area not seen in your mirrors

11 Objects hanging from your interior mirror may

Mark two answers
- [ ] **A.** restrict your view
- [ ] **B.** improve your driving
- [ ] **C.** distract your attention
- [ ] **D.** help your concentration

12 Which of the following may cause loss of concentration on a long journey?

Mark four answers
- [ ] **A.** Loud music
- [ ] **B.** Arguing with a passenger
- [ ] **C.** Using a mobile phone
- [ ] **D.** Putting in a cassette tape
- [ ] **E.** Stopping regularly to rest
- [ ] **F.** Pulling up to tune the radio

13 On a long motorway journey boredom can cause you to feel sleepy. You should

Mark two answers
- [ ] **A.** leave the motorway and find a safe place to stop
- [ ] **B.** keep looking around at the surrounding landscape
- [ ] **C.** drive faster to complete your journey sooner
- [ ] **D.** ensure a supply of fresh air into your vehicle
- [ ] **E.** stop on the hard shoulder for a rest

14 You are driving at dusk. You should switch your lights on

Mark two answers

A. even when street lights are not lit
B. so others can see you
C. only when others have done so
D. only when street lights are lit

15 You are most likely to lose concentration when driving if you

Mark two answers

A. use a mobile phone
B. listen to very loud music
C. switch on the heated rear window
D. look at the door mirrors

16 Which FOUR are most likely to cause you to lose concentration while you are driving?

Mark four answers

A. Using a mobile phone
B. Talking into a microphone
C. Tuning your car radio
D. Looking at a map
E. Checking the mirrors
F. Using the demisters

17 You should not use a mobile phone whilst driving

Mark one answer

A. until you are satisfied that no other traffic is near
B. unless you are able to drive one handed
C. because it might distract your attention from the road ahead
D. because reception is poor when the engine is running

18 Your vehicle is fitted with a hands-free phone system. Using this equipment whilst driving

Mark one answer

A. is quite safe as long as you slow down
B. could distract your attention from the road
C. is recommended by The Highway Code
D. could be very good for road safety

19 Using a hands-free phone is likely to

Mark one answer

A. improve your safety
B. increase your concentration
C. reduce your view
D. divert your attention

20 You should ONLY use a mobile phone when

Mark one answer

A. receiving a call
B. suitably parked
C. driving at less than 30mph
D. driving an automatic vehicle

21 Using a mobile phone while you are driving

Mark one answer

A. is acceptable in a vehicle with power steering
B. will reduce your field of vision
C. could distract your attention from the road
D. will affect your vehicle's electronic systems

22 What is the safest way to use a mobile phone in your vehicle?

Mark one answer

- A. Use hands-free equipment
- B. Find a suitable place to stop
- C. Drive slowly on a quiet road
- D. Direct your call through the operator

23 You are driving on a wet road. You have to stop your vehicle in an emergency. You should

Mark one answer

- A. apply the handbrake and footbrake together
- B. keep both hands on the wheel
- C. select reverse gear
- D. give an arm signal

24 When you are moving off from behind a parked car you should

Mark three answers

- A. look round before you move off
- B. use all the mirrors on the vehicle
- C. look round after moving off
- D. use the exterior mirrors only
- E. give a signal if necessary
- F. give a signal after moving off

25 You are travelling along this narrow country road. When passing the cyclist you should go

Mark one answer

- A. slowly, sounding the horn as you pass
- B. quickly, leaving plenty of room
- C. slowly, leaving plenty of room
- D. quickly, sounding the horn as you pass

26 Your vehicle is fitted with a hand-held telephone. To use the telephone you should

Mark one answer

- A. reduce your speed
- B. find a safe place to stop
- C. steer the vehicle with one hand
- D. be particularly careful at junctions

27 To answer a call on your mobile phone while travelling you should

Mark one answer

- A. reduce your speed wherever you are
- B. stop in a proper and convenient place
- C. keep the call time to a minimum
- D. slow down and allow others to overtake

TIP When following long vehicles, keep well back so that you are visible in the driver's mirrors. Take a look at the markers on the sides and the end. They are there to warn you of the length of the vehicle, and sometimes overhanging loads.

28 Your mobile phone rings while you are on the motorway. Before answering you should

Mark one answer **NI**

- [ ] **A.** reduce your speed to 50mph
- [ ] **B.** pull up on the hard shoulder
- [ ] **C.** move into the left-hand lane
- [ ] **D.** stop in a safe place

29 You are turning right on to a dual carriageway. What should you do before emerging?

Mark one answer

- [ ] **A.** Stop, apply the handbrake and then select a low gear
- [ ] **B.** Position your vehicle well to the left of the side road
- [ ] **C.** Check that the central reserve is wide enough for your vehicle
- [ ] **D.** Make sure that you leave enough room for a following vehicle

30 You lose your way on a busy road. What is the best action to take?

Mark one answer

- [ ] **A.** Stop at traffic lights and ask pedestrians
- [ ] **B.** Shout to other drivers to ask them the way
- [ ] **C.** Turn into a side road, stop and check a map
- [ ] **D.** Check a map, and keep going with the traffic flow

31 You are waiting to emerge from a junction. The screen pillar is restricting your view. What should you be particularly aware of?

Mark one answer

- [ ] **A.** Lorries
- [ ] **B.** Buses
- [ ] **C.** Motorcyclists
- [ ] **D.** Coaches

32 When emerging from junctions which is most likely to obstruct your view?

Mark one answer

- [ ] **A.** Windscreen pillars
- [ ] **B.** Steering wheel
- [ ] **C.** Interior mirror
- [ ] **D.** Windscreen wipers

33 Windscreen pillars can obstruct your view. You should take particular care when

Mark one answer

- [ ] **A.** driving on a motorway
- [ ] **B.** driving on a dual carriageway
- [ ] **C.** approaching a one-way street
- [ ] **D.** approaching bends and junctions

34 You cannot see clearly behind when reversing. What should you do?

Mark one answer

- [ ] **A.** Open your window to look behind
- [ ] **B.** Open the door and look behind
- [ ] **C.** Look in the nearside mirror
- [ ] **D.** Ask someone to guide you

35 At a pelican crossing the flashing amber light means you MUST

Mark one answer

- A. stop and wait for the green light
- B. stop and wait for the red light
- C. give way to pedestrians waiting to cross
- D. give way to pedestrians already on the crossing

36 You should never wave people across at pedestrian crossings because

Mark one answer

- A. there may be another vehicle coming
- B. they may not be looking
- C. it is safer for you to carry on
- D. they may not be ready to cross

37 At a puffin crossing what colour follows the green signal?

Mark one answer

- A. Steady red
- B. Flashing amber
- C. Steady amber
- D. Flashing green

38 You could use the 'Two-Second Rule'

Mark one answer

- A. before restarting the engine after it has stalled
- B. to keep a safe gap from the vehicle in front
- C. before using the 'Mirror-Signal-Manoeuvre' routine
- D. when emerging on wet roads

39 'Tailgating' means

Mark one answer

- A. using the rear door of a hatchback car
- B. reversing into a parking space
- C. following another vehicle too closely
- D. driving with rear fog lights on

40 Following this vehicle too closely is unwise because

Mark one answer

- A. your brakes will overheat
- B. your view ahead is increased
- C. your engine will overheat
- D. your view ahead is reduced

41 You are following a vehicle on a wet road. You should leave a time gap of at least

Mark one answer

- A. one second
- B. two seconds
- C. three seconds
- D. four seconds

42 You are in a line of traffic. The driver behind you is following very closely. What action should you take?

Mark one answer

- A. Ignore the following driver and continue to drive within the speed limit
- B. Slow down, gradually increasing the gap between you and the vehicle in front
- C. Signal left and wave the following driver past
- D. Move over to a position just left of the centre line of the road

43 A long, heavily laden lorry is taking a long time to overtake you. What should you do?

Mark one answer

- **A.** Speed up
- **B.** Slow down
- **C.** Hold your speed
- **D.** Change direction

44 Which of the following vehicles will use blue flashing beacons?

Mark three answers

- **A.** Motorway maintenance
- **B.** Bomb disposal
- **C.** Blood transfusion
- **D.** Police patrol
- **E.** Breakdown recovery

45 Which THREE of these emergency services might have blue flashing beacons?

Mark three answers

- **A.** Coastguard
- **B.** Bomb disposal
- **C.** Gritting lorries
- **D.** Animal ambulances
- **E.** Mountain rescue
- **F.** Doctors' cars

46 When being followed by an ambulance showing a flashing blue beacon you should

Mark one answer

- **A.** pull over as soon as safely possible to let it pass
- **B.** accelerate hard to get away from it
- **C.** maintain your speed and course
- **D.** brake harshly and immediately stop in the road

47 What type of emergency vehicle is fitted with a green flashing beacon?

Mark one answer

- **A.** Fire engine
- **B.** Road gritter
- **C.** Ambulance
- **D.** Doctor's car

48 A flashing green beacon on a vehicle means

Mark one answer

- **A.** police on non-urgent duties
- **B.** doctor on an emergency call
- **C.** road safety patrol operating
- **D.** gritting in progress

49 A vehicle has a flashing green beacon. What does this mean?

Mark one answer

- **A.** A doctor is answering an emergency call
- **B.** The vehicle is slow moving
- **C.** It is a motorway police patrol vehicle
- **D.** A vehicle is carrying hazardous chemicals

50 Diamond-shaped signs give instructions to

Mark one answer

- **A.** tram drivers
- **B.** bus drivers
- **C.** lorry drivers
- **D.** taxi drivers

TIP *The Highway Code* advises you *not* to use your mobile if you have an accident on a motorway. Use the (free) emergency phone; it connects directly with the police, who will then be able to identify your exact location.

51 On a road where trams operate, which of these vehicles will be most at risk from the tram rails?

Mark one answer

- [ ] **A.** Cars
- [ ] **B.** Cycles
- [ ] **C.** Buses
- [ ] **D.** Lorries

52 What should you use your horn for?

Mark one answer

- [ ] **A.** To alert others to your presence
- [ ] **B.** To allow you right of way
- [ ] **C.** To greet other road users
- [ ] **D.** To signal your annoyance

53 You are in a one-way street and want to turn right. You should position yourself

Mark one answer

- [ ] **A.** in the right-hand lane
- [ ] **B.** in the left-hand lane
- [ ] **C.** in either lane, depending on the traffic
- [ ] **D.** just left of the centre line

54 You wish to turn right ahead. Why should you take up the correct position in good time?

Mark one answer

- [ ] **A.** To allow other drivers to pull out in front of you
- [ ] **B.** To give a better view into the road that you're joining
- [ ] **C.** To help other road users know what you intend to do
- [ ] **D.** To allow drivers to pass you on the right

55 At which type of crossing are cyclists allowed to ride across with pedestrians?

Mark one answer

- [ ] **A.** Toucan
- [ ] **B.** Puffin
- [ ] **C.** Pelican
- [ ] **D.** Zebra

56 A bus is stopped at a bus stop ahead of you. Its right-hand indicator is flashing. You should

Mark one answer

- [ ] **A.** flash your headlights and slow down
- [ ] **B.** slow down and give way if it is safe to do so
- [ ] **C.** sound your horn and keep going
- [ ] **D.** slow down and then sound your horn

57 You are travelling at the legal speed limit. A vehicle comes up quickly behind, flashing its headlights. You should

Mark one answer

- [ ] **A.** accelerate to make a gap behind you
- [ ] **B.** touch the brakes sharply to show your brake lights
- [ ] **C.** maintain your speed to prevent the vehicle from overtaking
- [ ] **D.** allow the vehicle to overtake

58 You should ONLY flash your headlights to other road users

Mark one answer

- A. to show that you are giving way
- B. to show that you are about to turn
- C. to tell them that you have right of way
- D. to let them know that you are there

59 You are approaching unmarked crossroads. How should you deal with this type of junction?

Mark one answer

- A. Accelerate and keep to the middle
- B. Slow down and keep to the right
- C. Accelerate looking to the left
- D. Slow down and look both ways

60 You are approaching a pelican crossing. The amber light is flashing. You MUST

Mark one answer

- A. give way to pedestrians who are crossing
- B. encourage pedestrians to cross
- C. not move until the green light appears
- D. stop even if the crossing is clear

61 At puffin crossings which light will not show to a driver?

Mark one answer

- A. Flashing amber
- B. Red
- C. Steady amber
- D. Green

62 A two-second gap between yourself and the car in front is sufficient when conditions are

Mark one answer

- A. wet
- B. good
- C. damp
- D. foggy

63 You are driving on a clear night. There is a steady stream of oncoming traffic. The national speed limit applies. Which lights should you use?

Mark one answer

- A. Full beam headlights
- B. Sidelights
- C. Dipped headlights
- D. Fog lights

64 You are driving behind a large goods vehicle. It signals left but steers to the right. You should

Mark one answer

- A. slow down and let the vehicle turn
- B. drive on, keeping to the left
- C. overtake on the right of it
- D. hold your speed and sound your horn

TIP Remember **O A P:**
Observe
Anticipate
Plan

65 You are driving along this road. The red van cuts in close in front of you. What should you do?

Mark one answer

- [ ] **A.** Accelerate to get closer to the red van
- [ ] **B.** Give a long blast on the horn
- [ ] **C.** Drop back to leave the correct separation distance
- [ ] **D.** Flash your headlights several times

66 You are waiting in a traffic queue at night. To avoid dazzling following drivers you should

Mark one answer

- [ ] **A.** apply the handbrake only
- [ ] **B.** apply the footbrake only
- [ ] **C.** switch off your headlights
- [ ] **D.** use both the handbrake and footbrake

67 You are driving in traffic at the speed limit for the road. The driver behind is trying to overtake. You should

Mark one answer

- [ ] **A.** move closer to the car ahead, so the driver behind has no room to overtake
- [ ] **B.** wave the driver behind to overtake when it is safe
- [ ] **C.** keep a steady course and allow the driver behind to overtake
- [ ] **D.** accelerate to get away from the driver behind

68 You are driving at night on an unlit road following a slower-moving vehicle. You should

Mark one answer

- [ ] **A.** flash your headlights
- [ ] **B.** use dipped beam headlights
- [ ] **C.** switch off your headlights
- [ ] **D.** use full beam headlights

69 A bus lane on your left shows no times of operation. This means it is

Mark one answer

- [ ] **A.** not in operation at all
- [ ] **B.** only in operation at peak times
- [ ] **C.** in operation 24 hours a day
- [ ] **D.** only in operation in daylight hours

70 You are driving along a country road. A horse and rider are approaching. What should you do?

Mark two answers

- [ ] **A.** Increase your speed
- [ ] **B.** Sound your horn
- [ ] **C.** Flash your headlights
- [ ] **D.** Drive slowly past
- [ ] **E.** Give plenty of room
- [ ] **F.** Rev your engine

71 A person herding sheep asks you to stop. You should

Mark one answer

- A. ignore them as they have no authority
- B. stop and switch off your engine
- C. continue on but drive slowly
- D. try and get past quickly

72 When overtaking a horse and rider you should

Mark one answer

- A. sound your horn as a warning
- B. go past as quickly as possible
- C. flash your headlights as a warning
- D. go past slowly and carefully

73 You are approaching a zebra crossing. Pedestrians are waiting to cross. You should

Mark one answer

- A. give way to the elderly and infirm only
- B. slow down and prepare to stop
- C. use your headlights to indicate they can cross
- D. wave at them to cross the road

74 You are driving a slow-moving vehicle on a narrow winding road. You should

Mark one answer

- A. keep well out to stop vehicles overtaking dangerously
- B. wave following vehicles past you if you think they can overtake quickly
- C. pull in safely when you can, to let following vehicles overtake
- D. give a left signal when it is safe for vehicles to overtake you

75 You are driving a slow-moving vehicle on a narrow road. When traffic wishes to overtake you should

Mark one answer

- A. take no action
- B. put your hazard warning lights on
- C. stop immediately and wave it on
- D. pull in safely as soon as you can do so

76 You are driving a slow-moving vehicle on a narrow winding road. In order to let other vehicles overtake you should

Mark one answer

- A. wave to them to pass
- B. pull in when you can
- C. show a left turn signal
- D. keep left and hold your speed

77 A vehicle pulls out in front of you at a junction. What should you do?

Mark one answer

- A. Swerve past it and sound your horn
- B. Flash your headlights and drive up close behind
- C. Slow down and be ready to stop
- D. Accelerate past it immediately

78 You stop for pedestrians waiting to cross at a zebra crossing. They do not start to cross. What should you do?

Mark one answer

- A. Be patient and wait
- B. Sound your horn
- C. Carry on
- D. Wave them to cross

79 You are following this lorry. You should keep well back from it to

Mark one answer

- A. give you a good view of the road ahead
- B. stop following traffic from rushing through the junction
- C. prevent traffic behind you from overtaking
- D. allow you to hurry through the traffic lights if they change

80 You are approaching a red light at a puffin crossing. Pedestrians are on the crossing. The red light will stay on until

Mark one answer

- A. you start to edge forward on to the crossing
- B. the pedestrians have reached a safe position
- C. the pedestrians are clear of the front of your vehicle
- D. a driver from the opposite direction reaches the crossing

81 Which instrument panel warning light would show that headlights are on full beam?

Mark one answer

A. 　　　B.

C. 　　　D.

TIP Blue flashing lights are used by ambulances, fire engines and police vehicles, as well as other emergency services Doctors on call display green flashing lights. Gritting lorries, motorway maintenance and breakdown recovery vehicles display flashing amber lights.

Safety and Your Vehicle – Section 3

82 Which of these, if allowed to get low, could cause an accident?

Mark one answer

- [ ] **A.** Antifreeze level
- [ ] **B.** Brake fluid level
- [ ] **C.** Battery water level
- [ ] **D.** Radiator coolant level

83 Which TWO are badly affected if the tyres are under-inflated?

Mark two answers

- [ ] **A.** Braking
- [ ] **B.** Steering
- [ ] **C.** Changing gear
- [ ] **D.** Parking

84 Motor vehicles can harm the environment. This has resulted in

Mark three answers

- [ ] **A.** air pollution
- [ ] **B.** damage to buildings
- [ ] **C.** reduced health risks
- [ ] **D.** improved public transport
- [ ] **E.** less use of electrical vehicles
- [ ] **F.** using up natural resources

85 Excessive or uneven tyre wear can be caused by faults in which THREE?

Mark three answers

- [ ] **A.** The gearbox
- [ ] **B.** The braking system
- [ ] **C.** The accelerator
- [ ] **D.** The exhaust system
- [ ] **E.** Wheel alignment
- [ ] **F.** The suspension

86 You must NOT sound your horn

Mark one answer

- [ ] **A.** between 10pm and 6am in a built-up area
- [ ] **B.** at any time in a built-up area
- [ ] **C.** between 11.30pm and 7am in a built-up area
- [ ] **D.** between 11.30pm and 6am on any road

87 The pictured vehicle is 'environmentally friendly' because it

Mark three answers

- [ ] **A.** reduces noise pollution
- [ ] **B.** uses diesel fuel
- [ ] **C.** uses electricity
- [ ] **D.** uses unleaded fuel
- [ ] **E.** reduces parking spaces
- [ ] **F.** reduces town traffic

88 Supertrams or Light Rapid Transit (LRT) systems are environmentally friendly because

Mark one answer

- [ ] **A.** they use diesel power
- [ ] **B.** they use quieter roads
- [ ] **C.** they use electric power
- [ ] **D.** they do not operate during rush hour

TIP Large dogs should be in a secure area to the rear of a hatchback, with a screen to prevent them being thrown forward in the event of an accident.

89 'Red routes' in major cities have been introduced to

Mark one answer

- A. raise the speed limits
- B. help the traffic flow
- C. provide better parking
- D. allow lorries to load more freely

90 In some narrow residential streets you will find a speed limit of

Mark one answer

- A. 20mph
- B. 25mph
- C. 35mph
- D. 40mph

91 Road humps, chicanes, and narrowings are

Mark one answer

- A. always at major road works
- B. used to increase traffic speed
- C. at toll bridge approaches only
- D. traffic calming measures

92 The purpose of a catalytic converter is to reduce

Mark one answer

- A. fuel consumption
- B. the risk of fire
- C. toxic exhaust gases
- D. engine wear

93 Catalytic converters are fitted to make the

Mark one answer

- A. engine produce more power
- B. exhaust system easier to replace
- C. engine run quietly
- D. exhaust fumes cleaner

94 It is essential that tyre pressures are checked regularly. When should this be done?

Mark one answer

- A. After any lengthy journey
- B. After travelling at high speed
- C. When tyres are hot
- D. When tyres are cold

95 When should you NOT use your horn in a built-up area?

Mark one answer

- A. Between 8pm and 8am
- B. Between 9pm and dawn
- C. Between dusk and 8am
- D. Between 11.30pm and 7am

96 You will use more fuel if your tyres are

Mark one answer

- A. under-inflated
- B. of different makes
- C. over-inflated
- D. new and hardly used

97 How should you dispose of a used battery?

Mark two answers

- A. Take it to a local authority site
- B. Put it in the dustbin
- C. Break it up into pieces
- D. Leave it on waste land
- E. Take it to a garage
- F. Burn it on a fire

98 What is most likely to cause high fuel consumption?

Mark one answer

- A. Poor steering control
- B. Accelerating around bends
- C. Staying in high gears
- D. Harsh braking and accelerating

99 The fluid level in your battery is low. What should you top it up with?

Mark one answer

- A. Battery acid
- B. Distilled water
- C. Engine oil
- D. Engine coolant

100 You need top up your battery. What level should you fill to?

Mark one answer

- A. The top of the battery
- B. Half-way up the battery
- C. Just below the cell plates
- D. Just above the cell plates

101 You have too much oil in your engine. What could this cause?

Mark one answer

- A. Low oil pressure
- B. Engine overheating
- C. Chain wear
- D. Oil leaks

102 You are parking on a two-way road at night. The speed limit is 40mph. You should park on the

NI

Mark one answer

- A. left with parking lights on
- B. left with no lights on
- C. right with parking lights on
- D. right with dipped headlights on

103 You are parked on the road at night. Where must you use parking lights?

Mark one answer

- A. Where there are continuous white lines in the middle of the road
- B. Where the speed limit exceeds 30mph
- C. Where you are facing oncoming traffic
- D. Where you are near a bus stop

104 Which FOUR of these MUST be in good working order for your car to be roadworthy?

Mark four answers

- A. Temperature gauge
- B. Speedometer
- C. Windscreen washers
- D. Windscreen wiper
- E. Oil warning light
- F. Horn

105 New petrol-engined cars must be fitted with catalytic converters. The reason for this is to

Mark one answer

- A. control exhaust noise levels
- B. prolong the life of the exhaust system
- C. allow the exhaust system to be recycled
- D. reduce harmful exhaust emissions

106 What can cause heavy steering?

Mark one answer
- [ ] **A.** Driving on ice
- [ ] **B.** Badly worn brakes
- [ ] **C.** Over-inflated tyres
- [ ] **D.** Under-inflated tyres

107 Driving with under-inflated tyres can affect

Mark two answers
- [ ] **A.** engine temperature
- [ ] **B.** fuel consumption
- [ ] **C.** braking
- [ ] **D.** oil pressure

108 Excessive or uneven tyre wear can be caused by faults in the

Mark two answers
- [ ] **A.** gearbox
- [ ] **B.** braking system
- [ ] **C.** suspension
- [ ] **D.** exhaust system

109 The main cause of brake fade is

Mark one answer
- [ ] **A.** the brakes overheating
- [ ] **B.** air in the brake fluid
- [ ] **C.** oil on the brakes
- [ ] **D.** the brakes out of adjustment

110 Your anti-lock brakes warning light stays on. You should

Mark one answer
- [ ] **A.** check the brake fluid level
- [ ] **B.** check the footbrake free play
- [ ] **C.** check that the handbrake is released
- [ ] **D.** have the brakes checked immediately

111 What does this instrument panel light mean when lit?

Mark one answer
- [ ] **A.** Gear lever in park
- [ ] **B.** Gear lever in neutral
- [ ] **C.** Handbrake on
- [ ] **D.** Handbrake off

112 While driving, this warning light on your dashboard comes on. It means

Mark one answer
- [ ] **A.** a fault in the braking system
- [ ] **B.** the engine oil is low
- [ ] **C.** a rear light has failed
- [ ] **D.** your seat belt is not fastened

113 It is important to wear suitable shoes when you are driving. Why is this?

Mark one answer
- [ ] **A.** To prevent wear on the pedals
- [ ] **B.** To maintain control of the pedals
- [ ] **C.** To enable you to adjust your seat
- [ ] **D.** To enable you to walk for assistance if you break down

114 A properly adjusted head restraint will

Mark one answer
- [ ] **A.** make you more comfortable
- [ ] **B.** help you to avoid neck injury
- [ ] **C.** help you to relax
- [ ] **D.** help you to maintain your driving position

115 What will reduce the risk of neck injury resulting from a collision?

Mark one answer

- A. An air-sprung seat
- B. Anti-lock brakes
- C. A collapsible steering wheel
- D. A properly adjusted head restraint

116 You are driving a friend's children home from school. They are both under 14 years old. Who is responsible for making sure they wear a seat belt?

Mark one answer

- A. An adult passenger
- B. The children
- C. You, the driver
- D. Your friend

117 Car passengers MUST wear a seat belt if one is available, unless they are

Mark one answer

- A. under 14 years old
- B. under 1.5 metres (5 feet) in height
- C. sitting in the rear seat
- D. exempt for medical reasons

118 You are testing your suspension. You notice that your vehicle keeps bouncing when you press down on the front wing. What does this mean?

Mark one answer

- A. Worn tyres
- B. Tyres under-inflated
- C. Steering wheel not located centrally
- D. Worn shock absorbers

119 A roof rack fitted to your car will

Mark one answer

- A. reduce fuel consumption
- B. improve the road handling
- C. make your car go faster
- D. increase fuel consumption

120 It is illegal to drive with tyres that

Mark one answer

- A. have been bought second-hand
- B. have a large deep cut in the side wall
- C. are of different makes
- D. are of different tread patterns

121 The legal minimum depth of tread for car tyres over three quarters of the breadth is

Mark one answer

- A. 1mm
- B. 1.6mm
- C. 2.5mm
- D. 4mm

122 You are carrying two 13-year-old children and their parents in your car. Who is responsible for seeing that the children wear seat belts?

Mark one answer

- A. The children's parents
- B. You, the driver
- C. The front-seat passenger
- D. The children

123 When a roof rack is not in use it should be removed. Why is this?

Mark one answer

- [ ] **A.** It will affect the suspension
- [ ] **B.** It is illegal
- [ ] **C.** It will affect your braking
- [ ] **D.** It will waste fuel

124 You have a loose filler cap on your diesel fuel tank. This will

Mark two answers

- [ ] **A.** waste fuel and money
- [ ] **B.** make roads slippery for other road users
- [ ] **C.** improve your vehicle's fuel consumption
- [ ] **D.** increase the level of exhaust emissions

125 How can you, as a driver, help the environment?

Mark three answers

- [ ] **A.** By reducing your speed
- [ ] **B.** By gentle acceleration
- [ ] **C.** By using leaded fuel
- [ ] **D.** By driving faster
- [ ] **E.** By harsh acceleration
- [ ] **F.** By servicing your vehicle properly

126 To help the environment, you can avoid wasting fuel by

Mark three answers

- [ ] **A.** having your vehicle properly serviced
- [ ] **B.** making sure your tyres are correctly inflated
- [ ] **C.** not over-revving in the lower gears
- [ ] **D.** driving at higher speeds where possible
- [ ] **E.** keeping an empty roof rack properly fitted
- [ ] **F.** servicing your vehicle less regularly

127 To reduce the volume of traffic on the roads you could

Mark three answers

- [ ] **A.** use public transport more often
- [ ] **B.** share a car when possible
- [ ] **C.** walk or cycle on short journeys
- [ ] **D.** travel by car at all times
- [ ] **E.** use a car with a smaller engine
- [ ] **F.** drive in a bus lane

128 Which THREE of the following are most likely to waste fuel?

Mark three answers

- [ ] **A.** Reducing your speed
- [ ] **B.** Carrying unnecessary weight
- [ ] **C.** Using the wrong grade of fuel
- [ ] **D.** Under-inflated tyres
- [ ] **E.** Using different brands of fuel
- [ ] **F.** A fitted, empty roof rack

129 To avoid spillage after refuelling, you should make sure that

Mark one answer

- [ ] **A.** your tank is only ¾ full
- [ ] **B.** you have used a locking filler cap
- [ ] **C.** you check your fuel gauge is working
- [ ] **D.** your filler cap is securely fastened

130 Which THREE things can you, as a road user, do to help the environment?

Mark three answers

- [ ] **A.** Cycle when possible
- [ ] **B.** Drive on under-inflated tyres
- [ ] **C.** Use the choke for as long as possible on a cold engine
- [ ] **D.** Have your vehicle properly tuned and serviced
- [ ] **E.** Watch the traffic and plan ahead
- [ ] **F.** Brake as late as possible without skidding

131 As a driver you can cause MORE damage to the environment by

Mark three answers

- A. choosing a fuel-efficient vehicle
- B. making a lot of short journeys
- C. driving in as high a gear as possible
- D. accelerating as quickly as possible
- E. having your vehicle regularly serviced
- F. using leaded fuel

132 Extra care should be taken when refuelling, because diesel fuel when spilt is

Mark one answer

- A. sticky
- B. odourless
- C. clear
- D. slippery

133 To help protect the environment you should NOT

Mark one answer

- A. remove your roof rack when unloaded
- B. use your car for very short journeys
- C. walk, cycle, or use public transport
- D. empty the boot of unnecessary weight

134 Which THREE does the law require you to keep in good condition?

Mark three answers

- A. Gears
- B. Transmission
- C. Headlights
- D. Windscreen
- E. Seat belts

135 Driving at 70mph uses more fuel than driving at 50mph by up to

Mark one answer

- A. 10%
- B. 30%
- C. 75%
- D. 100%

136 Your vehicle pulls to one side when braking. You should

Mark one answer

- A. change the tyres around
- B. consult your garage as soon as possible
- C. pump the pedal when braking
- D. use your handbrake at the same time

137 As a driver you can help reduce pollution levels in town centres by

Mark one answer

- A. driving more quickly
- B. using leaded fuel
- C. walking or cycling
- D. driving short journeys

138 Unbalanced wheels on a car may cause

Mark one answer

- A. the steering to pull to one side
- B. the steering to vibrate
- C. the brakes to fail
- D. the tyres to deflate

139 Turning the steering wheel while your car is stationary can cause damage to the

Mark two answers

- A. gearbox
- B. engine
- C. brakes
- D. steering
- E. tyres

140 How can you reduce the chances of your car being broken into when leaving it unattended?

Mark one answer

A. Take all contents with you
B. Park near a taxi rank
C. Place any valuables on the floor
D. Park near a fire station

141 You have to leave valuables in your car. It would be safer to

Mark one answer

A. put them in a carrier bag
B. park near a school entrance
C. lock them out of sight
D. park near a bus stop

142 How could you deter theft from your car when leaving it unattended?

Mark one answer

A. Leave valuables in a carrier bag
B. Lock valuables out of sight
C. Put valuables on the seats
D. Leave valuables on the floor

143 Which of the following may help to deter a thief from stealing your car?

Mark one answer

A. Always keeping the headlights on
B. Fitting reflective glass windows
C. Always keeping the interior light on
D. Etching the car number on the windows

144 How can you help to prevent your car radio being stolen?

Mark one answer

A. Park in an unlit area
B. Hide the radio with a blanket
C. Park near a busy junction
D. Install a security coded radio

145 Which of the following should not be kept in your vehicle?

Mark one answer

A. A first aid kit
B. A road atlas
C. The tax disc
D. The vehicle documents

146 What should you do when leaving your vehicle?

Mark one answer

A. Put valuable documents under the seats
B. Remove all valuables
C. Cover valuables with a blanket
D. Leave the interior light on

147 You are parking your car. You have some valuables which you are unable to take with you. What should you do?

Mark one answer

A. Park near a police station
B. Put them under the driver's seat
C. Lock them out of sight
D. Park in an unlit side road

148 Which of these is most likely to deter the theft of your vehicle?

Mark one answer

- **A.** An immobiliser
- **B.** Tinted windows
- **C.** Locking wheel nuts
- **D.** A sun screen

149 Wherever possible, which one of the following should you do when parking at night?

Mark one answer

- **A.** Park in a quiet car park
- **B.** Park in a well-lit area
- **C.** Park facing against the flow of traffic
- **D.** Park next to a busy junction

150 When parking and leaving your car you should

Mark one answer

- **A.** park under a shady tree
- **B.** remove the tax disc
- **C.** park in a quiet road
- **D.** engage the steering lock

151 Rear facing baby seats should NEVER be used on a seat protected with

Mark one answer

- **A.** an airbag
- **B.** seat belts
- **C.** head restraints
- **D.** seat covers

152 When leaving your vehicle parked and unattended you should

Mark one answer

- **A.** park near a busy junction
- **B.** park in a housing estate
- **C.** remove the key and lock it
- **D.** leave the left indicator on

153 How can you lessen the risk of your vehicle being broken into at night?

Mark one answer

- **A.** Leave it in a well-lit area
- **B.** Park in a quiet side road
- **C.** Don't engage the steering lock
- **D.** Park in a poorly lit area

154 To help keep your car secure you could join a

Mark one answer

- **A.** vehicle breakdown organisation
- **B.** vehicle watch scheme
- **C.** advanced drivers scheme
- **D.** car maintenance class

155 Which TWO of the following will improve fuel consumption?

Mark two answers

- **A.** Reducing your road speed
- **B.** Planning well ahead
- **C.** Late and harsh braking
- **D.** Driving in lower gears
- **E.** Short journeys with a cold engine
- **F.** Rapid acceleration

156 You service your own vehicle. How should you get rid of the old engine oil?

Mark one answer
- A. Take it to a local authority site
- B. Pour it down a drain
- C. Tip it into a hole in the ground
- D. Put it into your dustbin

157 On your vehicle, where would you find a catalytic converter?

Mark one answer
- A. In the fuel tank
- B. In the air filter
- C. On the cooling system
- D. On the exhaust system

158 Why do MOT tests include a strict exhaust emission test?

Mark one answer
- A. To recover the cost of expensive garage equipment
- B. To help protect the environment against pollution
- C. To discover which fuel supplier is used the most
- D. To make sure diesel and petrol engines emit the same fumes

159 To reduce the damage your vehicle causes to the environment you should

Mark three answers
- A. use narrow side streets
- B. avoid harsh acceleration
- C. brake in good time
- D. anticipate well ahead
- E. use busy routes

160 Your vehicle has a catalytic converter. Its purpose is to reduce

Mark one answer
- A. exhaust noise
- B. fuel consumption
- C. exhaust emissions
- D. engine noise

161 A properly serviced vehicle will give

Mark two answers
- A. lower insurance premiums
- B. you a refund on your road tax
- C. better fuel economy
- D. cleaner exhaust emissions

162 You enter a road where there are road humps. What should you do?

Mark one answer
- A. Maintain a reduced speed throughout
- B. Accelerate quickly between each one
- C. Always keep to the maximum legal speed
- D. Drive slowly at school times only

TIP Do not drive with an empty roof rack on your car. By increasing drag, the roof rack can eat up more than 10% of your total fuel consumption.

163 When should you especially check the engine oil level?

Mark one answer

- A. Before a long journey
- B. When the engine is hot
- C. Early in the morning
- D. Every 6,000 miles

164 You are having difficulty finding a parking space in a busy town. You can see there is space on the zigzag lines of a zebra crossing. Can you park there?

Mark one answer

- A. No, unless you stay with your car
- B. Yes, in order to drop off a passenger
- C. Yes, if you do not block people from crossing
- D. No, not in any circumstances

165 When leaving your car unattended for a few minutes you should

Mark one answer

- A. leave the engine running
- B. switch the engine off but leave the key in
- C. lock it and remove the key
- D. park near a traffic warden

166 When parking and leaving your car for a few minutes you should

Mark one answer

- A. leave it unlocked
- B. lock it and remove the key
- C. leave the hazard warning lights on
- D. leave the interior light on

167 When leaving your car to help keep it secure you should

Mark one answer

- A. leave the hazard warning lights on
- B. lock it and remove the key
- C. park on a one-way street
- D. park in a residential area

168 When leaving your vehicle where should you park if possible?

Mark one answer

- A. Opposite a traffic island
- B. In a secure car park
- C. On a bend
- D. At or near a taxi rank

169 You are leaving your vehicle parked on a road. When may you leave the engine running?

Mark one answer

- A. If you will be parking for less than five minutes
- B. If the battery is flat
- C. When in a 20mph zone
- D. Never on any occasion

TIP If you have a petrol-fuelled car built after 1992, it will be fitted with a **catalytic converter**. *Catalyst* means something that enables a chemical change to take place; the catalytic converter, which is located in the car's exhaust system, converts pollutant gases into less harmful gases.

170 In which THREE places would parking your vehicle cause danger or obstruction to other road users?

Mark three answers

- [ ] **A.** In front of a property entrance
- [ ] **B.** At or near a bus stop
- [ ] **C.** On your driveway
- [ ] **D.** In a marked parking space
- [ ] **E.** On the approach to a level crossing

TIP Driving a four-wheel drive vehicle (4WD) demands different techniques; a 4WD has a higher centre of gravity, and is more likely to topple over if you are forced to swerve or drive too fast around a tight corner. The advantage of 4WD is that it has better road holding capabilities and is excellent over rough terrain.

171 In which THREE places would parking cause an obstruction to others?

Mark three answers

- [ ] **A.** Near the brow of a hill
- [ ] **B.** In a lay-by
- [ ] **C.** Where the kerb is raised
- [ ] **D.** Where the kerb has been lowered for wheelchairs
- [ ] **E.** At or near a bus stop

172 You are away from home and have to park your vehicle overnight. Where should you leave it?

Mark one answer

- [ ] **A.** Opposite another parked vehicle
- [ ] **B.** In a quiet road
- [ ] **C.** Opposite a traffic island
- [ ] **D.** In a secure car park

173 Braking distances on ice can be

Mark one answer
- [ ] A. twice the normal distance
- [ ] B. five times the normal distance
- [ ] C. seven times the normal distance
- [ ] D. ten times the normal distance

174 Freezing conditions will affect the distance it takes you to come to a stop. You should expect stopping distances to increase by up to

Mark one answer
- [ ] A. two times
- [ ] B. three times
- [ ] C. five times
- [ ] D. ten times

175 In very hot weather the road surface can get soft. Which TWO of the following will be affected most?

Mark two answers
- [ ] A. The suspension
- [ ] B. The grip of the tyres
- [ ] C. The braking
- [ ] D. The exhaust

176 Where are you most likely to be affected by a side wind?

Mark one answer
- [ ] A. On a narrow country lane
- [ ] B. On an open stretch of road
- [ ] C. On a busy stretch of road
- [ ] D. On a long, straight road

177 In windy conditions you need to take extra care when

Mark one answer
- [ ] A. using the brakes
- [ ] B. making a hill start
- [ ] C. turning into a narrow road
- [ ] D. passing pedal cyclists

178 What is the shortest stopping distance at 70mph?

Mark one answer
- [ ] A. 53 metres (175 feet)
- [ ] B. 60 metres (197 feet)
- [ ] C. 73 metres (240 feet)
- [ ] D. 96 metres (315 feet)

179 What is the shortest overall stopping distance on a dry road from 60mph?

Mark one answer
- [ ] A. 53 metres (175 feet)
- [ ] B. 58 metres (190 feet)
- [ ] C. 73 metres (240 feet)
- [ ] D. 96 metres (315 feet)

180 Your indicators may be difficult to see in bright sunlight. What should you do?

Mark one answer
- [ ] A. Put your indicator on earlier
- [ ] B. Give an arm signal as well as using your indicator
- [ ] C. Touch the brake several times to show the stop lights
- [ ] D. Turn as quickly as you can

181
In very hot weather the road surface can get soft. Which TWO of the following will be affected most?

Mark two answers
- A. The suspension
- B. The steering
- C. The braking
- D. The exhaust

182
When approaching a right-hand bend you should keep well to the left. Why is this?

Mark one answer
- A. To improve your view of the road
- B. To overcome the effect of the road's slope
- C. To let faster traffic from behind overtake
- D. To be positioned safely if you skid

183
You should not overtake when

Mark three answers
- A. intending to turn left shortly afterwards
- B. in a one-way street
- C. approaching a junction
- D. going up a long hill
- E. the view ahead is blocked

TIP Don't forget – you may have to deal with more than one hazard at a time!

184
You have just gone through deep water. To dry off the brakes you should

Mark one answer
- A. accelerate and keep to a high speed for a short time
- B. go slowly while gently applying the brakes
- C. avoid using the brakes at all for a few miles
- D. stop for at least an hour to allow them time to dry

185
You are on a fast, open road in good conditions. For safety, the distance between you and the vehicle in front should be

Mark one answer
- A. a two-second time gap
- B. one-car length
- C. 2 metres (6 feet 6 inches)
- D. two-car lengths

186
What is the most common cause of skidding?

Mark one answer
- A. Worn tyres
- B. Driver error
- C. Other vehicles
- D. Pedestrians

187
You are driving on an icy road. How can you avoid wheelspin?

Mark one answer
- A. Drive at a slow speed in as high a gear as possible
- B. Use the handbrake if the wheels start to slip
- C. Brake gently and repeatedly
- D. Drive in a low gear at all times

188 Skidding is mainly caused by

Mark one answer

- A. the weather
- B. the driver
- C. the vehicle
- D. the road

189 You are driving in freezing conditions. What should you do when approaching a sharp bend?

Mark two answers

- A. Slow down before you reach the bend
- B. Gently apply your handbrake
- C. Firmly use your footbrake
- D. Coast into the bend
- E. Avoid sudden steering movements

190 You are turning left on a slippery road. The back of your vehicle slides to the right. You should

Mark one answer

- A. brake firmly and not turn the steering wheel
- B. steer carefully to the left
- C. steer carefully to the right
- D. brake firmly and steer to the left

191 You are braking on a wet road. Your vehicle begins to skid. Your vehicle does not have anti-lock brakes. What is the FIRST thing you should do?

Mark one answer

- A. Quickly pull up the handbrake
- B. Release the footbrake fully
- C. Push harder on the brake pedal
- D. Gently use the accelerator

192 Coasting the vehicle

Mark one answer

- A. improves the driver's control
- B. makes steering easier
- C. reduces the driver's control
- D. uses more fuel

193 Before starting a journey in freezing weather you should clear ice and snow from your vehicle's

Mark four answers

- A. aerial
- B. windows
- C. bumper
- D. lights
- E. mirrors
- F. number plates

194 You are trying to move off on snow. You should use

Mark one answer

- A. the lowest gear you can
- B. the highest gear you can
- C. a high engine speed
- D. the handbrake and footbrake together

195 When driving in falling snow you should

Mark one answer

- A. brake firmly and quickly
- B. be ready to steer sharply
- C. use sidelights only
- D. brake gently in plenty of time

196 The MAIN benefit of having four-wheel drive is to improve

Mark one answer

- [ ] **A.** road holding
- [ ] **B.** fuel consumption
- [ ] **C.** stopping distances
- [ ] **D.** passenger comfort

197 You are about to go down a steep hill. To control the speed of your vehicle you should

Mark one answer

- [ ] **A.** select a high gear and use the brakes carefully
- [ ] **B.** select a high gear and use the brakes firmly
- [ ] **C.** select a low gear and use the brakes carefully
- [ ] **D.** select a low gear and avoid using the brakes

198 How can you use the engine of your vehicle as a brake?

Mark one answer

- [ ] **A.** By changing to a lower gear
- [ ] **B.** By selecting reverse gear
- [ ] **C.** By changing to a higher gear
- [ ] **D.** By selecting neutral gear

199 You wish to park facing DOWNHILL. Which TWO of the following should you do?

Mark two answers

- [ ] **A.** Turn the steering wheel towards the kerb
- [ ] **B.** Park close to the bumper of another car
- [ ] **C.** Park with two wheels on the kerb
- [ ] **D.** Put the handbrake on firmly
- [ ] **E.** Turn the steering wheel away from the kerb

200 You are driving in a built-up area. You approach a speed hump. You should

Mark one answer

- [ ] **A.** move across to the left-hand side of the road
- [ ] **B.** wait for any pedestrians to cross
- [ ] **C.** slow your vehicle right down
- [ ] **D.** stop and check both pavements

201 You are on a long, downhill slope. What should you do to help control the speed of your vehicle?

Mark one answer

- [ ] **A.** Select neutral
- [ ] **B.** Select a lower gear
- [ ] **C.** Grip the handbrake firmly
- [ ] **D.** Apply the parking brake gently

202 Your vehicle is fitted with anti-lock brakes. To stop quickly in an emergency you should

Mark one answer **NI**

- [ ] **A.** brake firmly and pump the brake pedal on and off
- [ ] **B.** brake rapidly and firmly without releasing the brake pedal
- [ ] **C.** brake gently and pump the brake pedal on and off
- [ ] **D.** brake rapidly once, and immediately release the brake pedal

203 Anti-lock brakes prevent wheels from locking. This means the tyres are less likely to

Mark one answer

- A. aquaplane
- B. skid
- C. puncture
- D. wear

204 Anti-lock brakes reduce the chances of a skid occurring particularly when

Mark one answer

- A. driving down steep hills
- B. braking during normal driving
- C. braking in an emergency
- D. driving on good road surfaces

205 Anti-lock brakes are most effective when you

Mark one answer **NI**

- A. keep pumping the footbrake to prevent skidding
- B. brake normally, but grip the steering wheel tightly
- C. brake rapidly and firmly until you have slowed down
- D. apply the handbrake to reduce the stopping distance

206 Your car is fitted with anti-lock brakes. You need to stop in an emergency. You should

Mark one answer **NI**

- A. brake normally and avoid turning the steering wheel
- B. press the brake pedal rapidly and firmly until you have stopped
- C. keep pushing and releasing the footbrake quickly to prevent skidding
- D. apply the handbrake to reduce the stopping distance

207 Vehicles fitted with anti-lock brakes

Mark one answer

- A. are impossible to skid
- B. can be steered while you are braking
- C. accelerate much faster
- D. are not fitted with a handbrake

208 Anti-lock brakes may not work as effectively if the road surface is

Mark two answers

- A. dry
- B. loose
- C. wet
- D. good
- E. firm

209 Anti-lock brakes are of most use when you are

Mark one answer

- A. braking gently
- B. driving on worn tyres
- C. braking excessively
- D. driving normally

210 Driving a vehicle fitted with anti-lock brakes allows you to

Mark one answer

- A. brake harder because it is impossible to skid
- B. drive at higher speeds
- C. steer and brake at the same time
- D. pay less attention to the road ahead

211 Anti-lock brakes can greatly assist with

Mark one answer

- A. a higher cruising speed
- B. steering control when braking
- C. control when accelerating
- D. motorway driving

212 When would an anti-lock braking system start to work?

Mark one answer

- A. After the parking brake has been applied
- B. Whenever pressure on the brake pedal is applied
- C. Just as the wheels are about to lock
- D. When the normal braking system fails to operate

213 You are driving a vehicle fitted with anti-lock brakes. You need to stop in an emergency. You should apply the footbrake

NI

Mark one answer

- A. slowly and gently
- B. slowly but firmly
- C. rapidly and gently
- D. rapidly and firmly

214 Your vehicle has anti-lock brakes, but they may not always prevent skidding. This is most likely to happen when driving

Mark two answers

- A. in foggy conditions
- B. on surface water
- C. on loose road surfaces
- D. on dry tarmac
- E. at night on unlit roads

215 Anti-lock brakes will take effect when

Mark one answer

- A. you do not brake quickly enough
- B. excessive brake pressure has been applied
- C. you have not seen a hazard ahead
- D. speeding on slippery road surfaces

216 When driving in fog, which of the following are correct?

Mark three answers

- A. Use dipped headlights
- B. Use headlights on full beam
- C. Allow more time for your journey
- D. Keep close to the car in front
- E. Slow down
- F. Use sidelights only

TIP Never coast downhill. Keep in a low gear so that you have engine braking as well as the footbrake. The lower the gear the stronger the engine braking.

217 You are driving along a country road. You see this sign. AFTER dealing safely with the hazard you should always

Mark one answer

- A. check your tyre pressures
- B. switch on your hazard warning lights
- C. accelerate briskly
- D. test your brakes

218 You are driving in heavy rain. Your steering suddenly becomes very light. You should

Mark one answer

- A. steer towards the side of the road
- B. apply gentle acceleration
- C. brake firmly to reduce speed
- D. ease off the accelerator

219 How can you tell when you are driving over black ice?

Mark one answer

- A. It is easier to brake
- B. The noise from your tyres sounds louder
- C. You see black ice on the road
- D. Your steering feels light

220 The roads are icy. You should drive slowly

Mark one answer

- A. in the highest gear possible
- B. in the lowest gear possible
- C. with the handbrake partly on
- D. with your left foot on the brake

221 You are driving along a wet road. How can you tell if your vehicle is aquaplaning?

Mark one answer

- A. The engine will stall
- B. The engine noise will increase
- C. The steering will feel very heavy
- D. The steering will feel very light

222 How can you tell if you are driving on ice?

Mark two answers

- A. The tyres make a rumbling noise
- B. The tyres make hardly any noise
- C. The steering becomes heavier
- D. The steering becomes lighter

223 You are driving along a wet road. How can you tell if your vehicle's tyres are losing their grip on the surface?

Mark one answer

- A. The engine will stall
- B. The steering will feel very heavy
- C. The engine noise will increase
- D. The steering will feel very light

224 You are travelling at 50mph on a good, dry road. What is your shortest overall stopping distance?

Mark one answer
- **A.** 36 metres (120 feet)
- **B.** 53 metres (175 feet)
- **C.** 75 metres (245 feet)
- **D.** 96 metres (315 feet)

225 Your overall stopping distance will be much longer when driving

Mark one answer
- **A.** in the rain
- **B.** in fog
- **C.** at night
- **D.** in strong winds

226 You have driven through a flood. What is the first thing you should do?

Mark one answer
- **A.** Stop and check the tyres
- **B.** Stop and dry the brakes
- **C.** Check your exhaust
- **D.** Test your brakes

227 You are on a good, dry road surface. Your vehicle has good brakes and tyres. What is the BRAKING distance at 50mph?

Mark one answer
- **A.** 38 metres (125 feet)
- **B.** 14 metres (46 feet)
- **C.** 24 metres (79 feet)
- **D.** 55 metres (180 feet)

228 You are on a good, dry, road surface and your vehicle has good brakes and tyres. What is the typical overall stopping distance at 40mph?

Mark one answer
- **A.** 23 metres (75 feet)
- **B.** 36 metres (120 feet)
- **C.** 53 metres (175 feet)
- **D.** 96 metres (315 feet)

TIP Remember the 'two-second rule'? Well you can 'Say it again when driving in rain!' In other words, you need to allow at least twice the distance for braking and stopping in wet weather.

229

You see this sign on the rear of a slow-moving lorry that you want to pass. It is travelling in the middle lane of a three-lane motorway. You should

Mark one answer

- [ ] **A.** cautiously approach the lorry then pass on either side
- [ ] **B.** follow the lorry until you can leave the motorway
- [ ] **C.** wait on the hard shoulder until the lorry has stopped
- [ ] **D.** approach with care and keep to the left of the lorry

230

Where would you expect to see these markers?

Mark two answers

- [ ] **A.** On a motorway sign
- [ ] **B.** At the entrance to a narrow bridge
- [ ] **C.** On a large goods vehicle
- [ ] **D.** On a builder's skip placed on the road

231

What does this signal from a police officer, mean to oncoming traffic?

Mark one answer

- [ ] **A.** Go ahead
- [ ] **B.** Stop
- [ ] **C.** Turn left
- [ ] **D.** Turn right

232

What is the main hazard shown in this picture?

Mark one answer

- [ ] **A.** Vehicles turning right
- [ ] **B.** Vehicles doing U-turns
- [ ] **C.** The cyclist crossing the road
- [ ] **D.** Parked cars around the corner

233 Which road user has caused a hazard?

Mark one answer

- **A.** The parked car (arrowed A)
- **B.** The pedestrian waiting to cross (arrowed B)
- **C.** The moving car (arrowed C)
- **D.** The car turning (arrowed D)

234 What should the driver of the car approaching the crossing do?

Mark one answer

- **A.** Continue at the same speed
- **B.** Sound the horn
- **C.** Drive through quickly
- **D.** Slow down and get ready to stop

235 What THREE things should the driver of the grey car (arrowed) be especially aware of?

Mark three answers

- **A.** Pedestrians stepping out between cars
- **B.** Other cars behind the grey car
- **C.** Doors opening on parked cars
- **D.** The bumpy road surface
- **E.** Cars leaving parking spaces
- **F.** Empty parking spaces

236 You think the driver of the vehicle in front has forgotten to cancel the right indicator. You should

Mark one answer

- **A.** flash your lights to alert the driver
- **B.** sound your horn before overtaking
- **C.** overtake on the left if there is room
- **D.** stay behind and not overtake

TIP If you are driving past parked cars, it is a good idea to leave as much space as the width of a car door – in case one opens suddenly. If you can't give that much space, slow down so that you could **stop** if necessary.

237 What is the main hazard the driver of the red car (arrowed) should be most aware of?

Mark one answer

- **A.** Glare from the sun may affect the driver's vision
- **B.** The black car may stop suddenly
- **C.** The bus may move out into the road
- **D.** Oncoming vehicles will assume the driver is turning right

238 In heavy motorway traffic you are being followed closely by the vehicle behind. How can you lower the risk of an accident?

Mark one answer

- **A.** Increase your distance from the vehicle in front
- **B.** Tap your foot on the brake pedal sharply
- **C.** Switch on your hazard lights
- **D.** Move on to the hard shoulder and stop

239 You see this sign ahead. You should expect the road to

Mark one answer

- **A.** go steeply uphill
- **B.** go steeply downhill
- **C.** bend sharply to the left
- **D.** bend sharply to the right

240 You are approaching this cyclist. You should

Mark one answer

- **A.** overtake before the cyclist gets to the junction
- **B.** flash your headlights at the cyclist
- **C.** slow down and allow the cyclist to turn
- **D.** overtake the cyclist on the left-hand side

241 Why must you take extra care when turning right at this junction?

Mark one answer
- **A.** Road surface is poor
- **B.** Footpaths are narrow
- **C.** Road markings are faint
- **D.** There is reduced visibility

242 This yellow sign on a vehicle indicates this is

Mark one answer
- **A.** a vehicle broken down
- **B.** a school bus
- **C.** an ice-cream van
- **D.** a private ambulance

243 When approaching this bridge you should give way to

Mark one answer
- **A.** bicycles
- **B.** buses
- **C.** motorcycles
- **D.** cars

244 What type of vehicle could you expect to meet in the middle of the road?

Mark one answer
- **A.** Lorry
- **B.** Bicycle
- **C.** Car
- **D.** Motorcycle

TIP Driver sleepiness is thought to cause at least 10% of all road accidents and one in five of accidents on motorways and major roads.

245 At this blind junction you must stop

Mark one answer

- **A.** behind the line, then edge forward to see clearly
- **B.** beyond the line at a point where you can see clearly
- **C.** only if there is traffic on the main road
- **D.** only if you are turning to the right

246 A driver pulls out of a side road in front of you. You have to brake hard. You should

Mark one answer

- **A.** ignore the error and stay calm
- **B.** flash your lights to show your annoyance
- **C.** sound your horn to show your annoyance
- **D.** overtake as soon as possible

247 An elderly person's driving ability could be affected because they may be unable to

Mark one answer

- **A.** obtain car insurance
- **B.** understand road signs
- **C.** react very quickly
- **D.** give signals correctly

248 You have just passed these warning lights. What hazard would you expect to see next?

Mark one answer

- **A.** A level crossing with no barrier
- **B.** An ambulance station
- **C.** A school crossing patrol
- **D.** An opening bridge

249 Why should you be especially cautious when going past this bus?

Mark two answers

- **A.** There is traffic approaching in the distance
- **B.** The driver may open the door
- **C.** It may suddenly move off
- **D.** People may cross the road in front of it
- **E.** There are bicycles parked on the pavement

250 In areas where there are 'traffic calming' measures you should

Mark one answer

- **A.** drive at a reduced speed
- **B.** always drive at the speed limit
- **C.** position in the centre of the road
- **D.** only slow down if pedestrians are near

251 You are planning a long journey. Do you need to plan rest stops?

Mark one answer

- **A.** Yes, you should plan to stop every half an hour
- **B.** Yes, regular stops help concentration
- **C.** No, you will be less tired if you get there as soon as possible
- **D.** No, only fuel stops will be needed

252 A driver does something that upsets you. You should

Mark one answer

- **A.** try not to react
- **B.** let them know how you feel
- **C.** flash your headlights several times
- **D.** sound your horn

253 The red lights are flashing. What should you do when approaching this level crossing?

Mark one answer

- **A.** Go through quickly
- **B.** Go through carefully
- **C.** Stop before the barrier
- **D.** Switch on hazard warning lights

254 What are TWO main hazards you should be aware of when going along this street?

Mark two answers

- **A.** Glare from the sun
- **B.** Car doors opening suddenly
- **C.** Lack of road markings
- **D.** The headlights on parked cars being switched on
- **E.** Large goods vehicles
- **F.** Children running out from between vehicles

255 What is the main hazard you should be aware of when following this cyclist?

Mark one answer

- **A.** The cyclist may move into the left and dismount
- **B.** The cyclist may swerve out into the road
- **C.** The contents of the cyclist's carrier may fall on to the road
- **D.** The cyclist may wish to turn right at the end of the road

256 When approaching this hazard why should you slow down?

Mark two answers

- **A.** Because of the bend
- **B.** Because it's hard to see to the right
- **C.** Because of approaching traffic
- **D.** Because of animals crossing
- **E.** Because of the level crossing

257 A driver's behaviour has upset you. It may help if you

Mark one answer

- **A.** stop and take a break
- **B.** shout abusive language
- **C.** gesture to them with your hand
- **D.** follow their car, flashing the headlights

258 You are on a dual carriageway. Ahead you see a vehicle with an amber flashing light. What will this be?

Mark one answer

- **A.** An ambulance
- **B.** A fire engine
- **C.** A doctor on call
- **D.** A disabled person's vehicle

259 You are approaching crossroads. The traffic lights have failed. What should you do?

Mark one answer

- **A.** Brake and stop only for large vehicles
- **B.** Brake sharply to a stop before looking
- **C.** Be prepared to brake sharply to a stop
- **D.** Be prepared to stop for any traffic.

260 Why are destination markings painted on the road surface?

Mark one answer

- **A.** To restrict the flow of traffic
- **B.** To warn you of oncoming traffic
- **C.** To enable you to change lanes early
- **D.** To prevent you changing lanes

261 What should the driver of the red car (arrowed) do?

Mark one answer

- **A.** Wave the pedestrians who are waiting to cross
- **B.** Wait for the pedestrian in the road to cross
- **C.** Quickly drive behind the pedestrian in the road
- **D.** Tell the pedestrian in the road she should not have crossed

262 You are following a slower-moving vehicle on a narrow country road. There is a junction just ahead on the right. What should you do?

Mark one answer

- A. Overtake after checking your mirrors and signalling
- B. Stay behind until you are past the junction
- C. Accelerate quickly to pass before the junction
- D. Slow down and prepare to overtake on the left

263 What should you do as you approach this overhead bridge?

Mark one answer

- A. Move out to the centre of the road before going through
- B. Find another route, this is only for high vehicles
- C. Be prepared to give way to large vehicles in the middle of the road
- D. Move across to the right-hand side before going through

264 Why are mirrors often slightly curved (convex)?

Mark one answer

- A. They give a wider field of vision
- B. They totally cover blind spots
- C. They make it easier to judge the speed of following traffic
- D. They make following traffic look bigger

265 What does the solid white line at the side of the road indicate?

Mark one answer

- A. Traffic lights ahead
- B. Edge of the carriageway
- C. Footpath on the left
- D. Cycle path

266 You are driving towards this level crossing. What would be the first warning of an approaching train?

Mark one answer

- A. Both half-barriers down
- B. A steady amber light
- C. One half-barrier down
- D. Twin flashing red lights

> **TIP** Leave sufficient room to allow for the mistakes of others. After all, if an accident occurs, the fact that it was not your fault will be little consolation.

267 You are driving along this motorway. It is raining. When following this lorry you should

Mark two answers

- **A.** allow at least a two-second gap
- **B.** move left and drive on the hard shoulder
- **C.** allow at least a four-second gap
- **D.** be aware of spray reducing your vision
- **E.** move right and stay in the right-hand lane

268 You are behind this cyclist. When the traffic lights change, what should you do?

Mark one answer

- **A.** Try to move off before the cyclist
- **B.** Allow the cyclist time and room
- **C.** Turn right but give the cyclist room
- **D.** Tap your horn and drive through first

269 You are driving towards this left-hand bend. What dangers should you be aware of?

Mark one answer

- **A.** A vehicle overtaking you
- **B.** No white lines in the centre of the road
- **C.** No sign to warn you of the bend
- **D.** Pedestrians walking towards you

270 While driving, you see this sign ahead. You should

Mark one answer

- **A.** stop at the sign
- **B.** slow, but continue around the bend
- **C.** slow to a crawl and continue
- **D.** stop and look for open farm gates

271 Why should the junction on the left be kept clear?

Mark one answer
- A. To allow vehicles to enter and emerge
- B. To allow the bus to reverse
- C. To allow vehicles to make a U-turn
- D. To allow vehicles to park

272 When the traffic lights change to green the white car should

Mark one answer
- A. wait for the cyclist to pull away
- B. move off quickly and turn in front of the cyclist
- C. move close up to the cyclist to beat the lights
- D. sound the horn to warn the cyclist

273 You intend to turn left at the traffic lights. Just before turning you should

Mark one answer
- A. check your right mirror
- B. move close up to the white car
- C. straddle the lanes
- D. check for bicycles on your left

274 You should reduce your speed when driving along this road because

Mark one answer
- A. there is a staggered junction ahead
- B. there is a low bridge ahead
- C. there is a change in the road surface
- D. the road ahead narrows

275 You are driving at 60mph. As you approach this hazard you should

Mark one answer

- [ ] **A.** maintain your speed
- [ ] **B.** reduce your speed
- [ ] **C.** take the next right turn
- [ ] **D.** take the next left turn

276 The traffic ahead of you in the left lane is slowing. You should

Mark two answers

- [ ] **A.** be wary of cars on your right cutting in
- [ ] **B.** accelerate past the vehicles in the left lane
- [ ] **C.** pull up on the left-hand verge
- [ ] **D.** move across and continue in the right-hand lane
- [ ] **E.** slow down keeping a safe separation distance

277 What might you expect to happen in this situation?

Mark one answer

- [ ] **A.** Traffic will move into the right-hand lane
- [ ] **B.** Traffic speed will increase
- [ ] **C.** Traffic will move into the left-hand lane
- [ ] **D.** Traffic will not need to change position

278 You are driving on a road with several lanes. You see these signs above the lanes. What do they mean?

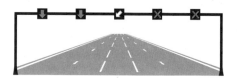

Mark one answer

- [ ] **A.** The two right lanes are open
- [ ] **B.** The two left lanes are open
- [ ] **C.** Traffic in the left lanes should stop
- [ ] **D.** Traffic in the right lanes should stop

279 As a provisional licence holder, you must not drive a motor car

Mark two answers **NI**

- A. at more than 50mph
- B. on your own
- C. on the motorway
- D. under the age of 18 years of age at night
- E. with passengers in the rear seats

280 After passing your driving test, you suffer from ill health. This affects your driving. You MUST

Mark one answer

- A. inform your local police station
- B. get on as best you can
- C. not inform anyone as you hold a full licence
- D. inform the licensing authority

281 You are invited to a pub lunch. You know that you will have to drive in the evening. What is your best course of action?

Mark one answer

- A. Avoid mixing your alcoholic drinks
- B. Not drink any alcohol at all
- C. Have some milk before drinking alcohol
- D. Eat a hot meal with your alcoholic drinks

282 You have been convicted of driving whilst unfit through drink or drugs. You will find this is likely to cause the cost of one of the following to rise considerably. Which one?

Mark one answer

- A. Road fund licence
- B. Insurance premiums
- C. Vehicle test certificate
- D. Driving licence

283 What advice should you give to a driver who has had a few alcoholic drinks at a party?

Mark one answer

- A. Have a strong cup of coffee and then drive home
- B. Drive home carefully and slowly
- C. Go home by public transport
- D. Wait a short while and then drive home

284 You have been taking medicine for a few days which made you feel drowsy. Today you feel better but still need to take the medicine. You should only drive

Mark one answer

- A. if your journey is necessary
- B. at night on quiet roads
- C. if someone goes with you
- D. after checking with your doctor

285
You are about to return home from holiday when you become ill. A doctor prescribes drugs which are likely to affect your driving. You should

Mark one answer

- A. drive only if someone is with you
- B. avoid driving on motorways
- C. not drive yourself
- D. never drive at more than 30mph

286
During periods of illness your ability to drive may be impaired. You MUST

Mark two answers

- A. see your doctor each time before you drive
- B. only take smaller doses of any medicines
- C. be medically fit to drive
- D. not drive after taking certain medicines
- E. take all your medicines with you when you drive

287
You feel drowsy when driving. You should

Mark two answers

- A. stop and rest as soon as possible
- B. turn the heater up to keep you warm and comfortable
- C. make sure you have a good supply of fresh air
- D. continue with your journey but drive more slowly
- E. close the car windows to help you concentrate

288
You are driving along a motorway and become tired. You should

Mark two answers

- A. stop at the next service area and rest
- B. leave the motorway at the next exit and rest
- C. increase your speed and turn up the radio volume
- D. close all your windows and set heating to warm
- E. pull up on the hard shoulder and change drivers

289
You are taking drugs that are likely to affect your driving. What should you do?

Mark one answer

- A. Seek medical advice before driving
- B. Limit your driving to essential journeys
- C. Only drive if accompanied by a full licence-holder
- D. Drive only for short distances

290
You are about to drive home. You feel very tired and have a severe headache. You should

Mark one answer

- A. wait until you are fit and well before driving
- B. drive home, but take a tablet for headaches
- C. drive home if you can stay awake for the journey
- D. wait for a short time, then drive home slowly

291 If you are feeling tired it is best to stop as soon as you can. Until then you should

Mark one answer
- [ ] **A.** increase your speed to find a stopping place quickly
- [ ] **B.** ensure a supply of fresh air
- [ ] **C.** gently tap the steering wheel
- [ ] **D.** keep changing speed to improve concentration

292 If your motorway journey seems boring and you feel drowsy whilst driving you should

Mark one answer
- [ ] **A.** open a window and drive to the next service area
- [ ] **B.** stop on the hard shoulder for a sleep
- [ ] **C.** speed up to arrive at your destination sooner
- [ ] **D.** slow down and let other drivers overtake

293 Driving long distances can be tiring. You can prevent this by

Mark three answers
- [ ] **A.** stopping every so often for a walk
- [ ] **B.** opening a window for some fresh air
- [ ] **C.** ensuring plenty of refreshment breaks
- [ ] **D.** completing the journey without stopping
- [ ] **E.** eating a large meal before driving

294 You go to a social event and need to drive a short time after. What precaution should you take?

Mark one answer
- [ ] **A.** Avoid drinking alcohol on an empty stomach
- [ ] **B.** Drink plenty of coffee after drinking alcohol
- [ ] **C.** Avoid drinking alcohol completely
- [ ] **D.** Drink plenty of milk before drinking alcohol

295 You take some cough medicine given to you by a friend. What should you do before driving?

Mark one answer
- [ ] **A.** Ask your friend if taking the medicine affected their driving
- [ ] **B.** Drink some strong coffee one hour before driving
- [ ] **C.** Check the label to see if the medicine will affect your driving
- [ ] **D.** Drive a short distance to see if the medicine is affecting your driving

296 You take the wrong route and find you are on a one-way street. You should

Mark one answer
- [ ] **A.** reverse out of the road
- [ ] **B.** turn round in a side road
- [ ] **C.** continue to the end of the road
- [ ] **D.** reverse into a driveway

TIP The reason motorcyclists have their headlamps on in daylight is to make them more visible to other road users.

297 Which THREE are likely to make you lose concentration while driving?

Mark three answers

- A. Looking at road maps
- B. Listening to loud music
- C. Using your windscreen washers
- D. Looking in your wing mirror
- E. Using a mobile phone

298 You are driving along this road. The driver on the left is reversing from a driveway. You should

Mark one answer

- A. move to the opposite side of the road
- B. drive through as you have priority
- C. sound your horn and be prepared to stop
- D. speed up and drive through quickly

299 You have been involved in an argument before starting your journey. This has made you feel angry. You should

Mark one answer

- A. start to drive, but open a window
- B. drive slower than normal and turn your radio on
- C. have an alcoholic drink to help you relax before driving
- D. calm down before you start to drive

300 You start to feel tired while driving. What should you do?

Mark one answer

- A. Increase your speed slightly
- B. Decrease your speed slightly
- C. Find a less busy route
- D. Pull over at a safe place to rest

301 You are driving on this dual carriageway. Why may you need to slow down?

Mark one answer

- A. There is a broken white line in the centre
- B. There are solid white lines either side
- C. There are road works ahead of you
- D. There are no footpaths

TIP It is tragic but true that people have been killed or seriously injured when struck by a vehicle being driven slowly in reverse gear. Young children, elderly and disabled people are especially vulnerable, often because they may not be aware of any danger. If in doubt get out and check!

302 You have just been overtaken by this motorcyclist who is cutting in sharply. You should

Mark one answer

- A. sound the horn
- B. brake firmly
- C. keep a safe gap
- D. flash your lights

303 You are about to drive home. You cannot find the glasses you need to wear. You should

Mark one answer

- A. drive home slowly, keeping to quiet roads
- B. borrow a friend's glasses and use those
- C. drive home at night, so that the lights will help you
- D. find a way of getting home without driving

304 Which THREE result from drinking alcohol?

Mark three answers

- A. Less control
- B. A false sense of confidence
- C. Faster reactions
- D. Poor judgement of speed
- E. Greater awareness of danger

305 Which THREE of these are likely effects of drinking alcohol?

Mark three answers

- A. Reduced co-ordination
- B. Increased confidence
- C. Poor judgement
- D. Increased concentration
- E. Faster reactions
- F. Colour blindness

306 How does alcohol affect you?

Mark one answer

- A. It speeds up your reactions
- B. It increases your awareness
- C. It improves your co-ordination
- D. It reduces your concentration

307 Your doctor has given you a course of medicine. Why should you ask how it will affect you?

Mark one answer

- A. Drugs make you a better driver by quickening your reactions
- B. You will have to let your insurance company know about the medicine
- C. Some types of medicine can cause your reactions to slow down
- D. The medicine you take may affect your hearing

308 You are not sure if your cough medicine will affect you. What TWO things could you do?

Mark two answers

- A. Ask your doctor
- B. Check the medicine label
- C. Drive if you feel alright
- D. Ask a friend or relative for advice

309 You are on a motorway. You feel tired. You should

Mark one answer

- A. carry on but go slowly
- B. leave the motorway at the next exit
- C. complete your journey as quickly as possible
- D. stop on the hard shoulder

310 You find that you need glasses to read vehicle number plates at the required distance. When MUST you wear them?

Mark one answer

- A. Only in bad weather conditions
- B. At all times when driving
- C. Only when you think it necessary
- D. Only in bad light or at night time

311 Which TWO things would help to keep you alert during a long journey?

Mark two answers

- A. Finishing your journey as fast as you can
- B. Keeping off the motorways and using country roads
- C. Making sure that you get plenty of fresh air
- D. Making regular stops for refreshments

312 Which of the following types of glasses should NOT be worn when driving at night?

Mark one answer

- A. Half-moon
- B. Round
- C. Bi-focal
- D. Tinted

313 Drinking any amount of alcohol is likely to

Mark three answers

- A. slow down your reactions to hazards
- B. increase the speed of your reactions
- C. worsen your judgement of speed
- D. improve your awareness of danger
- E. give a false sense of confidence

314 What else can seriously affect your concentration, other than alcoholic drinks?

Mark three answers

- A. Drugs
- B. Tiredness
- C. Tinted windows
- D. Contact lenses
- E. Loud music

315 As a driver you find that your eyesight has become very poor. Your optician says they cannot help you. The law says that you should tell

Mark one answer

- A. the licensing authority
- B. your own doctor
- C. the local police station
- D. another optician

316 For which of these may you use hazard warning lights?

Mark one answer

- [ ] **A.** When driving on a motorway to warn traffic behind of a hazard ahead
- [ ] **B.** When you are double-parked on a two-way road
- [ ] **C.** When your direction indicators are not working
- [ ] **D.** When warning oncoming traffic that you intend to stop

317 When should you use hazard warning lights?

Mark one answer

- [ ] **A.** When you are double-parked on a two-way road
- [ ] **B.** When your direction indicators are not working
- [ ] **C.** When warning oncoming traffic that you intend to stop
- [ ] **D.** When your vehicle has broken down and is causing an obstruction

> **TIP** A blind person will usually carry a **white stick** to alert you to their presence. If the stick has a **red band**, this means that the person is also deaf, so will have no warning of an approaching car either visually or from engine noise.

318 You want to turn left at this junction. The view of the main road is restricted. What should you do?

Mark one answer

- [ ] **A.** Stay well back and wait to see if something comes
- [ ] **B.** Build up your speed so that you can emerge quickly
- [ ] **C.** Stop and apply the handbrake even if the road is clear
- [ ] **D.** Approach slowly and edge out until you can see more clearly

319 You are driving on a motorway. The traffic ahead is braking sharply because of an accident. How could you warn following traffic?

Mark one answer

- [ ] **A.** Briefly use the hazard warning lights
- [ ] **B.** Switch on the hazard warning lights continuously
- [ ] **C.** Briefly use the rear fog lights
- [ ] **D.** Switch on the headlamps continuously

320 When may you use hazard warning lights?

Mark one answer

- **A.** To park alongside another car
- **B.** To park on double yellow lines
- **C.** When you are being towed
- **D.** When you have broken down

321 Hazard warning lights should be used when vehicles are

Mark one answer

- **A.** broken down and causing an obstruction
- **B.** faulty and moving slowly
- **C.** being towed along a road
- **D.** reversing into a side road

322 When driving a car fitted with automatic transmission what would you use 'kick down' for?

Mark one answer

- **A.** Cruise control
- **B.** Quick acceleration
- **C.** Slow braking
- **D.** Fuel economy

TIP Research shows that male drivers (aged 18–30) are more at risk of falling asleep at the wheel than other drivers. They may keep late hours and be lacking in sleep; they tend to drive fast and be over-confident of their ability; and they are less likely to stop and take a break.

323 Which sign means that there may be people walking along the road?

Mark one answer

A.

B.

C.

D.

324 You are turning left at a junction. Pedestrians have started to cross the road. You should

Mark one answer

A. go on, giving them plenty of room
B. stop and wave at them to cross
C. blow your horn and proceed
D. give way to them

325 You are turning left from a main road into a side road. People are already crossing the road into which you are turning. You should

Mark one answer

A. continue, as it is your right of way
B. signal to them to continue crossing
C. wait and allow them to cross
D. sound your horn to warn them of your presence

326 You are at a road junction, turning into a minor road. There are pedestrians crossing the minor road. You should

Mark one answer

A. stop and wave the pedestrians across
B. sound your horn to let the pedestrians know that you are there
C. give way to the pedestrians who are already crossing
D. carry on; the pedestrians should give way to you

327 You are turning left into a side road. What hazards should you be especially aware of?

Mark one answer
- **A.** One-way street
- **B.** Pedestrians
- **C.** Traffic congestion
- **D.** Parked vehicles

328 You intend to turn right into a side road. Just before turning you should check for motorcyclists who might be

Mark one answer
- **A.** overtaking on your left
- **B.** following you closely
- **C.** emerging from the side road
- **D.** overtaking on your right

329 A toucan crossing is different from other crossings because

Mark one answer
- **A.** moped riders can use it
- **B.** it is controlled by a traffic warden
- **C.** it is controlled by two flashing lights
- **D.** cyclists can use it

330 At toucan crossings

Mark two answers
- **A.** there is no flashing amber light
- **B.** cyclists are not permitted
- **C.** there is a continuously flashing amber beacon
- **D.** pedestrians and cyclists may cross
- **E.** you only stop if someone is waiting to cross

331 What does this sign tell you?

Mark one answer
- **A.** No cycling
- **B.** Cycle route ahead
- **C.** Route for cycles only
- **D.** End of cycle route

332 How will a school crossing patrol signal you to stop?

Mark one answer
- **A.** By pointing to children on the opposite pavement
- **B.** By displaying a red light
- **C.** By displaying a stop sign
- **D.** By giving you an arm signal

333 Where would you see this sign?

Mark one answer
- **A.** In the window of a car taking children to school
- **B.** At the side of the road
- **C.** At playground areas
- **D.** On the rear of a school bus or coach

334 Which sign tells you that pedestrians may be walking in the road as there is no pavement?

Mark one answer

A.

B.

C.

D.

335 What does this sign mean?

Mark one answer

A. No route for pedestrians and cyclists
B. A route for pedestrians only
C. A route for cyclists only
D. A route for pedestrians and cyclists

336 You see a pedestrian with a white stick and red band. This means that the person is

Mark one answer

A. physically disabled
B. deaf only
C. blind only
D. deaf and blind

337 What action would you take when elderly people are crossing the road?

Mark one answer

A. Wave them across so they know that you have seen them
B. Be patient and allow them to cross in their own time
C. Rev the engine to let them know that you are waiting
D. Tap the horn in case they are hard of hearing

338 You see two elderly pedestrians about to cross the road ahead. You should

Mark one answer

A. expect them to wait for you to pass
B. speed up to get past them quickly
C. stop and wave them across the road
D. be careful, they may misjudge your speed

339 What does this sign mean?

Mark one answer

A. Contraflow pedal cycle lane
B. With-flow pedal cycle lane
C. Pedal cycles and buses only
D. No pedal cycles or buses

340 You are coming up to a roundabout. A cyclist is signalling to turn right. What should you do?

Mark one answer

- A. Overtake on the right
- B. Give a horn warning
- C. Signal the cyclist to move across
- D. Give the cyclist plenty of room

341 You are approaching this roundabout and see the cyclist signal right. Why is the cyclist keeping to the left?

Mark one answer

- A. It is a quicker route for the cyclist
- B. The cyclist is going to turn left instead
- C. The cyclist thinks The Highway Code does not apply to bicycles
- D. The cyclist is slower and more vulnerable

342 When you are overtaking a cyclist you should leave as much room as you would give to a car. What is the main reason for this?

Mark one answer

- A. The cyclist might change lanes
- B. The cyclist might get off the bike
- C. The cyclist might swerve
- D. The cyclist might have to make a right turn

343 Which TWO should you allow extra room when overtaking?

Mark two answers

- A. Motorcycles
- B. Tractors
- C. Bicycles
- D. Road-sweeping vehicles

344 Why should you look particularly for motorcyclists and cyclists at junctions?

Mark one answer

- A. They may want to turn into the side road
- B. They may slow down to let you turn
- C. They are harder to see
- D. They might not see you turn

345 You are waiting to come out of a side road. Why should you watch carefully for motorcycles?

Mark one answer

- A. Motorcycles are usually faster than cars
- B. Police patrols often use motorcycles
- C. Motorcycles are small and hard to see
- D. Motorcycles have right of way

346 In daylight, an approaching motorcyclist is using a dipped headlight. Why?

Mark one answer

- A. So that the rider can be seen more easily
- B. To stop the battery overcharging
- C. To improve the rider's vision
- D. The rider is inviting you to proceed

347 Motorcyclists should wear bright clothing mainly because

Mark one answer
- A. they must do so by law
- B. it helps keep them cool in summer
- C. the colours are popular
- D. drivers often do not see them

348 There is a slow-moving motorcyclist ahead of you. You are unsure what the rider is going to do. You should

Mark one answer
- A. pass on the left
- B. pass on the right
- C. stay behind
- D. move closer

349 Motorcyclists will often look round over their right shoulder just before turning right. This is because

Mark one answer
- A. they need to listen for following traffic
- B. motorcycles do not have mirrors
- C. looking around helps them balance as they turn
- D. they need to check for traffic in their blind area

350 At road junctions which of the following are most vulnerable?

Mark three answers
- A. Cyclists
- B. Motorcyclists
- C. Pedestrians
- D. Car drivers
- E. Lorry drivers

351 Motorcyclists are particularly vulnerable

Mark one answer
- A. when moving off
- B. on dual carriageways
- C. when approaching junctions
- D. on motorways

352 An injured motorcyclist is lying unconscious in the road. You should

Mark one answer
- A. remove the safety helmet
- B. seek medical assistance
- C. move the person off the road
- D. remove the leather jacket

353 You notice horse riders in front. What should you do FIRST?

Mark one answer
- A. Pull out to the middle of the road
- B. Be prepared to slow down
- C. Accelerate around them
- D. Signal right

354 You are approaching a roundabout. There are horses just ahead of you. You should

Mark two answers

- **A.** be prepared to stop
- **B.** treat them like any other vehicle
- **C.** give them plenty of room
- **D.** accelerate past as quickly as possible
- **E.** sound your horn as a warning

355 Which THREE should you do when passing sheep on a road?

Mark three answers

- **A.** Allow plenty of room
- **B.** Go very slowly
- **C.** Pass quickly but quietly
- **D.** Be ready to stop
- **E.** Briefly sound your horn

356 At night you see a pedestrian wearing reflective clothing and carrying a bright red light. What does this mean?

Mark one answer

- **A.** You are approaching road works
- **B.** You are approaching an organised walk
- **C.** You are approaching a slow-moving vehicle
- **D.** You are approaching an accident black spot

357 As you approach a pelican crossing the lights change to green. Elderly people are half-way across. You should

Mark one answer

- **A.** wave them to cross as quickly as they can
- **B.** rev your engine to make them hurry
- **C.** flash your lights in case they have not heard you
- **D.** wait because they will take longer to cross

358 There are flashing amber lights under a school warning sign. What action should you take?

Mark one answer

- **A.** Reduce speed until you are clear of the area
- **B.** Keep up your speed and sound the horn
- **C.** Increase your speed to clear the area quickly
- **D.** Wait at the lights until they change to green

359 Which of the following types of crossing can detect when people are on them?

Mark one answer

- **A.** Pelican
- **B.** Toucan
- **C.** Zebra
- **D.** Puffin

TIP It's the motorist's responsibility to look out for hazards and give pedestrians plenty of room.

360 You are approaching this crossing. You should

Mark one answer
- **A.** prepare to slow down and stop
- **B.** stop and wave the pedestrians across
- **C.** speed up and pass by quickly
- **D.** drive on unless the pedestrians step out

361 You see a pedestrian with a dog. The dog has a bright orange lead and collar. This especially warns you that the pedestrian is

Mark one answer
- **A.** elderly
- **B.** dog training
- **C.** colour blind
- **D.** deaf

362 These road markings must be kept clear to allow

W-SCHOOL KEEP CLEAR-W

Mark one answer
- **A.** schoolchildren to be dropped off
- **B.** for teachers to park
- **C.** schoolchildren to be picked up
- **D.** a clear view of the crossing area

363 You must not stop on these road markings because you may obstruct

W-SCHOOL KEEP CLEAR-W

Mark one answer
- **A.** children's view of the crossing area
- **B.** teachers' access to the school
- **C.** delivery vehicles' access to the school
- **D.** emergency vehicles' access to the school

364 The left-hand pavement is closed due to street repairs. What should you do?

Mark one answer
- **A.** Watch out for pedestrians walking in the road
- **B.** Use your right-hand mirror more often
- **C.** Speed up to get past the road works quicker
- **D.** Position close to the left-hand kerb

365 Where would you see this sign?

Mark one answer
- **A.** Near a school crossing
- **B.** At a playground entrance
- **C.** On a school bus
- **D.** At a 'pedestrians only' area

366 You are following a motorcyclist on an uneven road. You should

Mark one answer

- **A.** allow less room so you can be seen in their mirrors
- **B.** overtake immediately
- **C.** allow extra room in case they swerve to avoid pot-holes
- **D.** allow the same room as normal because road surfaces do not affect motorcyclists

367 You are following two cyclists. They approach a roundabout in the left-hand lane. In which direction should you expect the cyclists to go?

Mark one answer

- **A.** Left
- **B.** Right
- **C.** Any direction
- **D.** Straight ahead

368 You are travelling behind a moped. You want to turn left just ahead. You should

Mark one answer

- **A.** overtake the moped before the junction
- **B.** pull alongside the moped and stay level until just before the junction
- **C.** sound your horn as a warning and pull in front of the moped
- **D.** stay behind until the moped has passed the junction

369 Which THREE of the following are hazards motorcyclists present in queues of traffic?

Mark three answers

- **A.** Cutting in just in front of you
- **B.** Riding in single file
- **C.** Passing very close to you
- **D.** Riding with their headlight on dipped beam
- **E.** Filtering between the lanes

370 You see a horse rider as you approach a roundabout. They are signalling right but keeping well to the left. You should

Mark one answer

- **A.** proceed as normal
- **B.** keep close to them
- **C.** cut in front of them
- **D.** stay well back

371 How would you react to drivers who appear to be inexperienced?

Mark one answer

- **A.** Sound your horn to warn them of your presence
- **B.** Be patient and prepare for them to react more slowly
- **C.** Flash your headlights to indicate that it is safe for them to proceed
- **D.** Overtake them as soon as possible

372 You are following a learner driver who stalls at a junction. You should

Mark one answer
- [ ] A. be patient as you expect them to make mistakes
- [ ] B. stay very close behind and flash your headlights
- [ ] C. start to rev your engine if they take too long to restart
- [ ] D. immediately steer around them and drive on

373 You are on a country road. What should you expect to see coming towards you on YOUR side of the road?

Mark one answer
- [ ] A. Motorcycles
- [ ] B. Bicycles
- [ ] C. Pedestrians
- [ ] D. Horse riders

374 You are turning left into a side road. Pedestrians are crossing the road near the junction. You must

Mark one answer
- [ ] A. wave them on
- [ ] B. sound your horn
- [ ] C. switch on your hazard lights
- [ ] D. wait for them to cross

375 You are following a car driven by an elderly driver. You should

Mark one answer
- [ ] A. expect the driver to drive badly
- [ ] B. flash your lights and overtake
- [ ] C. be aware that the driver's reactions may not be as fast as yours
- [ ] D. stay very close behind but be careful

376 You are following a cyclist. You wish to turn left just ahead. You should

Mark one answer
- [ ] A. overtake the cyclist before the junction
- [ ] B. pull alongside the cyclist and stay level until after the junction
- [ ] C. hold back until the cyclist has passed the junction
- [ ] D. go around the cyclist on the junction

377 A horse rider is in the left-hand lane approaching a roundabout. You should expect the rider to

Mark one answer
- [ ] A. go in any direction
- [ ] B. turn right
- [ ] C. turn left
- [ ] D. go ahead

378 You have just passed your test. How can you decrease your risk of accidents on the motorway?

Mark one answer

- [ ] **A.** By keeping up with the car in front
- [ ] **B.** By never going over 40mph
- [ ] **C.** By staying only in the left-hand lane
- [ ] **D.** By taking further training

379 Powered vehicles used by disabled people are small and hard to see. How do they give early warning when on a dual carriageway?

Mark one answer

- [ ] **A.** They will have a flashing red light
- [ ] **B.** They will have a flashing green light
- [ ] **C.** They will have a flashing blue light
- [ ] **D.** They will have a flashing amber light

380 You should never attempt to overtake a cyclist

Mark one answer

- [ ] **A.** just before you turn left
- [ ] **B.** on a left-hand bend
- [ ] **C.** on a one-way street
- [ ] **D.** on a dual carriageway

381 Ahead of you there is a moving vehicle with a flashing amber beacon. This means it is

Mark one answer

- [ ] **A.** slow moving
- [ ] **B.** broken down
- [ ] **C.** a doctor's car
- [ ] **D.** a school crossing patrol

382 You want to reverse into a side road. You are not sure that the area behind your car is clear. What should you do?

Mark one answer

- [ ] **A.** Look through the rear window only
- [ ] **B.** Get out and check
- [ ] **C.** Check the mirrors only
- [ ] **D.** Carry on, assuming it is clear

383 You are about to reverse into a side road. A pedestrian wishes to cross behind you. You should

Mark one answer

- [ ] **A.** wave to the pedestrian to stop
- [ ] **B.** give way to the pedestrian
- [ ] **C.** wave to the pedestrian to cross
- [ ] **D.** reverse before the pedestrian starts to cross

384 Who is especially in danger of not being seen as you reverse your car?

Mark one answer

- [ ] **A.** Motorcyclists
- [ ] **B.** Car drivers
- [ ] **C.** Cyclists
- [ ] **D.** Children

385 You are reversing around a corner when you notice a pedestrian walking behind you. What should you do?

Mark one answer

- [ ] **A.** Slow down and wave the pedestrian across
- [ ] **B.** Continue reversing and steer round the pedestrian
- [ ] **C.** Stop and give way
- [ ] **D.** Continue reversing and sound your horn

386

You want to turn right from a junction but your view is restricted by parked vehicles. What should you do?

Mark one answer

- A. Move out quickly, but be prepared to stop
- B. Sound your horn and pull out if there is no reply
- C. Stop, then move slowly forward until you have a clear view
- D. Stop, get out and look along the main road to check

387

You are at the front of a queue of traffic waiting to turn right into a side road. Why is it important to check your right mirror just before turning?

Mark one answer

- A. To look for pedestrians about to cross
- B. To check for overtaking vehicles
- C. To make sure the side road is clear
- D. To check for emerging traffic

388

What must a driver do at a pelican crossing when the amber light is flashing?

Mark one answer

- A. Signal the pedestrian to cross
- B. Always wait for the green light before proceeding
- C. Give way to any pedestrians on the crossing
- D. Wait for the red-and-amber light before proceeding

389

You have stopped at a pelican crossing. A disabled person is crossing slowly in front of you. The lights have now changed to green. You should

Mark two answers

- A. allow the person to cross
- B. drive in front of the person
- C. drive behind the person
- D. sound your horn
- E. be patient
- F. edge forward slowly

390

You are driving past parked cars. You notice a wheel of a bicycle sticking out between them. What should you do?

Mark one answer

- A. Accelerate past quickly and sound your horn
- B. Slow down and wave the cyclist across
- C. Brake sharply and flash your headlights
- D. Slow down and be prepared to stop for a cyclist

TIP **Pass Plus** is a scheme set up in 1995 by the Driving Standards Agency and the Department of the Environment, Transport and the Regions. Planned in consultation with driving instructors and the insurance industry, it's aimed at encouraging people to go on training to *improve* their standard of driving during the first year after they pass their test.

391
You are driving past a line of parked cars. You notice a ball bouncing out into the road ahead. What should you do?

Mark one answer

- **A.** Continue driving at the same speed and sound your horn
- **B.** Continue driving at the same speed and flash your headlights
- **C.** Slow down and be prepared to stop for children
- **D.** Stop and wave the children across to fetch their ball

392
You want to turn right from a main road into a side road. Just before turning you should

Mark one answer

- **A.** cancel your right-turn signal
- **B.** select first gear
- **C.** check for traffic overtaking on your right
- **D.** stop and set the handbrake

393
You are driving in slow-moving queues of traffic. Just before changing lane you should

Mark one answer

- **A.** sound the horn
- **B.** look for motorcyclists filtering through the traffic
- **C.** give a 'slowing down' arm signal
- **D.** change down to first gear

394
You are driving in town. There is a bus at the bus stop on the other side of the road. Why should you be careful?

Mark one answer

- **A.** The bus may have broken down
- **B.** Pedestrians may come from behind the bus
- **C.** The bus may move off suddenly
- **D.** The bus may remain stationary

395
How should you overtake horse riders?

Mark one answer

- **A.** Drive up close and overtake as soon as possible
- **B.** Speed is not important but allow plenty of room
- **C.** Use your horn just once to warn them
- **D.** Drive slowly and leave plenty of room

396
A friend wants to teach you to drive a car. They MUST

Mark one answer

- **A.** be over 21 and have held a full licence for at least two years
- **B.** be over 18 and hold an advanced driver's certificate
- **C.** be over 18 and have fully comprehensive insurance
- **D.** be over 21 and have held a full licence for at least three years

397
You are dazzled at night by a vehicle behind you. You should

Mark one answer

- **A.** set your mirror to anti-dazzle
- **B.** set your mirror to dazzle the other driver
- **C.** brake sharply to a stop
- **D.** switch your rear lights on and off

398 You have a collision whilst your car is moving. What is the first thing you must do?

Mark one answer
- A. Stop only if there are injured people
- B. Call the emergency services
- C. Stop at the scene of the accident
- D. Call your insurance company

399 Yellow zigzag lines on the road outside schools mean

W-SCHOOL KEEP CLEAR-W

Mark one answer
- A. sound your horn to alert other road users
- B. stop to allow children to cross
- C. you must not wait or park on these lines
- D. you must not drive over these lines

400 What do these road markings outside a school mean?

W-SCHOOL KEEP CLEAR-W

Mark one answer
- A. You may park here if you are a teacher
- B. Sound your horn before parking
- C. When parking use your hazard warning lights
- D. You must not wait or park your vehicle here

401 You are driving on a main road. You intend to turn right into a side road. Just before turning you should

Mark one answer
- A. adjust your interior mirror
- B. flash your headlamps
- C. steer over to the left
- D. check for traffic overtaking on your right

402 Why should you allow extra room when overtaking a motorcyclist on a windy day?

Mark one answer
- A. The rider may turn off suddenly to get out of the wind
- B. The rider may be blown across in front of you
- C. The rider may stop suddenly
- D. The rider may be travelling faster than normal

403 Which age group of drivers is most likely to be involved in a road accident?

Mark one answer
- A. 36 to 45-year-olds
- B. 55-year-olds and over
- C. 46 to 55-year-olds
- D. 17 to 25-year-olds

TIP Remember: part of learning to drive safely is being able to control the car at very slow speeds, as when following a cyclist.

404 You are driving towards a zebra crossing. Waiting to cross is a person in a wheelchair. You should

Mark one answer

- A. continue on your way
- B. wave to the person to cross
- C. wave to the person to wait
- D. be prepared to stop

405 Where in particular should you look out for motorcyclists?

Mark one answer

- A. In a filling station
- B. At a road junction
- C. Near a service area
- D. When entering a car park

406 Where should you take particular care to look out for motorcyclists and cyclists?

Mark one answer

- A. On dual carriageways
- B. At junctions
- C. At zebra crossings
- D. On one-way streets

407 The road outside this school is marked with yellow zigzag lines. What do these lines mean?

Mark one answer

- A. You may park on the lines when dropping off schoolchildren
- B. You may park on the lines when picking schoolchildren up
- C. You must not wait or park your vehicle here at all
- D. You must stay with your vehicle if you park here

TIP By far the greatest number of accidents occurs within 18 metres (20 yards) of a junction. T-junctions and staggered junctions have proved to be more dangerous than roundabouts, or even crossroads.

408
The road is wet. Why might a motorcyclist steer round drain covers on a bend?

Mark one answer

A. To avoid puncturing the tyres on the edge of the drain covers

B. To prevent the motorcycle sliding on the metal drain covers

C. To help judge the bend using the drain covers as marker points

D. To avoid splashing pedestrians on the pavement

409
You are about to overtake a slow-moving motorcyclist. Which one of these signs would make you take special care?

Mark one answer

A.

B.

C.

D.

410
You are waiting to emerge left from a minor road. A large vehicle is approaching from the right. You have time to turn, but you should wait. Why?

Mark one answer

A. The large vehicle can easily hide an overtaking vehicle

B. The large vehicle can turn suddenly

C. The large vehicle is difficult to steer in a straight line

D. The large vehicle can easily hide vehicles from the left

411
You are following a long vehicle. It approaches a crossroads and signals left, but moves out to the right. You should

Mark one answer

A. get closer in order to pass it quickly

B. stay well back and give it room

C. assume the signal is wrong and it is really turning right

D. overtake as it starts to slow down

> **TIP** If you cannot see the side mirrors of the long vehicle ahead, the driver is unaware you are there. Keep well back.

412

You are following a long vehicle approaching a crossroads. The driver signals right but moves close to the left-hand kerb. What should you do?

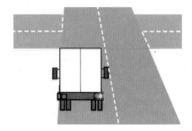

Mark one answer

- **A.** Warn the driver of the wrong signal
- **B.** Wait behind the long vehicle
- **C.** Report the driver to the police
- **D.** Overtake on the right-hand side

413

You are approaching a mini-roundabout. The long vehicle in front is signalling left but positioned over to the right. You should

Mark one answer

- **A.** sound your horn
- **B.** overtake on the left
- **C.** follow the same course as the lorry
- **D.** keep well back

414

Before overtaking a large vehicle you should keep well back. Why is this?

Mark one answer

- **A.** To give acceleration space to overtake quickly on blind bends
- **B.** To get the best view of the road ahead
- **C.** To leave a gap in case the vehicle stops and rolls back
- **D.** To offer other drivers a safe gap if they want to overtake you

415

Why is passing a lorry more risky than passing a car?

Mark one answer

- **A.** Lorries are longer than cars
- **B.** Lorries may suddenly pull up
- **C.** The brakes of lorries are not as good
- **D.** Lorries climb hills more slowly

416

You are travelling behind a bus that pulls up at a bus stop. What should you do?

Mark two answers

- **A.** Accelerate past the bus sounding your horn
- **B.** Watch carefully for pedestrians
- **C.** Be ready to give way to the bus
- **D.** Pull in closely behind the bus

TIP Watch carefully for speed limits marked on the road – not just on traffic signs.

417 When you approach a bus signalling to move off from a bus stop you should

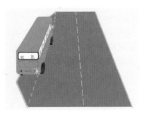

Mark one answer
- [ ] **A.** get past before it moves
- [ ] **B.** allow it to pull away, if it is safe to do so
- [ ] **C.** flash your headlights as you approach
- [ ] **D.** signal left and wave the bus on

418 Which of these vehicles is LEAST likely to be affected by crosswinds?

Mark one answer
- [ ] **A.** Cyclists
- [ ] **B.** Motorcyclists
- [ ] **C.** High-sided vehicles
- [ ] **D.** Cars

419 You are following a large lorry on a wet road. Spray makes it difficult to see. You should

Mark one answer
- [ ] **A.** drop back until you can see better
- [ ] **B.** put your headlights on full beam
- [ ] **C.** keep close to the lorry, away from the spray
- [ ] **D.** speed up and overtake quickly

420 Some two-way roads are divided into three lanes. Why are these particularly dangerous?

Mark one answer
- [ ] **A.** Traffic in both directions can use the middle lane to overtake
- [ ] **B.** Traffic can travel faster in poor weather conditions
- [ ] **C.** Traffic can overtake on the left
- [ ] **D.** Traffic uses the middle lane for emergencies only

421 What should you do as you approach this lorry?

Mark one answer
- [ ] **A.** Slow down and be prepared to wait
- [ ] **B.** Make the lorry wait for you
- [ ] **C.** Flash your lights at the lorry
- [ ] **D.** Move to the right-hand side of the road

TIP Box junctions were introduced to prevent blockages at crossroads and other junctions. The rule is: do not enter the box unless your exit is clear. Usually you will not stop in the yellow box unless, while your exit route is clear, you are caused to wait by oncoming traffic.

422 You are following a large articulated vehicle. It is going to turn left into a narrow road. What action should you take?

Mark one answer
- **A.** Move out and overtake on the right
- **B.** Pass on the left as the vehicle moves out
- **C.** Be prepared to stop behind
- **D.** Overtake quickly before the lorry moves out

423 You keep well back while waiting to overtake a large vehicle. A car fills the gap. You should

Mark one answer
- **A.** sound your horn
- **B.** drop back further
- **C.** flash your headlights
- **D.** start to overtake

424 At a junction you see this signal. It means

Mark one answer
- **A.** cars must stop
- **B.** trams must stop
- **C.** both trams and cars must stop
- **D.** both trams and cars can continue

425 You are following a large vehicle approaching crossroads. The driver signals to turn left. What should you do?

Mark one answer
- **A.** Overtake if you can leave plenty of room
- **B.** Overtake only if there are no oncoming vehicles
- **C.** Do not overtake until the vehicle begins to turn
- **D.** Do not overtake when at or approaching a junction

426 You are following a long lorry. The driver signals to turn left into a narrow road. What should you do?

Mark one answer
- **A.** Overtake on the left before the lorry reaches the junction
- **B.** Overtake on the right as soon as the lorry slows down
- **C.** Do not overtake unless you can see there is no oncoming traffic
- **D.** Do not overtake, stay well back and be prepared to stop

TIP Many drivers 'tailgate' in fog because the rear lights ahead give them a false sense of security. In fact, you should leave a much greater separation distance from the vehicle in front in any kind of adverse weather.

427 You wish to overtake a long, slow-moving vehicle on a busy road. You should

Mark one answer

- [ ] **A.** follow it closely and keep moving out to see the road ahead
- [ ] **B.** flash your headlights for the oncoming traffic to give way
- [ ] **C.** stay behind until the driver waves you past
- [ ] **D.** keep well back until you can see that it is clear

428 It is very windy. You are behind a motorcyclist who is overtaking a high-sided vehicle. What should you do?

Mark one answer

- [ ] **A.** Overtake the motorcyclist immediately
- [ ] **B.** Keep well back
- [ ] **C.** Stay level with the motorcyclist
- [ ] **D.** Keep close to the motorcyclist

429 It is very windy. You are about to overtake a motorcyclist. You should

Mark one answer

- [ ] **A.** overtake slowly
- [ ] **B.** allow extra room
- [ ] **C.** sound your horn
- [ ] **D.** keep close as you pass

430 You are towing a caravan. Which is the safest type of rear view mirror to use?

Mark one answer

- [ ] **A.** Interior wide-angle-view mirror
- [ ] **B.** Extended-arm side mirrors
- [ ] **C.** Ordinary door mirrors
- [ ] **D.** Ordinary interior mirror

431 You are driving downhill. There is a car parked on the other side of the road. Large, slow lorries are coming towards you. You should

Mark one answer

- [ ] **A.** keep going because you have the right of way
- [ ] **B.** slow down and give way
- [ ] **C.** speed up and get past quickly
- [ ] **D.** pull over on the right behind the parked car

432 You are driving in town. Ahead of you a bus is at a bus stop. Which TWO of the following should you do?

Mark two answers

- [ ] **A.** Be prepared to give way if the bus suddenly moves off
- [ ] **B.** Continue at the same speed but sound your horn as a warning
- [ ] **C.** Watch carefully for the sudden appearance of pedestrians
- [ ] **D.** Pass the bus as quickly as you possibly can

433 You are driving in heavy traffic on a wet road. Spray makes it difficult to be seen. You should use your

Mark two answers

- [ ] **A.** full beam headlights
- [ ] **B.** rear fog lights if visibility is less than 100 metres (328 feet)
- [ ] **C.** rear fog lights if visibility is more than 100 metres (328 feet)
- [ ] **D.** dipped headlights
- [ ] **E.** sidelights only

434 You are driving along this road. What should you be prepared to do?

Mark one answer

- **A.** Sound your horn and continue
- **B.** Slow down and give way
- **C.** Report the driver to the police
- **D.** Squeeze through the gap

435 You are on a wet motorway with surface spray. You should use

Mark one answer

- **A.** hazard flashers
- **B.** dipped headlights
- **C.** rear fog lights
- **D.** sidelights

436 As a driver why should you be more careful where trams operate?

Mark one answer

- **A.** Because they do not have a horn
- **B.** Because they do not stop for cars
- **C.** Because they do not have lights
- **D.** Because they cannot steer to avoid you

TIP If there's been a sudden downpour there may be water covering the road surface, making it difficult to control the car; and excessive speed may result in **aquaplaning**. It is rather like skidding, but on water, because the tyres cannot grip effectively. If you find yourself aquaplaning, take your foot off the accelerator and slow down gently. And keep a safe distance from the vehicle in front.

437 You are following a vehicle at a safe distance on a wet road. Another driver overtakes you and pulls into the gap you have left. What should you do?

Mark one answer

- [ ] **A.** Flash your headlights as a warning
- [ ] **B.** Try to overtake safely as soon as you can
- [ ] **C.** Drop back to regain a safe distance
- [ ] **D.** Stay close to the other vehicle until it moves on

438 In which THREE of these situations may you overtake another vehicle on the left?

Mark three answers

- [ ] **A.** When you are in a one-way street
- [ ] **B.** When approaching a motorway slip road where you will be turning off
- [ ] **C.** When the vehicle in front is signalling to turn right
- [ ] **D.** When a slower vehicle is travelling in the right-hand lane of a dual carriageway
- [ ] **E.** In slow-moving traffic queues when traffic in the right-hand lane is moving more slowly

439 You are travelling in very heavy rain. Your overall stopping distance is likely to be

Mark one answer

- [ ] **A.** doubled
- [ ] **B.** halved
- [ ] **C.** up to ten times greater
- [ ] **D.** no different

440 Which TWO of the following are correct? When overtaking at night you should

Mark two answers

- [ ] **A.** wait until a bend so that you can see the oncoming headlights
- [ ] **B.** sound your horn twice before moving out
- [ ] **C.** be careful because you can see less
- [ ] **D.** beware of bends in the road ahead
- [ ] **E.** put headlights on full beam

441 When may you wait in a box junction?

Mark one answer

- [ ] **A.** When you are stationary in a queue of traffic
- [ ] **B.** When approaching a pelican crossing
- [ ] **C.** When approaching a zebra crossing
- [ ] **D.** When oncoming traffic prevents you turning right

442 Which of these plates normally appear with this road sign?

Mark one answer

A.
> **Humps for ½ mile**

B.
> **Hump Bridge**

C.
> **Low Bridge**

D.
> **Soft Verge**

443 Areas reserved for trams may have

Mark three answers

A. metal studs around them
B. white line markings
C. zigzag markings
D. a different coloured surface
E. yellow hatch markings
F. a different surface texture

444 Traffic calming measures are used to

Mark one answer

A. stop road rage
B. help overtaking
C. slow traffic down
D. help parking

445 Why should you always reduce your speed when travelling in fog?

Mark one answer

A. Because the brakes do not work as well
B. Because you could be dazzled by other people's fog lights
C. Because the engine is colder
D. Because it is more difficult to see events ahead

446 You are on a motorway in fog. The left-hand edge of the motorway can be identified by reflective studs. What colour are they?

Mark one answer

A. Green
B. Amber
C. Red
D. White

447 A rumble device is designed to

Mark two answers

A. give directions
B. prevent cattle escaping
C. alert you to low tyre pressure
D. alert you to a hazard
E. encourage you to reduce speed

448 You are on a narrow road at night. A slower-moving vehicle ahead has been signalling right for some time. What should you do?

Mark one answer

- **A.** Overtake on the left
- **B.** Flash your headlights before overtaking
- **C.** Signal right and sound your horn
- **D.** Wait for the signal to be cancelled before overtaking

449 Why should you test your brakes after this hazard?

Mark one answer

- **A.** Because you will be on a slippery road
- **B.** Because your brakes will be soaking wet
- **C.** Because you will have gone down a long hill
- **D.** Because you will have just crossed a long bridge

450 You have to make a journey in foggy conditions. You should

Mark one answer

- **A.** follow other vehicles' tail-lights closely
- **B.** avoid using dipped headlights
- **C.** leave plenty of time for your journey
- **D.** keep two seconds behind other vehicles

451 You are overtaking a car at night. You must be sure that

Mark one answer

- **A.** you flash your headlights before overtaking
- **B.** you select a higher gear
- **C.** you have switched your lights to full beam before overtaking
- **D.** you do not dazzle other road users

452 You see a vehicle coming towards you on a single track road. You should

Mark one answer

- **A.** go back to the main road
- **B.** do an emergency stop
- **C.** stop at a passing place
- **D.** put on your hazard warning lights

453 You are on a road which has speed humps. A driver in front is travelling slower than you. You should

Mark one answer

- **A.** sound your horn
- **B.** overtake as soon as you can
- **C.** flash your headlights
- **D.** slow down and stay behind

454 You are following other vehicles in fog with your lights on. How else can you reduce the chances of being involved in an accident?

Mark one answer

- A. Keep close to the vehicle in front
- B. Use your main beam instead of dipped headlights
- C. Keep together with the faster vehicles
- D. Reduce your speed and increase the gap

455 You see these markings on the road. Why are they there?

Mark one answer

- A. To show a safe distance between vehicles
- B. To keep the area clear of traffic
- C. To make you aware of your speed
- D. To warn you to change direction

456 When MUST you use dipped headlights during the day?

Mark one answer

- A. All the time
- B. Along narrow streets
- C. In poor visibility
- D. When parking

457 What are TWO main reasons why coasting downhill is wrong?

Mark two answers

- A. Fuel consumption will be higher
- B. The vehicle will pick up speed
- C. It puts more wear and tear on the tyres
- D. You have less braking and steering control
- E. It damages the engine

458 Hills can affect the performance of your vehicle. Which TWO apply when driving up steep hills?

Mark two answers

- A. Higher gears will pull better
- B. You will slow down sooner
- C. Overtaking will be easier
- D. The engine will work harder
- E. The steering will feel heavier

459 Why is coasting wrong?

Mark one answer

- A. It will cause the car to skid
- B. It will make the engine stall
- C. The engine will run faster
- D. There is no engine braking

460 You are driving on the motorway in windy conditions. When passing high-sided vehicles you should

Mark one answer

- A. increase your speed
- B. be wary of a sudden gust
- C. drive alongside very closely
- D. expect normal conditions

461 To correct a rear wheel skid you should

Mark one answer

- A. not steer at all
- B. steer away from it
- C. steer into it
- D. apply your handbrake

462 You have to make a journey in fog. What are the TWO most important things you should do before you set out?

Mark two answers

- A. Top up the radiator with antifreeze
- B. Make sure that you have a warning triangle in the vehicle
- C. Check that your lights are working
- D. Check the battery
- E. Make sure that the windows are clean

463 You are driving in fog. Why should you keep well back from the vehicle in front?

Mark one answer

- A. In case it changes direction suddenly
- B. In case its fog lights dazzle you
- C. In case it stops suddenly
- D. In case its brake lights dazzle you

464 You should switch your rear fog lights on when visibility drops below

Mark one answer

- A. your overall stopping distance
- B. ten car lengths
- C. 200 metres (656 feet)
- D. 100 metres (328 feet)

465 Whilst driving, the fog clears and you can see more clearly. You must remember to

Mark one answer

- A. switch off the fog lights
- B. reduce your speed
- C. switch off the demister
- D. close any open windows

466 You have to park on the road in fog. You should

Mark one answer

- A. leave sidelights on
- B. leave dipped headlights and fog lights on
- C. leave dipped headlights on
- D. leave main beam headlights on

467 On a foggy day you unavoidably have to park your car on the road. You should

Mark one answer

- A. leave your headlights on
- B. leave your fog lights on
- C. leave your sidelights on
- D. leave your hazard lights on

468 You are travelling at night. You are dazzled by headlights coming towards you. You should

Mark one answer

- A. pull down your sun visor
- B. slow down or stop
- C. switch on your main beam headlights
- D. put your hand over your eyes

469 Which of the following may apply when dealing with this hazard?

Mark four answers

- ☐ **A.** It could be more difficult in winter
- ☐ **B.** Use a low gear and drive slowly
- ☐ **C.** Use a high gear to prevent wheelspin
- ☐ **D.** Test your brakes afterwards
- ☐ **E.** Always switch on fog lamps
- ☐ **F.** There may be a depth gauge

470 Front fog lights may be used ONLY if

Mark one answer

- ☐ **A.** visibility is seriously reduced
- ☐ **B.** they are fitted above the bumper
- ☐ **C.** they are not as bright as the headlights
- ☐ **D.** an audible warning device is used

471 Front fog lights may be used ONLY if

Mark one answer

- ☐ **A.** your headlights are not working
- ☐ **B.** they are operated with rear fog lights
- ☐ **C.** they were fitted by the vehicle manufacturer
- ☐ **D.** visibility is seriously reduced

472 You are driving with your front fog lights switched on. Earlier fog has now cleared. What should you do?

Mark one answer

- ☐ **A.** Leave them on if other drivers have their lights on
- ☐ **B.** Switch them off as long as visibility remains good
- ☐ **C.** Flash them to warn oncoming traffic that it is foggy
- ☐ **D.** Drive with them on instead of your headlights

473 Front fog lights should be used ONLY when

Mark one answer

- ☐ **A.** travelling in very light rain
- ☐ **B.** visibility is seriously reduced
- ☐ **C.** daylight is fading
- ☐ **D.** driving after midnight

474 Why is it dangerous to leave rear fog lights on when they are not needed?

NI

Mark two answers

- ☐ **A.** Brake lights are less clear
- ☐ **B.** Following drivers can be dazzled
- ☐ **C.** Electrical systems could be overloaded
- ☐ **D.** Direction indicators may not work properly
- ☐ **E.** The battery could fail

475

You are driving on a clear dry night with your rear fog lights switched on. This may

Mark two answers **NI**

- [ ] A. reduce glare from the road surface
- [ ] B. make other drivers think you are braking
- [ ] C. give a better view of the road ahead
- [ ] D. dazzle following drivers
- [ ] E. help your indicators to be seen more clearly

476

You have just driven out of fog. Visibility is now good. You MUST

Mark one answer **NI**

- [ ] A. switch off all your fog lights
- [ ] B. keep your rear fog lights on
- [ ] C. keep your front fog lights on
- [ ] D. leave fog lights on in case fog returns

477

You forget to switch off your rear fog lights when the fog has cleared. This may

Mark three answers

- [ ] A. dazzle other road users
- [ ] B. reduce battery life
- [ ] C. cause brake lights to be less clear
- [ ] D. be breaking the law
- [ ] E. seriously affect engine power

478

You have been driving in thick fog which has now cleared. You must switch OFF your rear fog lights because

Mark one answer **NI**

- [ ] A. they use a lot of power from the battery
- [ ] B. they make your brake lights less clear
- [ ] C. they will cause dazzle in your rear-view mirrors
- [ ] D. they may not be properly adjusted

479

Front fog lights should be used

Mark one answer

- [ ] A. when visibility is reduced to 100 metres (328 feet)
- [ ] B. as a warning to oncoming traffic
- [ ] C. when driving during the hours of darkness
- [ ] D. in any conditions and at any time

480

Using rear fog lights in clear daylight will

Mark one answer

- [ ] A. be useful when towing a trailer
- [ ] B. give extra protection
- [ ] C. dazzle other drivers
- [ ] D. make following drivers keep back

481

Using front fog lights in clear daylight will

Mark one answer

- [ ] A. flatten the battery
- [ ] B. dazzle other drivers
- [ ] C. improve your visibility
- [ ] D. increase your awareness

482

You may use front fog lights with headlights ONLY when visibility is reduced to less than

Mark one answer

- [ ] A. 100 metres (328 feet)
- [ ] B. 200 metres (656 feet)
- [ ] C. 300 metres (984 feet)
- [ ] D. 400 metres (1,312 feet)

483 You may drive with front fog lights switched on

N 512 CTW

Mark one answer

- [ ] **A.** when visibility is less than 100 metres (328 feet)
- [ ] **B.** at any time to be noticed
- [ ] **C.** instead of headlights on high-speed roads
- [ ] **D.** when dazzled by the lights of oncoming vehicles

484 Chains can be fitted to your wheels to help prevent

Mark one answer

- [ ] **A.** damage to the road surface
- [ ] **B.** wear to the tyres
- [ ] **C.** skidding in deep snow
- [ ] **D.** the brakes locking

485 Pressing the clutch pedal down or rolling in neutral for too long while driving will

Mark one answer

- [ ] **A.** use more fuel
- [ ] **B.** cause the engine to overheat
- [ ] **C.** reduce your control
- [ ] **D.** improve tyre wear

486 How can you use the engine of your vehicle to control your speed?

Mark one answer

- [ ] **A.** By changing to a lower gear
- [ ] **B.** By selecting reverse gear
- [ ] **C.** By changing to a higher gear
- [ ] **D.** By selecting neutral

487 You are driving down a steep hill. Why could keeping the clutch down or selecting neutral for too long be dangerous?

Mark one answer

- [ ] **A.** Fuel consumption will be higher
- [ ] **B.** Your vehicle will pick up speed
- [ ] **C.** It will damage the engine
- [ ] **D.** It will wear tyres out more quickly

488 Why could keeping the clutch down or selecting neutral for long periods of time be dangerous?

Mark one answer

- [ ] **A.** Fuel spillage will occur
- [ ] **B.** Engine damage may be caused
- [ ] **C.** You will have less steering and braking control
- [ ] **D.** It will wear tyres out more quickly

489
You are driving on an icy road. What distance should you drive from the car in front?

Mark one answer

- A. four times the normal distance
- B. six times the normal distance
- C. eight times the normal distance
- D. ten times the normal distance

490
You are on a well-lit motorway at night. You must

Mark one answer

- A. use only your sidelights
- B. always use your headlights
- C. always use rear fog lights
- D. use headlights only in bad weather

491
You are on a motorway at night with other vehicles just ahead of you. Which lights should you have on?

Mark one answer

- A. Front fog lights
- B. Main beam headlights
- C. Sidelights only
- D. Dipped headlights

492
Which THREE of the following will affect your stopping distance?

Mark three answers

- A. How fast you are going
- B. The tyres on your vehicle
- C. The time of day
- D. The weather
- E. The street lighting

493
You are on a motorway at night. You MUST have your headlights switched on unless

NI

Mark one answer

- A. there are vehicles close in front of you
- B. you are travelling below 50mph
- C. the motorway is lit
- D. your vehicle is broken down on the hard shoulder

494
You will feel the effects of engine braking when you

Mark one answer

- A. only use the handbrake
- B. only use neutral
- C. change to a lower gear
- D. change to a higher gear

495
Daytime visibility is poor but not seriously reduced. You should switch on

Mark one answer

- A. headlights and fog lights
- B. front fog lights
- C. dipped headlights
- D. rear fog lights

496
Why are vehicles fitted with rear fog lights?

Mark one answer

- A. To be seen when driving at high speed
- B. To use if broken down in a dangerous position
- C. To make them more visible in thick fog
- D. To warn drivers following closely to drop back

497 While you are driving in fog, it becomes necessary to use front fog lights. You should

Mark one answer

- [ ] **A.** only turn them on in heavy traffic conditions
- [ ] **B.** remember not to use them on motorways
- [ ] **C.** only use them on dual carriageways
- [ ] **D.** remember to switch them off as visibility improves

498 When snow is falling heavily you should

Mark one answer

- [ ] **A.** only drive with your hazard lights on
- [ ] **B.** not drive unless you have a mobile phone
- [ ] **C.** only drive when your journey is short
- [ ] **D.** not drive unless it is essential

499 You are driving down a long steep hill. You suddenly notice your brakes are not working as well as normal. What is the usual cause of this?

Mark one answer

- [ ] **A.** The brakes overheating
- [ ] **B.** Air in the brake fluid
- [ ] **C.** Oil on the brakes
- [ ] **D.** Badly adjusted brakes

TIP If you are being tailgated, gradually slow down to increase the gap between your vehicle and the one in front, allowing at least double the distance of the two-second rule. If you need to brake, allow for the following driver by braking early and gently, keeping an eye on the mirror. This is called **braking for two** – that is, for yourself and the tailgater.

500 Which FOUR of these must NOT use motorways?

Mark four answers

- [ ] **A.** Learner car drivers
- [ ] **B.** Motorcycles over 50cc
- [ ] **C.** Double-decker buses
- [ ] **D.** Farm tractors
- [ ] **E.** Horse riders
- [ ] **F.** Cyclists

501 Which FOUR of these must NOT use motorways?

Mark four answers

- [ ] **A.** Learner car drivers
- [ ] **B.** Motorcycles over 50cc
- [ ] **C.** Double-deck buses
- [ ] **D.** Farm tractors
- [ ] **E.** Learner motorcyclists
- [ ] **F.** Cyclists

502 Immediately after joining a motorway you should normally

Mark one answer

- [ ] **A.** try to overtake
- [ ] **B.** re-adjust your mirrors
- [ ] **C.** position your vehicle in the centre lane
- [ ] **D.** keep in the left lane

503 When joining a motorway you must always

Mark one answer

- [ ] **A.** use the hard shoulder
- [ ] **B.** stop at the end of the acceleration lane
- [ ] **C.** come to a stop before joining the motorway
- [ ] **D.** give way to traffic already on the motorway

504 What is the national speed limit for cars and motorcycles in the centre lane of a three-lane motorway?

Mark one answer

- [ ] **A.** 40mph
- [ ] **B.** 50mph
- [ ] **C.** 60mph
- [ ] **D.** 70mph

505 What is the national speed limit on motorways for cars and motorcycles?

Mark one answer

- [ ] **A.** 30mph
- [ ] **B.** 50mph
- [ ] **C.** 60mph
- [ ] **D.** 70mph

506 The left-hand lane on a three-lane motorway is for use by

Mark one answer

- [ ] **A.** any vehicle
- [ ] **B.** large vehicles only
- [ ] **C.** emergency vehicles only
- [ ] **D.** slow vehicles only

507 What is the right-hand lane used for on a three-lane motorway?

Mark one answer

- [ ] **A.** Emergency vehicles only
- [ ] **B.** Overtaking
- [ ] **C.** Vehicles towing trailers
- [ ] **D.** Coaches only

508 Which of these IS NOT allowed to travel in the right-hand lane of a three-lane motorway?

Mark one answer

- A. A small delivery van
- B. A motorcycle
- C. A vehicle towing a trailer
- D. A motorcycle and sidecar

509 You are travelling on a motorway. You decide you need a rest. You should

Mark two answers

- A. stop on the hard shoulder
- B. go to a service area
- C. park on the slip road
- D. park on the central reservation
- E. leave at the next exit

510 You break down on a motorway. You need to call for help. Why may it be better to use an emergency roadside telephone rather than a mobile phone?

Mark one answer **NI**

- A. It connects you to a local garage
- B. Using a mobile phone will distract other drivers
- C. It allows easy location by the emergency services
- D. Mobile phones do not work on motorways

511 What should you use the hard shoulder of a motorway for?

Mark one answer

- A. Stopping in an emergency
- B. Leaving the motorway
- C. Stopping when you are tired
- D. Joining the motorway

512 After a breakdown you need to rejoin the main carriageway of a motorway from the hard shoulder. You should

Mark one answer

- A. move out on to the carriageway then build up your speed
- B. move out on to the carriageway using your hazard lights
- C. gain speed on the hard shoulder before moving out on to the carriageway
- D. wait on the hard shoulder until someone flashes their headlights at you

513 A crawler lane on a motorway is found

Mark one answer

- A. on a steep gradient
- B. before a service area
- C. before a junction
- D. along the hard shoulder

Crawler lane

514 You are driving on a motorway. There are red flashing lights above every lane. You must

Mark one answer
- [ ] **A.** pull on to the hard shoulder
- [ ] **B.** slow down and watch for further signals
- [ ] **C.** leave at the next exit
- [ ] **D.** stop and wait

515 You are driving in the right-hand lane on a motorway. You see these overhead signs. This means

Mark one answer

- [ ] **A.** move to the left and reduce your speed to 50mph
- [ ] **B.** there are road works 50 metres (55 yards) ahead
- [ ] **C.** use the hard shoulder until you have passed the hazard
- [ ] **D.** leave the motorway at the next exit

516 What do these motorway signs show?

Mark one answer
- [ ] **A.** They are countdown markers to a bridge
- [ ] **B.** They are distance markers to the next telephone
- [ ] **C.** They are countdown markers to the next exit
- [ ] **D.** They warn of a police control ahead

517 On a motorway the amber reflective studs can be found between

Mark one answer
- [ ] **A.** the hard shoulder and the carriageway
- [ ] **B.** the acceleration lane and the carriageway
- [ ] **C.** the central reservation and the carriageway
- [ ] **D.** each pair of the lanes

518 What colour are the reflective studs between the lanes on a motorway?

Mark one answer
- [ ] **A.** Green
- [ ] **B.** Amber
- [ ] **C.** White
- [ ] **D.** Red

519 What colour are the reflective studs between a motorway and its slip road?

Mark one answer
- [ ] **A.** Amber
- [ ] **B.** White
- [ ] **C.** Green
- [ ] **D.** Red

520 You are allowed to stop on a motorway when you

Mark one answer
- [ ] **A.** need to walk and get fresh air
- [ ] **B.** wish to pick up hitch-hikers
- [ ] **C.** are told to do so by flashing red lights
- [ ] **D.** need to use a mobile telephone

521
You have broken down on a motorway. To find the nearest emergency telephone you should always walk

Mark one answer
- A. with the traffic flow
- B. facing oncoming traffic
- C. in the direction shown on the marker posts
- D. in the direction of the nearest exit

522
You are travelling along the left lane of a three-lane motorway. Traffic is joining from a slip road. You should

Mark one answer
- A. race the other vehicles
- B. move to another lane
- C. maintain a steady speed
- D. switch on your hazard flashers

523
You are joining a motorway. Why is it important to make full use of the slip road?

Mark one answer
- A. Because there is space available to turn round if you need to
- B. To allow you direct access to the overtaking lanes
- C. To build up a speed similar to traffic on the motorway
- D. Because you can continue on the hard shoulder

524
How should you use the emergency telephone on a motorway?

Mark one answer
- A. Stay close to the carriageway
- B. Face the oncoming traffic
- C. Keep your back to the traffic
- D. Stand on the hard shoulder

525
You are on a motorway. What colour are the reflective studs on the left of the carriageway?

Mark one answer
- A. Green
- B. Red
- C. White
- D. Amber

526
On a three-lane motorway which lane should you normally use?

Mark one answer
- A. Left
- B. Right
- C. Centre
- D. Either the right or centre

527
A basic rule when on motorways is

Mark one answer
- A. use the lane that has least traffic
- B. keep to the left lane unless overtaking
- C. overtake on the side that is clearest
- D. try to keep above 50mph to prevent congestion

TIP Never underestimate how dangerous the hard shoulder can be. As many as one in eight road deaths happen there.

528 When going through a contraflow system on a motorway you should

Mark one answer

- **A.** ensure that you do not exceed 30mph
- **B.** keep a good distance from the vehicle ahead
- **C.** switch lanes to keep the traffic flowing
- **D.** stay close to the vehicle ahead to reduce queues

529 You are on a three-lane motorway. There are red reflective studs on your left and white ones to your right. Where are you?

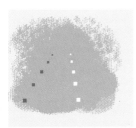

Mark one answer

- **A.** In the right-hand lane
- **B.** In the middle lane
- **C.** On the hard shoulder
- **D.** In the left-hand lane

530 When may you stop on a motorway?

Mark three answers

- **A.** If you have to read a map
- **B.** When you are tired and need a rest
- **C.** If red lights show above every lane
- **D.** When told to by the police
- **E.** If your mobile phone rings
- **F.** In an emergency or a breakdown

531 You are approaching road works on a motorway. What should you do?

Mark one answer

- **A.** Speed up to clear the area quickly
- **B.** Always use the hard shoulder
- **C.** Obey all speed limits
- **D.** Stay very close to the vehicle in front

532 On motorways you should never overtake on the left UNLESS

Mark one answer

- **A.** you can see well ahead that the hard shoulder is clear
- **B.** the traffic in the right-hand lane is signalling right
- **C.** you warn drivers behind by signalling left
- **D.** there is a queue of slow-moving traffic to your right that is moving slower than you are

533 You are towing a trailer on a motorway. What is your maximum speed limit?

Mark one answer

- **A.** 40mph
- **B.** 50mph
- **C.** 60mph
- **D.** 70mph

534 The left-hand lane of a motorway should be used for

Mark one answer

- A. breakdowns and emergencies only
- B. overtaking slower traffic in the other lanes
- C. slow vehicles only
- D. normal driving

535 You are driving on a motorway. You have to slow down quickly due to a hazard. You should

Mark one answer

- A. switch on your hazard lights
- B. switch on your headlights
- C. sound your horn
- D. flash your headlights

536 You get a puncture on the motorway. You manage to get your vehicle on to the hard shoulder. You should

Mark one answer

- A. change the wheel yourself immediately
- B. use the emergency telephone and call for assistance
- C. try to wave down another vehicle for help
- D. only change the wheel if you have a passenger to help you

537 You are driving on a motorway. By mistake, you go past the exit that you wanted to take. You should

Mark one answer

- A. carefully reverse on the hard shoulder
- B. carry on to the next exit
- C. carefully reverse in the left-hand lane
- D. make a U-turn at the next gap in the central reservation

538 Your vehicle breaks down on the hard shoulder of a motorway. You decide to use your mobile phone to call for help. You should

Mark one answer [NI]

- A. stand at the rear of the vehicle while making the call
- B. try to repair the vehicle yourself
- C. get out of the vehicle by the right-hand door
- D. check your location from the marker posts on the left

539 You are driving a car on a motorway. Unless signs show otherwise you must NOT exceed

Mark one answer

- A. 50mph
- B. 60mph
- C. 70mph
- D. 80mph

540 You are on a three-lane motorway towing a trailer. You may use the right-hand lane when

Mark one answer **NI**

- A. there are lane closures
- B. there is slow-moving traffic
- C. you can maintain a high speed
- D. large vehicles are in the left and centre lanes

541 You are on a motorway. There is a contraflow system ahead. What would you expect to find?

Mark one answer

- A. Temporary traffic lights
- B. Lower speed limits
- C. Wider lanes than normal
- D. Speed humps

542 You are driving at 70mph on a three-lane motorway. There is no traffic ahead. Which lane should you use?

Mark one answer

- A. Any lane
- B. Middle lane
- C. Right lane
- D. Left lane

543 Your vehicle has broken down on a motorway. You are not able to stop on the hard shoulder. What should you do?

Mark one answer

- A. Switch on your hazard warning lights
- B. Stop following traffic and ask for help
- C. Attempt to repair your vehicle quickly
- D. Stand behind your vehicle to warn others

544 Why is it particularly important to carry out a check on your vehicle before making a long motorway journey?

Mark one answer

- A. You will have to do more harsh braking on motorways
- B. Motorway service stations do not deal with breakdowns
- C. The road surface will wear down the tyres faster
- D. Continuous high speeds may increase the risk of your vehicle breaking down

545 For what reason may you use the right-hand lane of a motorway?

Mark one answer

- A. For keeping out of the way of lorries
- B. For driving at more than 70mph
- C. For turning right
- D. For overtaking other vehicles

546 On a motorway you may ONLY stop on the hard shoulder

Mark one answer

- **A.** in an emergency
- **B.** if you feel tired and need to rest
- **C.** if you accidentally go past the exit that you wanted to take
- **D.** to pick up a hitch-hiker

547 You are driving on a motorway. The car ahead shows its hazard lights for a short time. This tells you that

Mark one answer

- **A.** the driver wants you to overtake
- **B.** the other car is going to change lanes
- **C.** traffic ahead is slowing or stopping suddenly
- **D.** there is a police speed check ahead

548 The emergency telephones on a motorway are connected to the

Mark one answer

- **A.** ambulance service
- **B.** police control
- **C.** fire brigade
- **D.** breakdown service

549 You are intending to leave the motorway at the next exit. Before you reach the exit you should normally position your vehicle

Mark one answer

- **A.** in the middle lane
- **B.** in the left-hand lane
- **C.** on the hard shoulder
- **D.** in any lane

550 As a provisional licence holder you should not drive a car

Mark one answer

- **A.** over 30mph
- **B.** at night
- **C.** on the motorway
- **D.** with passengers in rear seats

TIP The first motorway sign-board, a mile before the exit, will only provide the road numbers and sometimes major town names. The half-mile sign gives major town names. Make sure you know in advance which junction number you're looking for.

551 What is the meaning of this sign?

Mark one answer
- **A.** Local speed limit applies
- **B.** No waiting on the carriageway
- **C.** National speed limit applies
- **D.** No entry to vehicular traffic

552 What is the national speed limit on a single carriageway road for cars and motorcycles?

Mark one answer
- **A.** 70mph
- **B.** 60mph
- **C.** 50mph
- **D.** 30mph

553 What is the national speed limit for cars and motorcycles on a dual carriageway?

Mark one answer
- **A.** 30mph
- **B.** 50mph
- **C.** 60mph
- **D.** 70mph

554 There are no speed limit signs on the road. How is a 30mph limit indicated?

Mark one answer
- **A.** By hazard warning lines
- **B.** By street lighting
- **C.** By pedestrian islands
- **D.** By double or single yellow lines

555 Where you see street lights but no speed limit signs the limit is usually

Mark one answer
- **A.** 30mph
- **B.** 40mph
- **C.** 50mph
- **D.** 60mph

556 What does this sign mean?

Mark one answer
- **A.** Minimum speed 30mph
- **B.** End of maximum speed
- **C.** End of minimum speed
- **D.** Maximum speed 30mph

557 There is a tractor ahead of you. You wish to overtake but you are NOT sure if it is safe to do so. You should

Mark one answer
- **A.** follow another overtaking vehicle through
- **B.** sound your horn to the slow vehicle to pull over
- **C.** speed through but flash your lights to oncoming traffic
- **D.** not overtake if you are in doubt

TIP When judging the probable actions of another vehicle at a junction, check for clues such as the position on the road of the other vehicle and the angle of the wheels.

558 Which three of the following are most likely to take an unusual course at roundabouts?

Mark three answers
- A. Horse riders
- B. Milk floats
- C. Delivery vans
- D. Long vehicles
- E. Estate cars
- F. Cyclists

559 In which FOUR places must you NOT park or wait?

Mark four answers
- A. On a dual carriageway
- B. At a bus stop
- C. On the slope of a hill
- D. Opposite a traffic island
- E. In front of someone else's drive
- F. On the brow of a hill

560 In which TWO places must you NOT park?

Mark two answers
- A. Near a school entrance
- B. Near a police station
- C. In a side road
- D. At a bus stop
- E. In a one-way street

561 On a clearway you must not stop

Mark one answer
- A. at any time
- B. when it is busy
- C. in the rush hour
- D. during daylight hours

562 What is the meaning of this sign?

Mark one answer
- A. No entry
- B. Waiting restrictions
- C. National speed limit
- D. School crossing patrol

563 You can park on the right-hand side of a road at night

Mark one answer
- A. in a one-way street
- B. with your sidelights on
- C. more than 10 metres (32 feet) from a junction
- D. under a lamppost

564 On a three-lane dual carriageway the right-hand lane can be used for

Mark one answer
- A. overtaking only, never turning right
- B. overtaking or turning right
- C. fast-moving traffic only
- D. turning right only, never overtaking

565
You are approaching a busy junction. There are several lanes with road markings. At the last moment you realise that you are in the wrong lane. You should

Mark one answer
- A. continue in that lane
- B. force your way across
- C. stop until the area has cleared
- D. use clear arm signals to cut across

566
Where may you overtake on a one-way street?

Mark one answer
- A. Only on the left-hand side
- B. Overtaking is not allowed
- C. Only on the right-hand side
- D. Either on the right or the left

567
When going straight ahead at a roundabout you should

Mark one answer
- A. indicate left before leaving the roundabout
- B. not indicate at any time
- C. indicate right when approaching the roundabout
- D. indicate left when approaching the roundabout

568
Which vehicle might have to use a different course to normal at roundabouts?

Mark one answer
- A. Sports car
- B. Van
- C. Estate car
- D. Long vehicle

569
You are going straight ahead at a roundabout. How should you signal?

Mark one answer
- A. Signal right on the approach and then left to leave the roundabout
- B. Signal left as you leave the roundabout
- C. Signal left on the approach to the roundabout and keep the signal on until you leave
- D. Signal left just after you pass the exit before the one you will take

570
You may only enter a box junction when

Mark one answer
- A. there are less than two vehicles in front of you
- B. the traffic lights show green
- C. your exit road is clear
- D. you need to turn left

> **TIP** In your driving test, where there are lanes the examiner will check your position on the road; it's important not to be straddling two lanes at a time.

571 You may wait in a yellow box junction when

Mark one answer

- [ ] **A.** oncoming traffic is preventing you from turning right
- [ ] **B.** you are in a queue of traffic turning left
- [ ] **C.** you are in a queue of traffic to go ahead
- [ ] **D.** you are on a roundabout

572 You MUST stop when signalled to do so by which THREE of these?

Mark three answers

- [ ] **A.** A police officer
- [ ] **B.** A pedestrian
- [ ] **C.** A school crossing patrol
- [ ] **D.** A bus driver
- [ ] **E.** A red traffic light

TIP Did you know that you are allowed to have your seat belt unfastened when you are reversing? It's the only time you can do so when driving.

573 You will see these markers when approaching

Mark one answer

- [ ] **A.** the end of a motorway
- [ ] **B.** a concealed level crossing
- [ ] **C.** a concealed speed limit sign
- [ ] **D.** the end of a dual carriageway

574 Someone is waiting to cross at a zebra crossing. They are standing on the pavement. You should normally

Mark one answer

- [ ] **A.** go on quickly before they step on to the crossing
- [ ] **B.** stop before you reach the zigzag lines and let them cross
- [ ] **C.** stop, let them cross, wait patiently
- [ ] **D.** ignore them as they are still on the pavement

575 At toucan crossings, apart from pedestrians you should be aware of

Mark one answer

- [ ] **A.** emergency vehicles emerging
- [ ] **B.** buses pulling out
- [ ] **C.** trams crossing in front
- [ ] **D.** cyclists riding across

576 Who can use a toucan crossing?

Mark two answers

- **A.** Trains
- **B.** Cyclists
- **C.** Buses
- **D.** Pedestrians
- **E.** Trams

577 At a pelican crossing, what does a flashing amber light mean?

Mark one answer

- **A.** You must not move off until the lights stop flashing
- **B.** You must give way to pedestrians still on the crossing
- **C.** You can move off, even if pedestrians are still on the crossing
- **D.** You must stop because the lights are about to change to red

578 You are waiting at a pelican crossing. The red light changes to flashing amber. This means you must

Mark one answer

- **A.** wait for pedestrians on the crossing to clear
- **B.** move off immediately without any hesitation
- **C.** wait for the green light before moving off
- **D.** get ready and go when the continuous amber light shows

579 You are travelling on a well-lit road at night in a built-up area. By using dipped headlights you will be able to

Mark one answer

- **A.** see further along the road
- **B.** go at a much faster speed
- **C.** switch to main beam quickly
- **D.** be easily seen by others

580 When can you park on the left opposite these road markings?

Mark one answer

- **A.** If the line nearest to you is broken
- **B.** When there are no yellow lines
- **C.** To pick up or set down passengers
- **D.** During daylight hours only

581 You are intending to turn right at a crossroads. An oncoming driver is also turning right. It will normally be safer to

Mark one answer

- **A.** keep the other vehicle to your RIGHT and turn behind it (offside to offside)
- **B.** keep the other vehicle to your LEFT and turn in front of it (nearside to nearside)
- **C.** carry on and turn at the next junction instead
- **D.** hold back and wait for the other driver to turn first

582 You are on a road that has no traffic signs. There are street lights. What is the speed limit?

Mark one answer

- **A.** 20mph
- **B.** 30mph
- **C.** 40mph
- **D.** 60mph

583
You are going along a street with parked vehicles on the left-hand side. For which THREE reasons should you keep your speed down?

Mark three answers
- [ ] **A.** So that oncoming traffic can see you more clearly
- [ ] **B.** You may set off car alarms
- [ ] **C.** Vehicles may be pulling out
- [ ] **D.** Drivers' doors may open
- [ ] **E.** Children may run out from between the vehicles

584
You meet an obstruction on your side of the road. You should

Mark one answer
- [ ] **A.** carry on, you have priority
- [ ] **B.** give way to oncoming traffic
- [ ] **C.** wave oncoming vehicles through
- [ ] **D.** accelerate to get past first

585
You are on a two-lane dual carriageway. For which TWO of the following would you use the right-hand lane?

Mark two answers
- [ ] **A.** Turning right
- [ ] **B.** Normal progress
- [ ] **C.** Staying at the minimum allowed speed
- [ ] **D.** Constant high speed
- [ ] **E.** Overtaking slower traffic
- [ ] **F.** Mending punctures

586
Who has priority at an unmarked crossroads?

Mark one answer
- [ ] **A.** The larger vehicle
- [ ] **B.** No one has priority
- [ ] **C.** The faster vehicle
- [ ] **D.** The smaller vehicle

587
What is the nearest you may park to a junction?

Mark one answer **NI**
- [ ] **A.** 10 metres (32 feet)
- [ ] **B.** 12 metres (39 feet)
- [ ] **C.** 15 metres (49 feet)
- [ ] **D.** 20 metres (66 feet)

588
In which THREE places must you NOT park?

Mark three answers **NI**
- [ ] **A.** Near the brow of a hill
- [ ] **B.** At or near a bus stop
- [ ] **C.** Where there is no pavement
- [ ] **D.** Within 10 metres (32 feet) of a junction
- [ ] **E.** On a 40mph road

589
You are waiting at a level crossing. A train has passed but the lights keep flashing. You must

Mark one answer
- [ ] **A.** carry on waiting
- [ ] **B.** phone the signal operator
- [ ] **C.** edge over the stop line and look for trains
- [ ] **D.** park and investigate

590

You park overnight on a road with a 40mph speed limit. You should park

Mark one answer
- [ ] **A.** facing the traffic
- [ ] **B.** with parking lights on
- [ ] **C.** with dipped headlights on
- [ ] **D.** near a street light

591

The dual carriageway you are turning right on to has a very narrow central reserve. What should you do?

Mark one answer
- [ ] **A.** Proceed to the central reserve and wait
- [ ] **B.** Wait until the road is clear in both directions
- [ ] **C.** Stop in the first lane so that other vehicles give way
- [ ] **D.** Emerge slightly to show your intentions

592

At a crossroads there are no signs or road markings. Two vehicles approach. Which has priority?

Mark one answer
- [ ] **A.** Neither of the vehicles
- [ ] **B.** The vehicle travelling the fastest
- [ ] **C.** Oncoming vehicles turning right
- [ ] **D.** Vehicles approaching from the right

593

What does this sign tell you?

Mark one answer
- [ ] **A.** That it is a no-through road
- [ ] **B.** End of traffic calming zone
- [ ] **C.** Free parking zone ends
- [ ] **D.** No waiting zone ends

594

You are entering an area of road works. There is a temporary speed limit displayed. You should

Mark one answer
- [ ] **A.** not exceed the speed limit
- [ ] **B.** obey the limit only during rush hour
- [ ] **C.** ignore the displayed limit
- [ ] **D.** obey the limit except at night

595

You may drive over a footpath

Mark one answer
- [ ] **A.** to overtake slow-moving traffic
- [ ] **B.** when the pavement is very wide
- [ ] **C.** if no pedestrians are near
- [ ] **D.** to get into a property

596

A single-carriageway road has this sign. What is the maximum permitted speed for a car towing a trailer?

Mark one answer

A. 30mph
B. 40mph
C. 50mph
D. 60mph

597

You are towing a small caravan on a dual carriageway. You must not exceed

Mark one answer

A. 50mph
B. 40mph
C. 70mph
D. 60mph

598

You want to park and you see this sign. On the days and times shown you should

Mark one answer

A. park in a bay and not pay
B. park on yellow lines and pay
C. park on yellow lines and not pay
D. park in a bay and pay

Meter
ZONE

Mon - Fri
8.30 am - 6.30 pm
Saturday
8.30 am - 1.30 pm

599

As a car driver which THREE lanes are you NOT normally allowed to use?

Mark three answers

A. Crawler lane
B. Bus lane
C. Overtaking lane
D. Acceleration lane
E. Cycle lane
F. Tram lane

600

You are driving along a road that has a cycle lane. The lane is marked by a solid white line. This means that during its period of operation

Mark one answer

A. the lane may be used for parking your car
B. you may drive in that lane at any time
C. the lane may be used when necessary
D. you must not drive in that lane

601

A cycle lane is marked by a solid white line. You must not drive or park in it

Mark one answer

A. at any time
B. during the rush hour
C. if a cyclist is using it
D. during its period of operation

602

While driving, you intend to turn left into a minor road. On the approach you should

Mark one answer

A. keep just left of the middle of the road
B. keep in the middle of the road
C. swing out wide just before turning
D. keep well to the left of the road

603

You are waiting at a level crossing. The red warning lights continue to flash after a train has passed by. What should you do?

Mark one answer

- **A.** Get out and investigate
- **B.** Telephone the signal operator
- **C.** Continue to wait
- **D.** Drive across carefully

604

You are driving over a level crossing. The warning lights come on and a bell rings. What should you do?

Mark one answer

- **A.** Get everyone out of the vehicle immediately
- **B.** Stop and reverse back to clear the crossing
- **C.** Keep going and clear the crossing
- **D.** Stop immediately and use your hazard warning lights

605

You are on a busy main road and find that you are travelling in the wrong direction. What should you do?

Mark one answer

- **A.** Turn into a side road on the right and reverse into the main road
- **B.** Make a U-turn in the main road
- **C.** Make a 'three-point' turn in the main road
- **D.** Turn round in a side road

606

You may remove your seat belt when carrying out a manoeuvre that involves

Mark one answer

- **A.** reversing
- **B.** a hill start
- **C.** an emergency stop
- **D.** driving slowly

607

You must not reverse

Mark one answer

- **A.** for longer than necessary
- **B.** for more than a car's length
- **C.** into a side road
- **D.** in a built-up area

608

You are parked in a busy high street. What is the safest way to turn your vehicle around to go the opposite way?

Mark one answer

- **A.** Find a quiet side road to turn round in
- **B.** Drive into a side road and reverse into the main road
- **C.** Get someone to stop the traffic
- **D.** Do a U-turn

609 When you are NOT sure that it is safe to reverse your vehicle you should

Mark one answer

- A. use your horn
- B. rev your engine
- C. get out and check
- D. reverse slowly

610 When may you reverse from a side road into a main road?

Mark one answer

- A. Only if both roads are clear of traffic
- B. Not at any time
- C. At any time
- D. Only if the main road is clear of traffic

611 You want to turn right at a box junction. There is oncoming traffic. You should

Mark one answer

- A. wait in the box junction if your exit is clear
- B. wait before the junction until it is clear of all traffic
- C. drive on, you cannot turn right at a box junction
- D. drive slowly into the box junction when signalled by oncoming traffic

612 You are reversing your vehicle into a side road. When would the greatest hazard to passing traffic occur?

Mark one answer

- A. After you've completed the manoeuvre
- B. Just before you actually begin to manoeuvre
- C. After you've entered the side road
- D. When the front of your vehicle swings out

613 You are driving on a road that has a cycle lane. The lane is marked by a broken white line. This means that

Mark two answers

- A. you should not drive in the lane unless it is unavoidable
- B. you should not park in the lane unless it is unavoidable
- C. you can drive in the lane at any time
- D. the lane must be used by motorcyclists in heavy traffic

614 Where is the safest place to park your vehicle at night?

Mark one answer

- A. In a garage
- B. On a busy road
- C. In a quiet car park
- D. Near a red route

615 To help keep your vehicle secure at night where should you park?

Mark one answer

- A. Near a police station
- B. In a quiet road
- C. On a red route
- D. In a well-lit area

616
You are in the right-hand lane of a dual carriageway. You see signs showing that the right lane is closed 800 yards ahead. You should

GET IN LANE

800 yards

Mark one answer

- [ ] A. keep in that lane until you reach the queue
- [ ] B. move to the left immediately
- [ ] C. wait and see which lane is moving faster
- [ ] D. move to the left in good time

617
You are driving on an urban clearway. You may stop only to

Mark one answer

- [ ] A. set down and pick up passengers
- [ ] B. use a mobile telephone
- [ ] C. ask for directions
- [ ] D. load or unload goods

618
You are looking for somewhere to park your vehicle. The area is full EXCEPT for spaces marked 'disabled use'. You can

Mark one answer

- [ ] A. use these spaces when elsewhere is full
- [ ] B. park if you stay with your vehicle
- [ ] C. use these spaces, disabled or not
- [ ] D. not park there unless permitted

619
Your vehicle is parked on the road at night. When must you use sidelights?

Mark one answer

- [ ] A. Where there are continuous white lines in the middle of the road
- [ ] B. Where the speed limit exceeds 30mph
- [ ] C. Where you are facing oncoming traffic
- [ ] D. Where you are near a bus stop

620
On which THREE occasions MUST you stop your vehicle?

Mark three answers

- [ ] A. When involved in an accident
- [ ] B. At a red traffic light
- [ ] C. When signalled to do so by a police officer
- [ ] D. At a junction with double broken white lines
- [ ] E. At a pelican crossing when the amber light is flashing and no pedestrians are crossing

621
You are on a road that is only wide enough for one vehicle. There is a car coming towards you. What should you do?

Mark one answer

- [ ] A. Pull into a passing place on your right
- [ ] B. Force the other driver to reverse
- [ ] C. Pull into a passing place if your vehicle is wider
- [ ] D. Pull into a passing place on your left

622 What MUST you have to park in a disabled space?

Mark one answer
- [ ] **A.** An orange or blue badge
- [ ] **B.** A wheelchair
- [ ] **C.** An advanced driver certificate
- [ ] **D.** A modified vehicle

623 You are driving at night with full beam headlights on. A vehicle is overtaking you. You should dip your lights

Mark one answer
- [ ] **A.** some time after the vehicle has passed you
- [ ] **B.** before the vehicle starts to pass you
- [ ] **C.** only if the other driver dips their headlights
- [ ] **D.** as soon as the vehicle passes you

TIP You can recognise a car driven by someone who is disabled because they display a **Blue Card** (formerly an Orange Badge). This gives them the right to park in a space with disabilities.

624 When may you drive a motor car in this bus lane?

local
taxi

Mon - Fri
7 - 10 am
4.00 - 6.30 pm

Mark one answer
- [ ] **A.** Outside its hours of operation
- [ ] **B.** To get to the front of a traffic queue
- [ ] **C.** You may not use it at any time
- [ ] **D.** To overtake slow-moving traffic

625 Signals are normally given by direction indicators and

Mark one answer
- [ ] **A.** brake lights
- [ ] **B.** sidelights
- [ ] **C.** fog lights
- [ ] **D.** interior lights

626 You MUST obey signs giving orders. These signs are mostly in

Mark one answer

- A. green rectangles
- B. red triangles
- C. blue rectangles
- D. red circles

627 Traffic signs giving orders are generally which shape?

Mark one answer

- A.
- B.
- C.
- D.

628 Which type of sign tells you NOT to do something?

Mark one answer

- A.
- B.
- C.
- D.

629 What does this sign mean?

Mark one answer

- A. Maximum speed limit with traffic calming
- B. Minimum speed limit with traffic calming
- C. '20 cars only' parking zone
- D. Only 20 cars allowed at any one time

20 ZONE *symbol* Place Name

630 Which sign means no motor vehicles are allowed?

Mark one answer

- A.
- B.
- C.
- D.

631 Which of these signs means no motor vehicles?

Mark one answer

- A.
- B.
- C.
- D.

632 What does this sign mean?

Mark one answer

- **A.** New speed limit 20mph
- **B.** No vehicles over 30 tonnes
- **C.** Minimum speed limit 30mph
- **D.** End of 20mph zone

633 What does this sign mean?

Mark one answer

- **A.** No overtaking
- **B.** No motor vehicles
- **C.** Clearway (no stopping)
- **D.** Cars and motorcycles only

634 What does this sign mean?

Mark one answer

- **A.** No parking
- **B.** No road markings
- **C.** No through road
- **D.** No entry

635 What does this sign mean?

Mark one answer

- **A.** Bend to the right
- **B.** Road on the right closed
- **C.** No traffic from the right
- **D.** No right turn

636 Which sign means 'no entry'?

Mark one answer

- **A.**
- **B.**
- **C.**
- **D.**

637 What does this sign mean?

Mark one answer

- **A.** Route for trams only
- **B.** Route for buses only
- **C.** Parking for buses only
- **D.** Parking for trams only

638 Which type of vehicle does this sign apply to?

Mark one answer

- [ ] A. Wide vehicles
- [ ] B. Long vehicles
- [ ] C. High vehicles
- [ ] D. Heavy vehicles

4.4 m
14′-6″

639 Which sign means NO motor vehicles allowed?

Mark one answer

- [ ] A.
- [ ] B.
- [ ] C.
- [ ] D.

640 What does this sign mean?

Mark one answer

- [ ] A. You have priority
- [ ] B. No motor vehicles
- [ ] C. Two-way traffic
- [ ] D. No overtaking

641 What does this sign mean?

Mark one answer

- [ ] A. Keep in one lane
- [ ] B. Give way to oncoming traffic
- [ ] C. Do not overtake
- [ ] D. Form two lanes

642 Which sign means no overtaking?

Mark one answer

- [ ] A.
- [ ] B.
- [ ] C.
- [ ] D.

643 What does this sign mean?

Mark one answer

- [ ] A. Waiting restrictions apply
- [ ] B. Waiting permitted
- [ ] C. National speed limit applies
- [ ] D. Clearway (no stopping)

644 What does this sign mean?

Mark one answer
- A. End of restricted speed area
- B. End of restricted parking area
- C. End of clearway
- D. End of cycle route

Zone ENDS

645 Which sign means 'no stopping'?

Mark one answer
- A.
- B.
- C.
- D.

646 What does this sign mean?

Mark one answer
- A. Roundabout
- B. Crossroads
- C. No stopping
- D. No entry

647 You see this sign ahead. It means

Mark one answer
- A. national speed limit applies
- B. waiting restrictions apply
- C. no stopping
- D. no entry

648 What does this sign mean?

Mark one answer
- A. Distance to parking place ahead
- B. Distance to public telephone ahead
- C. Distance to public house ahead
- D. Distance to passing place ahead

P 1 mile

649 What does this sign mean?

P

Mark one answer
- A. Vehicles may not park on the verge or footway
- B. Vehicles may park on the left-hand side of the road only
- C. Vehicles may park fully on the verge or footway
- D. Vehicles may park on the right-hand side of the road only

TIP Remember that where there are street lamps spaced less than 185 metres (202 yards) apart, a 30mph speed limit applies unless signs on the posts state otherwise.

650 What does this traffic sign mean?

Mark one answer
- A. No overtaking allowed
- B. Give priority to oncoming traffic
- C. Two-way traffic
- D. One-way traffic only

651 What is the meaning of this traffic sign?

Mark one answer
- A. End of two-way road
- B. Give priority to vehicles coming towards you
- C. You have priority over vehicles coming towards you
- D. Bus lane ahead

652 What MUST you do when you see this sign?

Mark one answer
- A. Stop, ONLY if traffic is approaching
- B. Stop, even if the road is clear
- C. Stop, ONLY if children are waiting to cross
- D. Stop, ONLY if a red light is showing

653 What does this sign mean?

Mark one answer
- A. No overtaking
- B. You are entering a one-way street
- C. Two-way traffic ahead
- D. You have priority over vehicles from the opposite direction

654 What shape is a STOP sign at a junction?

Mark one answer

- A.
- B.
- C.
- D.

655 At a junction you see this sign partly covered by snow. What does it mean?

Mark one answer
- A. Crossroads
- B. Give way
- C. Stop
- D. Turn right

656 Which shape is used for a GIVE WAY sign?

Mark one answer

A.

B.

C.

D.

657 What does this sign mean?

Mark one answer

A. Service area 30 miles ahead

B. Maximum speed 30mph

C. Minimum speed 30mph

D. Lay-by 30 miles ahead

658 Which of these signs means turn left ahead?

Mark one answer

A.

B.

C.

D.

659 What does this sign mean?

Mark one answer

A. Buses turning

B. Ring road

C. Mini-roundabout

D. Keep right

660 What does this sign mean?

Mark one answer

A. Give way to oncoming vehicles

B. Approaching traffic passes you on both sides

C. Turn off at the next available junction

D. Pass either side to get to the same destination

661 What does this sign mean?

Mark one answer

A. Route for trams

B. Give way to trams

C. Route for buses

D. Give way to buses

662 What does a circular traffic sign with a blue background do?

Mark one answer

- **A.** Give warning of a motorway ahead
- **B.** Give directions to a car park
- **C.** Give motorway information
- **D.** Give an instruction

663 Which of these signs means that you are entering a one-way street?

Mark one answer

- **A.**
- **B.**
- **C.**
- **D.**

664 Where would you see a contraflow bus and cycle lane?

Mark one answer

- **A.** On a dual carriageway
- **B.** On a roundabout
- **C.** On an urban motorway
- **D.** On a one-way street

665 What does this sign mean?

Mark one answer

- **A.** Bus station on the right
- **B.** Contraflow bus lane
- **C.** With-flow bus lane
- **D.** Give way to buses

666 What does this sign mean?

Mark one answer

- **A.** With-flow bus and cycle lane
- **B.** Contraflow bus and cycle lane
- **C.** No buses and cycles allowed
- **D.** No waiting for buses and cycles

667 What does a sign with a brown background show?

Mark one answer

- **A.** Tourist directions
- **B.** Primary roads
- **C.** Motorway routes
- **D.** Minor routes

668 This sign means

Mark one answer

- **A.** tourist attraction
- **B.** beware of trains
- **C.** level crossing
- **D.** beware of trams

669 What are triangular signs for?

Mark one answer

- **A.** To give warnings
- **B.** To give information
- **C.** To give orders
- **D.** To give directions

670 What does this sign mean?

Mark one answer

- **A.** Turn left ahead
- **B.** T-junction
- **C.** No through road
- **D.** Give way

671 What does this sign mean?

Mark one answer

- **A.** Multi-exit roundabout
- **B.** Risk of ice
- **C.** Six roads converge
- **D.** Place of historical interest

672 What does this sign mean?

Mark one answer

- **A.** Crossroads
- **B.** Level crossing with gate
- **C.** Level crossing without gate
- **D.** Ahead only

673 What does this sign mean?

Mark one answer

- **A.** Ring road
- **B.** Mini-roundabout
- **C.** No vehicles
- **D.** Roundabout

674 Which FOUR of these would be indicated by a triangular road sign?

Mark four answers

- A. Road narrows
- B. Ahead only
- C. Low bridge
- D. Minimum speed
- E. Children crossing
- F. T-junction

675 What does this sign mean?

Mark one answer

- A. Cyclists must dismount
- B. Cycles are not allowed
- C. Cycle route ahead
- D. Cycle in single file

676 Which sign means that pedestrians may be walking along the road?

Mark one answer

- A.
- B.
- C.
- D.

677 Which of these signs warn you of a pedestrian crossing?

Mark one answer

- A.
- B.
- C.
- D.

678 What does this sign mean?

Mark one answer

- A. No footpath ahead
- B. Pedestrians only ahead
- C. Pedestrian crossing ahead
- D. School crossing ahead

679 What does this sign mean?

Mark one answer

- A. School crossing patrol
- B. No pedestrians allowed
- C. Pedestrian zone – no vehicles
- D. Pedestrian crossing ahead

680 Which of these signs means there is a double bend ahead?

Mark one answer

- [ ] A.
- [ ] B.
- [ ] C.
- [ ] D.

681 What does this sign mean?

Mark one answer

- [ ] A. Wait at the barriers
- [ ] B. Wait at the crossroads
- [ ] C. Give way to trams
- [ ] D. Give way to farm vehicles

682 What does this sign mean?

Mark one answer

- [ ] A. Humpback bridge
- [ ] B. Humps in the road
- [ ] C. Entrance to tunnel
- [ ] D. Soft verges

683 What does this sign mean?

Mark one answer

- [ ] A. Low bridge ahead
- [ ] B. Tunnel ahead
- [ ] C. Ancient monument ahead
- [ ] D. Accident black spot ahead

684 What does this sign mean?

Mark one answer

- [ ] A. Two-way traffic straight ahead
- [ ] B. Two-way traffic crossing a one-way street
- [ ] C. Two-way traffic over a bridge
- [ ] D. Two-way traffic crosses a two-way road

685 Which sign means 'two-way traffic crosses a one-way road'?

Mark one answer

- [ ] A.
- [ ] B.
- [ ] C.
- [ ] D.

686 Which of these signs means the end of a dual carriageway?

Mark one answer

A.

B.

C.

D.

687 What does this sign mean?

Mark one answer

A. End of dual carriageway
B. Tall bridge
C. Road narrows
D. End of narrow bridge

688 What does this sign mean?

Mark one answer

A. Two-way traffic ahead across a one-way street
B. Traffic approaching you has priority
C. Two-way traffic straight ahead
D. Motorway contraflow system ahead

689 What does this sign mean?

Mark one answer

A. Crosswinds
B. Road noise
C. Airport
D. Adverse camber

690 What does this traffic sign mean?

Mark one answer

A. Slippery road ahead
B. Tyres liable to punctures ahead
C. Danger ahead
D. Service area ahead

691 You are about to overtake when you see this sign. You should

Mark one answer

A. overtake the other driver as quickly as possible
B. move to the right to get a better view
C. switch your headlights on before overtaking
D. hold back until you can see clearly ahead

Hidden dip

692 What does this sign mean?

Mark one answer

- **A.** Level crossing with gate or barrier
- **B.** Gated road ahead
- **C.** Level crossing without gate or barrier
- **D.** Cattle grid ahead

693 What does this sign mean?

Mark one answer

- **A.** No trams ahead
- **B.** Oncoming trams
- **C.** Trams crossing ahead
- **D.** Trams only

694 What does this sign mean?

Mark one answer

- **A.** Adverse camber
- **B.** Steep hill downwards
- **C.** Uneven road
- **D.** Steep hill upwards

695 What does this sign mean?

Mark one answer

- **A.** Uneven road surface
- **B.** Bridge over the road
- **C.** Road ahead ends
- **D.** Water across the road

696 What does this sign mean?

Mark one answer

- **A.** Humpback bridge
- **B.** Traffic calming hump
- **C.** Low bridge
- **D.** Uneven road

697 What does this sign mean?

Mark one answer

- **A.** Turn left for parking area
- **B.** No through road on the left
- **C.** No entry for traffic turning left
- **D.** Turn left for ferry terminal

698 What does this sign mean?

Mark one answer
- [ ] **A.** T-junction
- [ ] **B.** No through road
- [ ] **C.** Telephone box ahead
- [ ] **D.** Toilet ahead

699 Which sign means 'no through road'?

Mark one answer
- [ ] **A.**
- [ ] **B.**
- [ ] **C.**
- [ ] **D.**

700 Which of the following signs informs you that you are coming to a No Through Road?

Mark one answer
- [ ] **A.**
- [ ] **B.**
- [ ] **C.**
- [ ] **D.**

701 What does this sign mean?

Mark one answer
- [ ] **A.** Direction to park and ride car park
- [ ] **B.** No parking for buses or coaches
- [ ] **C.** Directions to bus and coach park
- [ ] **D.** Parking area for cars and coaches

702 You are driving through a tunnel and you see this sign. What does it mean?

Mark one answer
- [ ] **A.** Direction to emergency pedestrian exit
- [ ] **B.** Beware of pedestrians, no footpath ahead
- [ ] **C.** No access for pedestrians
- [ ] **D.** Beware of pedestrians crossing ahead

703 Which is the sign for a ring road?

Mark one answer
- [ ] **A.**
- [ ] **B.**
- [ ] **C.**
- [ ] **D.**

704 What does this sign mean?

Mark one answer

- A. Route for lorries
- B. Ring road
- C. Rest area
- D. Roundabout

705 What does this sign mean?

Mark one answer

- A. Hilly road
- B. Humps in road
- C. Holiday route
- D. Hospital route

706 What does this sign mean?

Mark one answer

- A. The right-hand lane ahead is narrow
- B. Right-hand lane for buses only
- C. Right-hand lane for turning right
- D. The right-hand lane is closed

707 What does this sign mean?

Mark one answer

- A. Change to the left lane
- B. Leave at the next exit
- C. Contraflow system
- D. One-way street

708 To avoid an accident when entering a contraflow system, you should

Mark three answers

- A. reduce speed in good time
- B. switch lanes any time to make progress
- C. choose an appropriate lane early
- D. keep the correct separation distance
- E. increase speed to pass through quickly
- F. follow other motorists closely to avoid long queues

709 What does this sign mean?

Mark one answer

- A. Leave motorway at next exit
- B. Lane for heavy and slow vehicles
- C. All lorries use the hard shoulder
- D. Rest area for lorries

710 You are approaching a red traffic light. The signal will change from red to

Mark one answer

- A. red and amber, then green
- B. green, then amber
- C. amber, then green
- D. green and amber, then green

711 A red traffic light means

Mark one answer

- A. you should stop unless turning left
- B. stop, if you are able to brake safely
- C. you must stop and wait behind the stop line
- D. proceed with caution

712 At traffic lights, amber on its own means

Mark one answer

- A. prepare to go
- B. go if the way is clear
- C. go if no pedestrians are crossing
- D. stop at the stop line

713 You are approaching traffic lights. Red and amber are showing. This means

Mark one answer

- A. pass the lights if the road is clear
- B. there is a fault with the lights – take care
- C. wait for the green light before you pass the lights
- D. the lights are about to change to red

714 You are at a junction controlled by traffic lights. When should you NOT proceed at green?

Mark one answer

- A. When pedestrians are waiting to cross
- B. When your exit from the junction is blocked
- C. When you think the lights may be about to change
- D. When you intend to turn right

715 You are in the left-hand lane at traffic lights. You are waiting to turn left. At which of these traffic lights must you NOT move on?

Mark one answer

- A.
- B.
- C.
- D.

716 What does this sign mean?

Mark one answer

- A. Traffic lights out of order
- B. Amber signal out of order
- C. Temporary traffic lights ahead
- D. New traffic lights ahead

717 When traffic lights are out of order, who has priority?

Mark one answer

- A. Traffic going straight on
- B. Traffic turning right
- C. Nobody
- D. Traffic turning left

718 These flashing red lights mean STOP. In which THREE of the following places could you find them?

Mark three answers

- A. Pelican crossings
- B. Lifting bridges
- C. Zebra crossings
- D. Level crossings
- E. Motorway exits
- F. Fire stations

719 What do these zigzag lines at pedestrian crossings mean?

Mark one answer

- A. No parking at any time
- B. Parking allowed only for a short time
- C. Slow down to 20mph
- D. Sounding horns is not allowed

720 When may you cross a double solid white line in the middle of the road?

Mark one answer

- A. To pass traffic that is queuing back at a junction
- B. To pass a car signalling to turn left ahead
- C. To pass a road maintenance vehicle travelling at 10mph or less
- D. To pass a vehicle that is towing a trailer

721 What does this road marking mean?

Mark one answer
- A. Do not cross the line
- B. No stopping allowed
- C. You are approaching a hazard
- D. No overtaking allowed

722 This marking appears on the road just before a

Mark one answer
- A. no entry sign
- B. give way sign
- C. stop sign
- D. no through road sign

723 Where would you see this road marking?

Mark one answer
- A. At traffic lights
- B. On road humps
- C. Near a level crossing
- D. At a box junction

724 Which is a hazard warning line?

Mark one answer
- A.

- B.

- C.

- D.

725 At this junction there is a stop sign with a solid white line on the road surface. Why is there a stop sign here?

Mark one answer
- A. Speed on the major road is de-restricted
- B. It is a busy junction
- C. Visibility along the major road is restricted
- D. There are hazard warning lines in the centre of the road

726 You see this line across the road at the entrance to a roundabout. What does it mean?

Mark one answer
- [ ] **A.** Give way to traffic from the right
- [ ] **B.** Traffic from the left has right of way
- [ ] **C.** You have right of way
- [ ] **D.** Stop at the line

727 Where would you find this road marking?

Mark one answer
- [ ] **A.** At a railway crossing
- [ ] **B.** At a junction
- [ ] **C.** On a motorway
- [ ] **D.** On a pedestrian crossing

728 How will a police officer in a patrol vehicle normally get you to stop?

Mark one answer
- [ ] **A.** Flash the headlights, indicate left and point to the left
- [ ] **B.** Wait until you stop, then approach you
- [ ] **C.** Use the siren, overtake, cut in front and stop
- [ ] **D.** Pull alongside you, use the siren and wave you to stop

729 There is a police car following you. The police officer flashes the headlights and points to the left. What should you do?

Mark one answer
- [ ] **A.** Turn at the next left
- [ ] **B.** Pull up on the left
- [ ] **C.** Stop immediately
- [ ] **D.** Move over to the left

730 You approach a junction. The traffic lights are not working. A police officer gives this signal. You should

Mark one answer
- [ ] **A.** turn left only
- [ ] **B.** turn right only
- [ ] **C.** stop level with the officer's arm
- [ ] **D.** stop at the stop line

731 The driver of the car in front is giving this arm signal. What does it mean?

Mark one answer
- [ ] **A.** The driver is slowing down
- [ ] **B.** The driver intends to turn right
- [ ] **C.** The driver wishes to overtake
- [ ] **D.** The driver intends to turn left

732 Where would you see these road markings?

Mark one answer
- [ ] **A.** At a level crossing
- [ ] **B.** On a motorway slip road
- [ ] **C.** At a pedestrian crossing
- [ ] **D.** On a single-track road

733 When may you NOT overtake on the left?

Mark one answer
- [ ] **A.** On a free-flowing motorway or dual carriageway
- [ ] **B.** When the traffic is moving slowly in queues
- [ ] **C.** On a one-way street
- [ ] **D.** When the car in front is signalling to turn right

734 What does this motorway sign mean?

Mark one answer
- [ ] **A.** Change to the lane on your left
- [ ] **B.** Leave the motorway at the next exit
- [ ] **C.** Change to the opposite carriageway
- [ ] **D.** Pull up on the hard shoulder

735 What does this motorway sign mean?

Mark one answer
- [ ] **A.** Temporary minimum speed 50mph
- [ ] **B.** No services for 50 miles
- [ ] **C.** Obstruction 50 metres (164 feet) ahead
- [ ] **D.** Temporary maximum speed 50mph

736 What does this sign mean?

Mark one answer
- [ ] **A.** Through traffic to use left lane
- [ ] **B.** Right-hand lane T-junction only
- [ ] **C.** Right-hand lane closed ahead
- [ ] **D.** 11 tonne weight limit

737 On a motorway this sign means

Mark one answer
- [ ] **A.** move over on to the hard shoulder
- [ ] **B.** overtaking on the left only
- [ ] **C.** leave the motorway at the next exit
- [ ] **D.** move to the lane on your left

738 What does '25' mean on this motorway sign?

Nottingham
A46
25

Mark one answer
- A. The distance to the nearest town
- B. The route number of the road
- C. The number of the next junction
- D. The speed limit on the slip road

739 The right-hand lane of a three-lane motorway is

Mark one answer
- A. for lorries only
- B. an overtaking lane
- C. the right-turn lane
- D. an acceleration lane

740 Where can you find reflective amber studs on a motorway?

Mark one answer
- A. Separating the slip road from the motorway
- B. On the left-hand edge of the road
- C. On the right-hand edge of the road
- D. Separating the lanes

741 Where on a motorway would you find green reflective studs?

Mark one answer
- A. Separating driving lanes
- B. Between the hard shoulder and the carriageway
- C. At slip road entrances and exits
- D. Between the carriageway and the central reservation

742 You are travelling along a motorway. You see this sign. You should

Mark one answer
- A. leave the motorway at the next exit
- B. turn left immediately
- C. change lane
- D. move on to the hard shoulder

743 What does this sign mean?

Mark one answer
- A. No motor vehicles
- B. End of motorway
- C. No through road
- D. End of bus lane

744 Which of these signs means that the national speed limit applies?

Mark one answer

A.

B.

C.

D.

745 What is the maximum speed on a single carriageway road?

Mark one answer

A. 50mph

B. 60mph

C. 40mph

D. 70mph

746 What does this sign mean?

Mark one answer

A. End of motorway

B. End of restriction

C. Lane ends ahead

D. Free recovery ends

747 This sign is advising you to

Mark one answer

A. follow the route diversion

B. follow the signs to the picnic area

C. give way to pedestrians

D. give way to cyclists

748 Why would this temporary speed limit sign be shown?

Mark one answer

A. To warn of the end of the motorway

B. To warn you of a low bridge

C. To warn you of a junction ahead

D. To warn of road works ahead

50
¾ mile ahead

749 This traffic sign means there is

Mark one answer

A. a compulsory maximum speed limit

B. an advisory maximum speed limit

C. a compulsory minimum speed limit

D. an advised separation distance

750 You see this sign at a crossroads. You should

Mark one answer

- [ ] **A.** maintain the same speed
- [ ] **B.** carry on with great care
- [ ] **C.** find another route
- [ ] **D.** telephone the police

751 You are signalling to turn right in busy traffic. How would you confirm your intention safely?

Mark one answer

- [ ] **A.** Sound the horn
- [ ] **B.** Give an arm signal
- [ ] **C.** Flash your headlights
- [ ] **D.** Position over the centre line

752 What does this sign mean?

Mark one answer

- [ ] **A.** Motorcycles only
- [ ] **B.** No cars
- [ ] **C.** Cars only
- [ ] **D.** No motorcycles

753 You are on a motorway. You see this sign on a lorry that has stopped in the right-hand lane. You should

Mark one answer

- [ ] **A.** move into the right-hand lane
- [ ] **B.** stop behind the flashing lights
- [ ] **C.** pass the lorry on the left
- [ ] **D.** leave the motorway at the next exit

754 You are on a motorway. Red flashing lights appear above your lane only. What should you do?

Mark one answer

- [ ] **A.** Continue in that lane and look for further information
- [ ] **B.** Move into another lane in good time
- [ ] **C.** Pull on to the hard shoulder
- [ ] **D.** Stop and wait for an instruction to proceed

755 A red traffic light means

Mark one answer

- [ ] **A.** you must stop behind the white stop line
- [ ] **B.** you may go straight on if there is no other traffic
- [ ] **C.** you may turn left if it is safe to do so
- [ ] **D.** you must slow down and prepare to stop if traffic has started to cross

756 The driver of this car is giving an arm signal. What are they about to do?

Mark one answer

- A. Turn to the right
- B. Turn to the left
- C. Go straight ahead
- D. Let pedestrians cross

757 Which arm signal tells you that the car you are following is going to turn left?

Mark one answer

- A.
- B.
- C.
- D.

758 When may you sound the horn?

Mark one answer

- A. To give you right of way
- B. To attract a friend's attention
- C. To warn others of your presence
- D. To make slower drivers move over

759 You must not use your horn when you are stationary

Mark one answer

- A. unless a moving vehicle may cause you danger
- B. at any time whatsoever
- C. unless it is used only briefly
- D. except for signalling that you have just arrived

760 What does this sign mean?

URBAN CLEARWAY
Monday to Friday

am	pm
8.00 - 9.30	4.30 - 6.30

Mark one answer

- A. You can park on the days and times shown
- B. No parking on the days and times shown
- C. No parking at all from Monday to Friday
- D. End of the urban clearway restrictions

761 What does this sign mean?

Mark one answer

- A. Quayside or river bank
- B. Steep hill downwards
- C. Uneven road surface
- D. Road liable to flooding

762 You see this amber traffic light ahead. Which light(s) will come on next?

Mark one answer

- A. Red alone
- B. Red and amber together
- C. Green and amber together
- D. Green alone

763 The white line painted in the centre of the road means

Mark one answer

- A. oncoming vehicles have priority over you
- B. you should give priority to oncoming vehicles
- C. there is a hazard ahead of you
- D. the area is a national speed limit zone

764 Which sign means you have priority over oncoming vehicles?

Mark one answer

- A.
- B.
- C.
- D.

765 You see this signal overhead on the motorway. What does it mean?

Mark one answer

- A. Leave the motorway at the next exit
- B. All vehicles use the hard shoulder
- C. Sharp bend to the left ahead
- D. Stop, all lanes ahead closed

766 A white line like this along the centre of the road is a

Mark one answer

- A. bus lane marking
- B. hazard warning
- C. give way marking
- D. lane marking

TIP The outside lane of a motorway can't be used by vehicles weighing over 7.5 tonnes, and passenger vehicles over 7.5 tonnes or over 12 metres in length, or adapted to carry more than 8 passengers.

767 What is the purpose of these yellow criss-cross lines on the road?

Mark one answer

- **A.** To make you more aware of the traffic lights
- **B.** To guide you into position as you turn
- **C.** To prevent the junction from becoming blocked
- **D.** To show you where to stop when the lights change

768 What is the reason for the yellow criss-cross lines painted on the road here?

Mark one answer

- **A.** To mark out an area for trams only
- **B.** To prevent queuing traffic from blocking the junction on the left
- **C.** To mark the entrance lane to a car park
- **D.** To warn you of the tram lines crossing the road

769 What is the reason for the area marked in red and white along the centre of this road?

Mark one answer

- **A.** It is to separate traffic flowing in opposite directions
- **B.** It marks an area to be used by overtaking motorcyclists
- **C.** It is a temporary marking to warn of the road works
- **D.** It is separating the two sides of the dual carriageway

770 Other drivers may sometimes flash their headlights at you. In which situation are they allowed to do this?

Mark one answer

- **A.** To warn of a radar speed trap ahead
- **B.** To show that they are giving way to you
- **C.** To warn you of their presence
- **D.** To let you know there is a fault with your vehicle

771 At road works which of the following can control traffic flow?

Mark three answers

- **A.** A STOP–GO board
- **B.** Flashing amber lights
- **C.** A police officer
- **D.** Flashing red lights
- **E.** Temporary traffic lights

772 You are approaching a zebra crossing where pedestrians are waiting. Which arm signal might you give?

Mark one answer

A.

B.

C.

D.

773 The white line along the side of the road

Mark one answer

A. shows the edge of the carriageway
B. shows the approach to a hazard
C. means no parking
D. means no overtaking

774 You see this white arrow on the road ahead. It means

Mark one answer

A. entrance on the left
B. all vehicles turn left
C. keep left of the hatched markings
D. road bending to the left

775 How should you give an arm signal to turn left?

Mark one answer

A.

B.

C.

D.

776 You are waiting at a T-junction. A vehicle is coming from the right with the left signal flashing. What should you do?

Mark one answer

A. Move out and accelerate hard
B. Wait until the vehicle starts to turn in
C. Pull out before the vehicle reaches the junction
D. Move out slowly

777 When may you use hazard warning lights when driving?

Mark one answer

- [ ] **A.** Instead of sounding the horn in a built-up area between 11.30pm and 7am
- [ ] **B.** On a motorway or unrestricted dual carriageway, to warn of a hazard ahead
- [ ] **C.** On rural routes, after a warning sign of animals
- [ ] **D.** On the approach to toucan crossings where cyclists are waiting to cross

778 You are driving on a motorway. There is a slow-moving vehicle ahead. On the back you see this sign. You should

Mark one answer

- [ ] **A.** pass on the right
- [ ] **B.** pass on the left
- [ ] **C.** leave at the next exit
- [ ] **D.** drive no further

TIP *The Highway Code* states that the only reason for flashing your lights is **to let others know you are there**. Many people flash their lights to indicate they are **letting another motorist go first**. But in general, you should not assume it is safe to proceed on the basis of such a signal – the lights may not be flashed at you but at someone else.

779 You should NOT normally stop on these markings near schools

M-SCHOOL KEEP CLEAR-M

Mark one answer

- [ ] **A.** except when picking up children
- [ ] **B.** under any circumstances
- [ ] **C.** unless there is nowhere else available
- [ ] **D.** except to set down children

780 Why should you make sure that your indicators are cancelled after turning?

Mark one answer

- [ ] **A.** To avoid flattening the battery
- [ ] **B.** To avoid misleading other road users
- [ ] **C.** To avoid dazzling other road users
- [ ] **D.** To avoid damage to the indicator relay

781 You are driving in busy traffic. You want to pull up on the left just after a junction on the left. When should you signal?

Mark one answer

- [ ] **A.** As you are passing or just after the junction
- [ ] **B.** Just before you reach the junction
- [ ] **C.** Well before you reach the junction
- [ ] **D.** It would be better not to signal at all

782 An MOT certificate is normally valid for

Mark one answer

- A. three years after the date it was issued
- B. 10,000 miles
- C. one year after the date it was issued
- D. 30,000 miles

783 A cover note is a document issued before you receive your

Mark one answer

- A. driving licence
- B. insurance certificate
- C. registration document
- D. MOT certificate

784 A police officer asks to see your documents. You do not have them with you. You may produce them at a police station within

Mark one answer **NI**

- A. five days
- B. seven days
- C. 14 days
- D. 21 days

785 You have just passed your practical test. You do not hold a full licence in another category. Within two years you get six penalty points on your licence. What will you have to do?

Mark two answers

- A. Retake only your theory test
- B. Retake your theory and practical tests
- C. Retake only your practical test
- D. Reapply for your full licence immediately
- E. Reapply for your provisional licence

786 To drive on the road learners MUST

Mark one answer

- A. have NO penalty points on their licence
- B. have taken professional instruction
- C. have a signed, valid provisional licence
- D. apply for a driving test within 12 months

787 Before driving anyone else's motor vehicle you should make sure that

Mark one answer

- A. the vehicle owner has third party insurance cover
- B. your own vehicle has insurance cover
- C. the vehicle is insured for your use
- D. the owner has left the insurance documents in the vehicle

788 Your car needs an MOT certificate. If you drive without one this could invalidate your

Mark one answer

- A. vehicle service record
- B. insurance
- C. road tax disc
- D. vehicle registration document

TIP Remember, a fine for speeding leads to penalty points on your licence. If you accumulate six penalty points within two years of passing your test, your licence will be revoked.

789 When is it legal to drive a car over three years old without an MOT certificate?

Mark one answer   **NI**

- A. Up to seven days after the old certificate has run out
- B. When driving to an MOT centre to arrange an appointment
- C. Just after buying a second-hand car with no MOT
- D. When driving to an appointment at an MOT centre

790 To supervise a learner driver you must

Mark two answers

- A. have held a full licence for at least 3 years
- B. be at least 21
- C. be an approved driving instructor
- D. hold an advanced driving certificate

791 The cost of your insurance may be reduced if

Mark one answer

- A. your car is large and powerful
- B. you are using the car for work purposes
- C. you have penalty points on your licence
- D. you are over 25 years old

792 How old must you be to supervise a learner driver?

Mark one answer

- A. 18 years old
- B. 19 years old
- C. 20 years old
- D. 21 years old

793 A newly qualified driver must

Mark one answer

- A. display green 'L' plates
- B. not exceed 40mph for 12 months
- C. be accompanied on a motorway
- D. have valid motor insurance

794 What is the legal minimum insurance cover you must have to drive on public roads?

Mark one answer

- A. Third party, fire and theft
- B. Fully comprehensive
- C. Third party only
- D. Personal injury cover

795 You have third party insurance. What does this cover?

Mark three answers

- A. Damage to your own vehicle
- B. Damage to your vehicle by fire
- C. Injury to another person
- D. Damage to someone's property
- E. Damage to other vehicles
- F. Injury to yourself

796 For which TWO of these must you show your motor insurance certificate?

Mark two answers

- A. When you are taking your driving test
- B. When buying or selling a vehicle
- C. When a police officer asks you for it
- D. When you are taxing your vehicle
- E. When having an MOT inspection

797 Vehicle excise duty is often called 'Road Tax' or 'The Tax Disc'. You must

Mark one answer

- **A.** keep it with your registration document
- **B.** display it clearly on your vehicle
- **C.** keep it concealed safely in your vehicle
- **D.** carry it on you at all times

798 Motor cars must FIRST have an MOT test certificate when they are

Mark one answer **NI**

- **A.** one year old
- **B.** three years old
- **C.** five years old
- **D.** seven years old

799 Your vehicle needs a current MOT certificate. You do not have one. Until you do have one you will not be able to renew your

Mark one answer

- **A.** driving licence
- **B.** vehicle insurance
- **C.** road tax disc
- **D.** vehicle registration document

800 Which THREE pieces of information are found on a vehicle registration document?

Mark three answers

- **A.** Registered keeper
- **B.** Make of the vehicle
- **C.** Service history details
- **D.** Date of the MOT
- **E.** Type of insurance cover
- **F.** Engine size

801 You have a duty to contact the licensing authority when

Mark three answers

- **A.** you go abroad on holiday
- **B.** you change your vehicle
- **C.** you change your name
- **D.** your job status is changed
- **E.** your permanent address changes
- **F.** your job involves travelling abroad

802 You must notify the licensing authority when

Mark three answers

- **A.** your health affects your driving
- **B.** your eyesight does not meet a set standard
- **C.** you intend lending your vehicle
- **D.** your vehicle requires an MOT certificate
- **E.** you change your vehicle

803 Your vehicle is insured third party only. This covers

Mark two answers

- **A.** damage to your vehicle
- **B.** damage to other vehicles
- **C.** injury to yourself
- **D.** injury to others
- **E.** all damage and injury

804 Your motor insurance policy has an excess of £100. What does this mean?

Mark one answer

- [ ] **A.** The insurance company will pay the first £100 of any claim
- [ ] **B.** You will be paid £100 if you do not have an accident
- [ ] **C.** Your vehicle is insured for a value of £100 if it is stolen
- [ ] **D.** You will have to pay the first £100 of any claim

805 When you apply to renew your vehicle excise licence (tax disc) you must produce

Mark one answer

- [ ] **A.** a valid insurance certificate
- [ ] **B.** the old tax disc
- [ ] **C.** the vehicle handbook
- [ ] **D.** a valid driving licence

806 What is the legal minimum insurance cover you must have to drive on public roads?

Mark one answer

- [ ] **A.** Fire and theft
- [ ] **B.** Theft only
- [ ] **C.** Third party
- [ ] **D.** Fire only

807 Which THREE of the following do you need before you can drive legally?

Mark three answers

- [ ] **A.** A valid driving licence with signature
- [ ] **B.** A valid tax disc displayed on your vehicle
- [ ] **C.** A vehicle service record
- [ ] **D.** Proper insurance cover
- [ ] **E.** Breakdown cover
- [ ] **F.** A vehicle handbook

808 The cost of your insurance may reduce if you

Mark one answer **NI**

- [ ] **A.** are under 25 years old
- [ ] **B.** do not wear glasses
- [ ] **C.** pass the driving test first time
- [ ] **D.** take the Pass Plus scheme

809 Which of the following may reduce the cost of your insurance?

Mark one answer **NI**

- [ ] **A.** Having a valid MOT certificate
- [ ] **B.** Taking a Pass Plus course
- [ ] **C.** Driving a powerful car
- [ ] **D.** Having penalty points on your licence

810 The Pass Plus scheme has been created for new drivers. What is its main purpose?

Mark one answer **NI**

- [ ] **A.** To allow you to drive faster
- [ ] **B.** To allow you to carry passengers
- [ ] **C.** To improve your basic skills
- [ ] **D.** To let you drive on motorways

811 At the scene of an accident you should

Mark one answer

- [ ] **A.** not put yourself at risk
- [ ] **B.** go to those casualties who are screaming
- [ ] **C.** pull everybody out of their vehicles
- [ ] **D.** leave vehicle engines switched on

812 You are the first to arrive at the scene of an accident. Which FOUR of these should you do?

Mark four answers

- [ ] **A.** Leave as soon as another motorist arrives
- [ ] **B.** Switch off the vehicle engine(s)
- [ ] **C.** Move uninjured people away from the vehicle(s)
- [ ] **D.** Call the emergency services
- [ ] **E.** Warn other traffic

813 An accident has just happened. An injured person is lying in the busy road. What is the FIRST thing you should do to help?

Mark one answer

- [ ] **A.** Treat the person for shock
- [ ] **B.** Warn other traffic
- [ ] **C.** Place them in the recovery position
- [ ] **D.** Make sure the injured person is kept warm

TIP At the scene of an accident remain calm and assess the situation. Ensure safety at the scene by controlling the traffic and checking that engines are switched off.

814 You are the first person to arrive at an accident where people are badly injured. Which THREE should you do?

Mark three answers

- [ ] **A.** Switch on your own hazard warning lights
- [ ] **B.** Make sure that someone telephones for an ambulance
- [ ] **C.** Try and get people who are injured to drink something
- [ ] **D.** Move the people who are injured clear of their vehicles
- [ ] **E.** Get people who are not injured clear of the scene

815 You arrive at the scene of a motorcycle accident. The rider is injured. When should the helmet be removed?

Mark one answer

- [ ] **A.** Only when it is essential
- [ ] **B.** Always straight away
- [ ] **C.** Only when the motorcyclist asks
- [ ] **D.** Always, unless they are in shock

816 You arrive at a serious motorcycle accident. The motorcyclist is unconscious and bleeding. Your main priorities should be to

Mark three answers

- [ ] **A.** try to stop the bleeding
- [ ] **B.** make a list of witnesses
- [ ] **C.** check the casualty's breathing
- [ ] **D.** take the numbers of the vehicles involved
- [ ] **E.** sweep up any loose debris
- [ ] **F.** check the casualty's airways

817
You arrive at an accident. A motorcyclist is unconscious. Your FIRST priority is the casualty's

Mark one answer
- [ ] **A.** breathing
- [ ] **B.** bleeding
- [ ] **C.** broken bones
- [ ] **D.** bruising

818
At an accident a casualty is unconscious. Which THREE of the following should you check urgently?

Mark three answers
- [ ] **A.** Circulation
- [ ] **B.** Airway
- [ ] **C.** Shock
- [ ] **D.** Breathing
- [ ] **E.** Broken bones

819
You arrive at the scene of an accident. It has just happened and someone is unconscious. Which of the following should be given urgent priority to help them?

Mark three answers
- [ ] **A.** Clear the airway and keep it open
- [ ] **B.** Try to get them to drink water
- [ ] **C.** Check that they are breathing
- [ ] **D.** Look for any witnesses
- [ ] **E.** Stop any heavy bleeding
- [ ] **F.** Take the numbers of vehicles involved

820
At an accident someone is unconscious. Your main priorities should be to

Mark three answers
- [ ] **A.** sweep up the broken glass
- [ ] **B.** take the names of witnesses
- [ ] **C.** count the number of vehicles involved
- [ ] **D.** check the airway is clear
- [ ] **E.** make sure they are breathing
- [ ] **F.** stop any heavy bleeding

821
You have stopped at the scene of an accident to give help. Which THREE things should you do?

Mark three answers
- [ ] **A.** Keep injured people warm and comfortable
- [ ] **B.** Keep injured people calm by talking to them reassuringly
- [ ] **C.** Keep injured people on the move by walking them around
- [ ] **D.** Give injured people a warm drink
- [ ] **E.** Make sure that injured people are not left alone

822
You arrive at the scene of an accident. It has just happened and someone is injured. Which THREE of the following should be given urgent priority?

Mark three answers
- [ ] **A.** Stop any severe bleeding
- [ ] **B.** Get them a warm drink
- [ ] **C.** Check that their breathing is OK
- [ ] **D.** Take numbers of vehicles involved
- [ ] **E.** Look for witnesses
- [ ] **F.** Clear their airway and keep it open

823
At an accident a casualty has stopped breathing. You should

Mark two answers
- [ ] A. remove anything that is blocking the mouth
- [ ] B. keep the head tilted forwards as far as possible
- [ ] C. raise the legs to help with circulation
- [ ] D. try to give the casualty something to drink
- [ ] E. keep the head tilted back as far as possible

824
You are at the scene of an accident. Someone is suffering from shock. You should

Mark four answers
- [ ] A. reassure them constantly
- [ ] B. offer them a cigarette
- [ ] C. keep them warm
- [ ] D. avoid moving them if possible
- [ ] E. loosen any tight clothing
- [ ] F. give them a warm drink

825
Which of the following should you NOT do at the scene of an accident?

Mark one answer
- [ ] A. Warn other traffic by switching on your hazard warning lights
- [ ] B. Call the emergency services immediately
- [ ] C. Offer someone a cigarette to calm them down
- [ ] D. Ask drivers to switch off their engines

826
There has been an accident. The driver is suffering from shock. You should

Mark two answers
- [ ] A. give them a drink
- [ ] B. reassure them
- [ ] C. not leave them alone
- [ ] D. offer them a cigarette
- [ ] E. ask who caused the accident

827
You are at the scene of an accident. Someone is suffering from shock. You should

Mark three answers
- [ ] A. offer them a cigarette
- [ ] B. offer them a warm drink
- [ ] C. keep them warm
- [ ] D. loosen any tight clothing
- [ ] E. reassure them constantly

828
You have to treat someone for shock at the scene of an accident. You should

Mark one answer
- [ ] A. reassure them constantly
- [ ] B. walk them around to calm them down
- [ ] C. give them something cold to drink
- [ ] D. cool them down as soon as possible

829 You arrive at the scene of a motorcycle accident. No other vehicle is involved. The rider is unconscious, lying in the middle of the road. The first thing you should do is

Mark one answer
- [ ] **A.** move the rider out of the road
- [ ] **B.** warn other traffic
- [ ] **C.** clear the road of debris
- [ ] **D.** give the rider reassurance

830 At an accident a small child is not breathing. When giving mouth to mouth you should breathe

Mark one answer
- [ ] **A.** sharply
- [ ] **B.** gently
- [ ] **C.** heavily
- [ ] **D.** rapidly

831 To start mouth to mouth on a casualty you should

Mark three answers
- [ ] **A.** tilt their head forward
- [ ] **B.** clear the airway
- [ ] **C.** turn them on their side
- [ ] **D.** tilt their head back
- [ ] **E.** pinch the nostrils together
- [ ] **F.** put their arms across their chest

832 When you are giving mouth to mouth you should only stop when

Mark one answer
- [ ] **A.** you think the casualty is dead
- [ ] **B.** the casualty can breathe without help
- [ ] **C.** the casualty has turned blue
- [ ] **D.** you think the ambulance is coming

833 You arrive at the scene of an accident. There has been an engine fire and someone's hands and arms have been burnt. You should NOT

Mark one answer
- [ ] **A.** douse the burn thoroughly with cool liquid
- [ ] **B.** lay the casualty down
- [ ] **C.** remove anything sticking to the burn
- [ ] **D.** reassure them constantly

834 You arrive at an accident where someone is suffering from severe burns. You should

Mark one answer
- [ ] **A.** apply lotions to the injury
- [ ] **B.** burst any blisters
- [ ] **C.** remove anything stuck to the burns
- [ ] **D.** douse the burns with cool liquid

835 You arrive at the scene of an accident. A pedestrian has a severe bleeding wound on their leg, although it is not broken. What should you do?

Mark two answers
- [ ] **A.** Dab the wound to stop bleeding
- [ ] **B.** Keep both legs flat on the ground
- [ ] **C.** Apply firm pressure to the wound
- [ ] **D.** Raise the leg to lessen bleeding
- [ ] **E.** Fetch them a warm drink

TIP Remember the **ABC** of First Aid:
A is for Airway
B is for Breathing
C is for Circulation

836
You arrive at the scene of an accident. A passenger is bleeding badly from an arm wound. What should you do?

Mark one answer
- **A.** Apply pressure over the wound and keep the arm down
- **B.** Dab the wound
- **C.** Get them a drink
- **D.** Apply pressure over the wound and raise the arm

837
You arrive at the scene of an accident. A pedestrian is bleeding heavily from a leg wound but the leg is not broken. What should you do?

Mark one answer
- **A.** Dab the wound to stop the bleeding
- **B.** Keep both legs flat on the ground
- **C.** Apply firm pressure to the wound
- **D.** Fetch them a warm drink

838
At an accident a casualty is unconscious but still breathing. You should only move them if

Mark one answer
- **A.** an ambulance is on its way
- **B.** bystanders advise you to
- **C.** there is further danger
- **D.** bystanders will help you to

839
At an accident you suspect a casualty has back injuries. The area is safe. You should

Mark one answer
- **A.** offer them a drink
- **B.** not move them
- **C.** raise their legs
- **D.** offer them a cigarette

840
At an accident it is important to look after the casualty. When the area is safe, you should

Mark one answer
- **A.** get them out of the vehicle
- **B.** give them a drink
- **C.** give them something to eat
- **D.** keep them in the vehicle

841
A tanker is involved in an accident. Which sign would show that the tanker is carrying dangerous goods?

Mark one answer
- **A.** LONG VEHICLE
- **B.** 2YE 1089
- **C.**
- **D.**

842 The police may ask you to produce which three of these documents following an accident?

Mark three answers
- A. Vehicle registration document
- B. Driving licence
- C. Theory test certificate
- D. Insurance certificate
- E. MOT test certificate
- F. Road tax disc

843 At a railway level crossing the red light signal continues to flash after a train has gone by. What should you do?

Mark one answer
- A. Phone the signal operator
- B. Alert drivers behind you
- C. Wait
- D. Proceed with caution

844 You see a car on the hard shoulder of a motorway with a HELP pennant displayed. This means the driver is most likely to be

Mark one answer
- A. a disabled person
- B. first aid trained
- C. a foreign visitor
- D. a rescue patrol person

845 On the motorway the hard shoulder should be used

Mark one answer
- A. to answer a mobile phone
- B. when an emergency arises
- C. for a short rest when tired
- D. to check a road atlas

846 For which TWO should you use hazard warning lights?

Mark two answers
- A. When you slow down quickly on a motorway because of a hazard ahead
- B. When you have broken down
- C. When you wish to stop on double yellow lines
- D. When you need to park on the pavement

847 When are you allowed to use hazard warning lights?

Mark one answer
- A. When stopped and temporarily obstructing traffic
- B. When travelling during darkness without headlights
- C. When parked for shopping on double yellow lines
- D. When travelling slowly because you are lost

848 You are on a motorway. A large box falls on to the road from a lorry. The lorry does not stop. You should

Mark one answer

- A. go to the next emergency telephone and inform the police
- B. catch up with the lorry and try to get the driver's attention
- C. stop close to the box until the police arrive
- D. pull over to the hard shoulder, then remove the box

849 There has been an accident. A motorcyclist is lying injured and unconscious. Why should you usually not attempt to remove their helmet?

Mark one answer

- A. Because they may not want you to
- B. This could result in more serious injury
- C. They will get too cold if you do this
- D. Because you could scratch the helmet

850 After an accident, someone is unconscious in their vehicle. When should you call the emergency services?

Mark one answer

- A. Only as a last resort
- B. As soon as possible
- C. After you have woken them up
- D. After checking for broken bones

851 An accident casualty has an injured arm. They can move it freely, but it is bleeding. Why should you get them to keep it in a raised position?

Mark one answer

- A. Because it will ease the pain
- B. It will help them to be seen more easily
- C. To stop them touching other people
- D. It will help to reduce the bleeding

852 You are going through a congested tunnel and have to stop. What should you do?

Mark one answer

- A. Pull up very close to the vehicle in front to save space
- B. Ignore any message signs as they are never up to date
- C. Keep a safe distance from the vehicle in front
- D. Make a U-turn and find another route

853 You are going through a tunnel. What should you look out for that warns of accidents or congestion?

Mark one answer

- A. Hazard warning lines
- B. Other drivers flashing their lights
- C. Variable message signs
- D. Areas marked with hatch markings

854 You are going through a tunnel. What systems are provided to warn of any accidents or congestion?

Mark one answer

- A. Double white centre lines
- B. Variable message signs
- C. Chevron 'distance markers'
- D. Rumble strips

TIP Don't give casualties anything to eat or drink, or offer them a cigarette. Reassure any injured person and keep them warm while waiting for the ambulance to arrive.

855 While driving, a warning light on your vehicle's instrument panel comes on. You should

Mark one answer

- A. continue if the engine sounds alright
- B. hope that it is just a temporary electrical fault
- C. deal with the problem when there is more time
- D. check out the problem quickly and safely

856 You have broken down on a two-way road. You have a warning triangle. You should place the warning triangle at least how far from your vehicle?

Mark one answer

- A. 5 metres (16 feet)
- B. 25 metres (82 feet)
- C. 45 metres (147 feet)
- D. 100 metres (328 feet)

857 You break down on a level crossing. The lights have not yet begun to flash. Which THREE things should you do?

Mark three answers

- A. Telephone the signal operator
- B. Leave your vehicle and get everyone clear
- C. Walk down the track and signal the next train
- D. Move the vehicle if a signal operator tells you to
- E. Tell drivers behind what has happened

858 Your vehicle has broken down on an automatic railway level crossing. What should you do FIRST?

Mark one answer

- A. Get everyone out of the vehicle and clear of the crossing
- B. Phone the signal operator so that trains can be stopped
- C. Walk along the track to give warning to any approaching trains
- D. Try to push the vehicle clear of the crossing as soon as possible

859 Your tyre bursts while you are driving. Which TWO things should you do?

Mark two answers

- A. Pull on the handbrake
- B. Brake as quickly as possible
- C. Pull up slowly at the side of the road
- D. Hold the steering wheel firmly to keep control
- E. Continue on at a normal speed

860 Which TWO things should you do when a front tyre bursts?

Mark two answers

- A. Apply the handbrake to stop the vehicle
- B. Brake firmly and quickly
- C. Let the vehicle roll to a stop
- D. Hold the steering wheel lightly
- E. Grip the steering wheel firmly

861
Your vehicle has a puncture on a motorway. What should you do?

Mark one answer

- A. Drive slowly to the next service area to get assistance
- B. Pull up on the hard shoulder. Change the wheel as quickly as possible
- C. Pull up on the hard shoulder. Use the emergency phone to get assistance
- D. Switch on your hazard lights. Stop in your lane

862
Which of these items should you carry in your vehicle for use in the event of an accident?

Mark three answers

- A. Road map
- B. Can of petrol
- C. Jump leads
- D. Fire extinguisher
- E. First aid kit
- F. Warning triangle

863
You are in an accident on a two-way road. You have a warning triangle with you. At what distance before the obstruction should you place the warning triangle?

Mark one answer

- A. 25 metres (82 feet)
- B. 45 metres (147 feet)
- C. 100 metres (328 feet)
- D. 150 metres (492 feet)

864
You have broken down on a two-way road. You have a warning triangle. It should be displayed

Mark one answer

- A. on the roof of your vehicle
- B. at least 150 metres (492 feet) behind your vehicle
- C. at least 45 metres (147 feet) behind your vehicle
- D. just behind your vehicle

865
You have stalled in the middle of a level crossing and cannot restart the engine. The warning bell starts to ring. You should

Mark one answer

- A. get out and clear of the crossing
- B. run down the track to warn the signal operator
- C. carry on trying to restart the engine
- D. push the vehicle clear of the crossing

866
You are on the motorway. Luggage falls from your vehicle. What should you do?

Mark one answer

- A. Stop at the next emergency telephone and contact the police
- B. Stop on the motorway and put on hazard lights whilst you pick it up
- C. Walk back up the motorway to pick it up
- D. Pull up on the hard shoulder and wave traffic down

867 You are on a motorway. When can you use hazard warning lights?

Mark two answers

A. When a vehicle is following too closely
B. When you slow down quickly because of danger ahead
C. When you are towing another vehicle
D. When driving on the hard shoulder
E. When you have broken down on the hard shoulder

868 You are involved in an accident with another vehicle. Someone is injured. Your vehicle is damaged. Which FOUR of the following should you find out?

Mark four answers

A. Whether the driver owns the other vehicle involved
B. The other driver's name, address and telephone number
C. The make and registration number of the other vehicle
D. The occupation of the other driver
E. The details of the other driver's vehicle insurance
F. Whether the other driver is licensed to drive

869 You have broken down on a motorway. When you use the emergency telephone you will be asked

Mark three answers

A. for the number on the telephone that you are using
B. for your driving licence details
C. for the name of your vehicle insurance company
D. for details of yourself and your vehicle
E. whether you belong to a motoring organisation

870 You lose control of your car and damage a garden wall. No one is around. What must you do?

Mark one answer **NI**

A. Report the accident to the police within 24 hours
B. Go back to tell the house owner the next day
C. Report the accident to your insurance company when you get home
D. Find someone in the area to tell them about it immediately

871 Your engine catches fire. What should you do first?

Mark one answer

A. Lift the bonnet and disconnect the battery
B. Lift the bonnet and warn other traffic
C. Call the breakdown service
D. Call the fire brigade

872 Before driving through a tunnel what should you do?

Mark one answer

A. Switch your radio off
B. Remove any sun-glasses
C. Close your sunroof
D. Switch on windscreen wipers

873 You are driving through a tunnel and the traffic is flowing normally. What should you do?

Mark one answer

A. Use parking lights
B. Use front spotlights
C. Use dipped headlights
D. Use rear fog lights

874 Before entering a tunnel it is good advice to

Mark one answer

- A. put on your sun-glasses
- B. check tyre pressures
- C. change to a lower gear
- D. tune your radio to a local channel

875 You are driving through a tunnel. Your vehicle breaks down. What should you do?

Mark one answer

- A. Switch on hazard warning lights
- B. Remain in your vehicle
- C. Wait for the police to find you
- D. Rely on CCTV cameras seeing you

876 Your vehicle breaks down in a tunnel. What should you do?

Mark one answer

- A. Stay in your vehicle and wait for the police
- B. Stand in the lane behind your vehicle to warn others
- C. Stand in front of your vehicle to warn oncoming drivers
- D. Switch on hazard lights then go and call for help immediately

877 You have an accident while driving through a tunnel. You are not injured but your vehicle cannot be driven. What should you do first?

Mark one answer

- A. Rely on other drivers phoning for the police
- B. Switch off the engine and switch on hazard lights
- C. Take the names of witnesses and other drivers
- D. Sweep up any debris that is in the road

878 When driving through a tunnel you should

Mark one answer

- A. Look out for variable message signs
- B. Use your air-conditioning system
- C. Switch on your rear fog lights
- D. Always use your windscreen wipers

879 What TWO safeguards could you take against fire risk to your vehicle?

Mark two answers

- A. Keep water levels above maximum
- B. Carry a fire extinguisher
- C. Avoid driving with a full tank of petrol
- D. Use unleaded petrol
- E. Check out any strong smell of petrol
- F. Use low-octane fuel

TIP To be confident that you could be of help in an accident, consider taking a course in First Aid from St John Ambulance or St Andrew's Ambulance Association, or from the British Red Cross. You can find local contact numbers in the phone book.

880
You are towing a small trailer on a busy three-lane motorway. All the lanes are open. You must

Mark two answers
- **A.** not exceed 60mph
- **B.** not overtake
- **C.** have a stabilizer fitted
- **D.** use only the left and centre lanes

881
Any load that is carried on a roof rack MUST be

Mark one answer
- **A.** securely fastened when driving
- **B.** carried only when strictly necessary
- **C.** as light as possible
- **D.** covered with plastic sheeting

882
You are planning to tow a caravan. Which of these will mostly help to aid the vehicle handling?

Mark one answer
- **A.** A jockey-wheel fitted to the tow bar
- **B.** Power steering fitted to the towing vehicle
- **C.** Anti-lock brakes fitted to the towing vehicle
- **D.** A stabilizer fitted to the tow bar

883
If a trailer swerves or snakes when you are towing it you should

Mark one answer
- **A.** ease off the accelerator and reduce your speed
- **B.** let go of the steering wheel and let it correct itself
- **C.** brake hard and hold the pedal down
- **D.** increase your speed as quickly as possible

884
How can you stop a caravan snaking from side to side?

Mark one answer
- **A.** Turn the steering wheel slowly to each side
- **B.** Accelerate to increase your speed
- **C.** Stop as quickly as you can
- **D.** Slow down very gradually

885
On which TWO occasions might you inflate your tyres to more than the recommended normal pressure?

Mark two answers
- **A.** When the roads are slippery
- **B.** When driving fast for a long distance
- **C.** When the tyre tread is worn below 2mm
- **D.** When carrying a heavy load
- **E.** When the weather is cold
- **F.** When the vehicle is fitted with anti-lock brakes

886
A heavy load on your roof rack will

Mark one answer
- **A.** improve the road holding
- **B.** reduce the stopping distance
- **C.** make the steering lighter
- **D.** reduce stability

887
Are passengers allowed to ride in a caravan that is being towed?

Mark one answer
- **A.** Yes if they are over 14
- **B.** No not at any time
- **C.** Only if all the seats in the towing vehicle are full
- **D.** Only if a stabilizer is fitted

888 You are towing a caravan along a motorway. The caravan begins to swerve from side to side. What should you do?

Mark one answer

- A. Ease off the accelerator slowly
- B. Steer sharply from side to side
- C. Do an emergency stop
- D. Speed up very quickly

889 A trailer must stay securely hitched-up to the towing vehicle. What additional safety device can be fitted to the trailer braking system?

Mark one answer

- A. Stabilizer
- B. Jockey wheel
- C. Corner steadies
- D. Breakaway cable

890 Overloading your vehicle can seriously affect the

Mark two answers

- A. gearbox
- B. steering
- C. handling
- D. battery life
- E. journey time

891 Who is responsible for making sure that a vehicle is not overloaded?

Mark one answer

- A. The driver of the vehicle
- B. The owner of the items being carried
- C. The person who loaded the vehicle
- D. The licensing authority

892 Which of these is a suitable restraint for a child under three years?

Mark one answer

- A. A child seat
- B. An adult holding a child
- C. An adult seat belt
- D. A lap belt

893 A child under three years is being carried in your vehicle. They should be secured in a restraint. Which of these is suitable?

Mark one answer

- A. An adult holding a child
- B. A lap belt
- C. A baby carrier
- D. An adult seat belt

TIP There isn't any room for argument here – passengers can't travel in a vehicle that's being towed.

TIP A stabilizer attached to the tow bar can help in making your tow load or trailer more secure.

Part 5

Glossary

Glossary

Accelerate

To make the vehicle move faster by pressing the right-hand pedal.

Advanced stop lines

A marked area on the road at traffic lights, which permits cyclists or buses to wait in front of other traffic.

Adverse weather

Bad weather that makes driving difficult or dangerous.

Alert

Quick to notice possible hazards.

Anticipation

Looking out for hazards and taking action before a problem starts.

Anti-lock brakes

Brakes that stop the wheels locking so that you are less likely to skid on a slippery road.

Aquaplane

To slide out of control on a wet road surface.

Articulated vehicle

A long vehicle that is divided into two or more sections joined by cables.

Attitude

The way you think or feel, which affects the way you drive. Especially, whether you are patient and polite, or impatient and aggressive.

Automatic

A vehicle with gears that change by themselves as you speed up or slow down.

Awareness

Taking notice of the road and traffic conditions around you at all times.

Black ice

An invisible film of ice that forms over the road surface, creating very dangerous driving conditions.

Blind spot

The section of road behind you which you cannot see in your mirrors. You 'cover' your blind spot by looking over your shoulder before moving off or overtaking.

Brake fade

Loss of power to the brakes when you have been using them for a long time without taking your foot off the brake pedal. For example, when driving down a steep hill. The brakes will overheat and not work properly.

Braking distance

The distance you must allow to slow the vehicle in order to come to a stop.

Brow

The highest point of a hill.

Built-up area

A town, or place with lots of buildings.

Carriageway

One side of a road or motorway. A 'dual carriageway' has two lanes on each side of a central reservation.

Catalytic converter

A piece of equipment fitted in the exhaust system that changes harmful gases into less harmful ones.

Chicane

A sharp double bend that has been put into a road to make traffic slow down.

Child restraint

A child seat or special seat belt for children. It keeps them safe and stops them moving around in the car.

Clearway

A road where no stopping is allowed at any time. The sign for a clearway is a red cross in a red circle on a blue background.

Coasting

Driving a vehicle without using any of the gears. That is, with your foot on the clutch pedal and the car in neutral.

Commentary driving

Talking to yourself about what you see on the road ahead and what action you are going to take – an aid to concentration.

Comprehensive insurance

A motor insurance policy that pays for repairs even if you cause an accident.

Concentration

Keeping all your attention on your driving.

Conditions

How good or bad the road surface is, volume of traffic on the road, and what the weather is like.

Congestion

Heavy traffic that makes it difficult to get to where you want to go.

Consideration

Thinking about other road users and not just yourself. For example, letting another driver go first at a junction, or stopping at a zebra crossing to let pedestrians cross over.

Contraflow

When traffic on a motorway follows signs to move to the opposite carriageway for a short distance because of roadworks. (During a contraflow, there is traffic driving in both directions on the same side of the motorway.)

Coolant

Liquid in the radiator that removes heat from the engine.

Defensive driving

Driving safely without taking risks, looking out for hazards and thinking for others.

Disqualified

Stopped from doing something (eg driving) by law, because you have broken the law.

Distraction

Anything that stops you concentrating on your driving, such as chatting to passengers or on your mobile phone.

Document

An official paper or card, eg your driving licence.

Dual carriageway

One side of a road or motorway, with two lanes on each side of a central reservation.

Engine braking – see also gears

Using the low gears to keep your speed down. For example, when you are driving down a steep hill and you want to stop the vehicle running away. Using the gears instead of braking will help to prevent brake fade.

Environment

The world around us and the air we breathe.

Exceed

Go higher than an upper limit.

Exhaust emissions

Gases that come out of the exhaust pipe to form part of the outside air.

Field of vision

How far you can see in front and around you when you are driving.

Filler cap

Provides access to the vehicle's fuel tank, for filling up with petrol or diesel.

Fog lights

Extra bright rear (and sometimes front) lights which may be switched on in conditions of very poor visibility. You must remember to switch them off when visibility improves, as they can dazzle and distract other drivers.

Ford

A place in a stream or river which is shallow enough to drive across with care.

Four-wheel drive (4WD)

On a conventional vehicle, steering and engine speed affect just two 'drive' wheels. On 4WD, they affect all four wheels, ensuring optimum grip on loose ground.

Frustration

Feeling annoyed because you cannot drive as fast as you want to because of other drivers or heavy traffic.

Fuel consumption

The amount of fuel (petrol or diesel) that your vehicle uses. Different vehicles have different rates of consumption. Increased fuel consumption means using more fuel. Decreased fuel consumption means using less fuel.

Fuel gauge

A display or dial on the instrument panel that tells you how much fuel (petrol or diesel) you have left.

Glossary

Gantry

An overhead platform like a high narrow bridge that displays electric signs on a motorway.

Gears

Control the speed of the engine in relation to the vehicle's speed. May be hand operated (manual) or automatically controlled. In a low gear (such as first or second) the engine runs more slowly. In a high gear (such as fourth or fifth), it runs more quickly. Putting the car into a lower gear as you drive can create the effect of engine braking – forcing the engine to run more slowly.

Handling

How well your vehicle moves or responds when you steer or brake.

Harass

To drive in a way that makes other road users afraid.

Hard shoulder

The single lane to the left of the inside lane on a motorway, which is for emergency use only. You should not drive on the hard shoulder except in an emergency, or when there are signs telling you to use the hard shoulder because of roadworks.

Harsh braking (or harsh acceleration)

Using the brake or accelerator too hard so as to cause wear on the engine.

Hazard warning lights

Flashing amber lights which you should use only when you have broken down. On a motorway you can use them to warn other drivers behind of a hazard ahead.

High-sided vehicle

A van or truck with tall sides, or a tall trailer such as a caravan or horse-box, that is at risk of being blown off-course in strong winds.

Impatient

Not wanting to wait for pedestrians and other road users.

Inflate

To blow up – to put air in your tyres until they are at the right pressures.

Instrument panel

The car's electrical controls and gauges, set behind the steering wheel. Also called the dashboard.

Intimidate

To make someone feel afraid.

Involved

Being part of something. For example, being one of the drivers in an accident.

Jump leads

A pair of thick electric cables with clips at either end. You use it to charge a flat battery by connecting it to the live battery in another vehicle.

Junction

A place where two or more roads join.

Liability

Being legally responsible.

Manoeuvre

Using the controls to make your car move in a particular direction. For example turning, reversing or parking.

Manual

By hand. In a car that is a 'manual' or has manual gears, you have to change the gears yourself.

Maximum

The largest possible; 'maximum speed' is the highest speed allowed.

Minimum

The smallest possible.

Mirrors

Modern cars have a minimum of three rear view mirrors: one in the centre of the windscreen, and one on each front door. Additional mirrors may be required on longer vehicles, or when towing a high trailer such as a caravan. Some mirrors may be curved (convex or concave) to increase the field of vision. The mirror on the windscreen can be turned to anti-dazzle position, if glare from headlights behind creates a distraction.

Mobility

The ability to move around easily.

Monotonous

Boring. For example, a long stretch of motorway with no variety and nothing interesting to see.

MOT

The test that proves your car is safe to drive. Your MOT certificate is one of the important documents for your vehicle.

Motorway

A fast road that has two or more lanes on each side and a hard shoulder. Drivers must join or leave it on the left, via a motorway junction. Many kinds of slower vehicles – such as bicycles – are not allowed on motorways.

Multiple-choice questions

Questions with several possible answers where you have to try to choose the right one.

Observation

The ability to notice important information, such as hazards developing ahead.

Obstruct

To get in the way of another road user.

Octagonal

Having eight sides.

Oil level

The amount of oil needed for the engine to run effectively.The oil level should be checked as part of your regular maintenance routine, and the oil replaced as necessary.

Pedestrian

A person walking.

Pegasus crossing

An unusual kind of crossing. It has a button high up for horse riders to push (Pegasus was a flying horse in Greek legend).

Pelican crossing

A crossing with traffic lights that pedestrians can use by pushing a button. Cars must give way to pedestrians on the crossing while the amber light is flashing. You must give pedestrians enough time to get to the other side of the road.

Perception

Seeing or noticing (as in Hazard Perception).

Peripheral vision

The area around the edges of your field of vision.

Positive attitude

Being sensible and obeying the law when you drive.

Priority

The vehicle or other road user that is allowed by law to go first is the one that has priority.

Provisional licence

A first driving licence. all learner drivers must get one before they start having lessons.

Puffin crossing

A type of pedestrian crossing that does not have a flashing amber light phase.

Reaction time

The amount of time it takes you to see a hazard and decide what to do about it.

Red route

You see these in London and some other cities. Double red lines at the edge of the road tell you that you must not stop or park there at any time. Single red lines have notices with times when you must not stop or park. Some red routes have marked bays for either parking or loading at certain times.

Red warning triangle

An item of safety equipment to carry in your car in case you break down. You can place the triangle 45m behind your car on the same side of the road. It warns traffic that your vehicle is causing an obstruction. (Do not use these on motorways.)

Residential areas

Areas of housing where people live. The speed limit is 30mph or sometimes 20mph.

Road hump

A low bump built across the road to slow vehicles down. Also called 'sleeping policemen'.

Rumble strips

Raised strips across the road near a roundabout or junction that change the sound the tyres make on the road surface, warning drivers to slow down. They are also used on motorways to separate the main carriageway from the hard shoulder.

Glossary

Safety margin

The amount of space you need to leave between your vehicle and the one in front so that you are not in danger of crashing into it if the driver slows down suddenly or stops. Safety margins have to be longer in wet or icy conditions.

Separation distance

The amount of space you need to leave between your vehicle and the one in front so that you are not in danger of crashing into it if the driver slows down suddenly or stops. The separation distance must be longer in wet or icy conditions.

Security coded radio

To deter thieves, a radio or CD unit which requires a security code (or pin number) to operate it.

Single carriageway

Generally, a road with one lane in each direction.

Skid

When the tyres fail to grip the surface of the road, the subsequent loss of control of the vehicle's movement is called a skid. Usually caused by harsh or fierce braking, steering or acceleration.

Snaking

Moving from side to side. This sometimes happens with caravans or trailers when you drive too fast, or they are not properly loaded.

Staggered junction

Where you drive cross another road. Instead of going straight across, you have to go a bit to the right or left.

Steering

Control of the direction of the vehicle. May be affected by road surface conditions: when the steering wheel turns very easily, steering is 'light', and when you have to pull hard on the wheel it is described as 'heavy'.

Sterile

Clean and free from bacteria.

Stopping distance

The time it takes for you to stop your vehicle – made up of 'thinking distance' and 'braking distance'.

Supervisor

Someone who sits in the passenger seat with a learner driver. They must be over 21 and have held a full driving licence for at least three years.

Tailgating

Driving too closely behind another vehicle – either to harass the driver in front or to help you in thick fog.

Tax disc

The disc you display on your windscreen to show that you have taxed your car (see Vehicle Excise Duty, below).

Thinking distance

The time it takes you to notice something and take the right action. You need to add thinking distance to your braking distance to make up your total stopping distance.

Third party insurance

An insurance policy that insures you against any claim by passengers or other persons for damage or injury to their person or property.

Toucan crossing

A type of pedestrian crossing that does not have a flashing amber light phase, and cyclists are allowed to ride across.

Tow

To pull something behind your vehicle. It could be a caravan or trailer.

Traffic calming measures

Speed humps, chicanes and other devices placed in roads to slow traffic down.

Tram

A public transport vehicle which moves along the streets on fixed rails, usually electrically powered by overhead lines.

Tread depth

The depth of the grooves in a car's tyres that help them grip the road surface. The grooves must all be at least 1.6mm deep.

Turbulence

Strong movement of air. For example, when a large vehicle passes a much smaller one.

Two-second rule

> In normal driving, the ideal minimum distance between you and the vehicle in front can be timed using the 'two-second' rule. As the vehicle in front passes a fixed object (such as a signpost), say to yourself 'Only a fool breaks the two second rule'. It takes two seconds to say it. If you have passed the same object before you finish, you are too close – pull back.

Tyre pressures

> The amount of air which must be pumped into a tyre in order for it to be correctly blown up.

Vehicle Excise Duty

> The tax you pay for your vehicle so that you may drive it on public roads.

Vehicle Registration Document

> A record of details about a vehicle and its owner.

Vehicle watch scheme

> A system for identifying vehicles that may have been stolen.

Vulnerable

> At risk of harm or injury.

Waiting restrictions

> Times when you may not park or load your vehicle in a particular area.

Wheel balancing

> To ensure smooth rotation at all speeds, wheels need to be 'balanced' correctly. This is a procedure done at a garage or tyre centre, when each wheel is removed for testing. Balancing may involve minor adjustment with the addition of small weights, to avoid wheel wobble.

Wheel spin

> When the vehicle's wheels spin round out of control with no grip on the road surface.

Zebra crossing

> A pedestrian crossing without traffic lights. It has an orange light, and is marked by black and white stripes on the road. Drivers must stop for pedestrians to cross.

Part 6

The Answers to the Theory Test Questions

ALERTNESS – SECTION 1

1 C	2 BDF	3 C	4 D	5 C	6 C	7 C	8 C	9 B
10 D	11 AC	12 ABCD	13 AD	14 AB	15 AB	16 ABCD	17 C	18 B
19 D	20 B	21 C	22 B	23 B	24 ABE	25 C	26 B	27 B
28 D	29 C	30 C	31 C	32 A	33 D	34 D		

ATTITUDE – SECTION 2

35 D	36 A	37 C	38 B	39 C	40 D	41 D	42 B	43 B
44 BCD	45 ABE	46 A	47 D	48 B	49 A	50 A	51 B	52 A
53 A	54 C	55 A	56 B	57 D	58 D	59 D	60 A	61 A
62 B	63 C	64 A	65 C	66 A	67 C	68 B	69 C	70 DE
71 B	72 D	73 B	74 C	75 D	76 B	77 C	78 A	79 A
80 B	81 A							

SAFETY AND YOUR VEHICLE – SECTION 3

82 B	83 AB	84 ABF	85 BEF	86 C	87 ACF	88 C	89 B	90 A
91 D	92 C	93 D	94 D	95 D	96 A	97 AE	98 D	99 B
100 D	101 D	102 A	103 B	104 BCDF	105 D	106 D	107 BC	108 BC
109 A	110 D	111 C	112 A	113 B	114 B	115 D	116 C	117 D
118 D	119 D	120 B	121 B	122 B	123 D	124 AB	125 ABF	126 ABC
127 ABC	128 BDF	129 D	130 ADE	131 BDF	132 D	133 B	134 CDE	135 B
136 B	137 C	138 B	139 DE	140 A	141 C	142 B	143 D	144 D
145 D	146 B	147 C	148 A	149 B	150 D	151 A	152 C	153 A
154 B	155 AB	156 A	157 D	158 B	159 BCD	160 C	161 CD	162 A
163 A	164 D	165 C	166 B	167 B	168 B	169 D	170 ABE	171 ADE
172 D								

SAFETY MARGINS – SECTION 4

173 D	174 D	175 BC	176 B	177 D	178 D	179 C	180 B	181 BC
182 A	183 ACE	184 B	185 A	186 B	187 A	188 B	189 AE	190 C
191 B	192 C	193 BDEF	194 B	195 D	196 A	197 C	198 A	199 AD
200 C	201 B	202 B	203 B	204 C	205 C	206 B	207 B	208 BC
209 C	210 C	211 B	212 C	213 D	214 BC	215 B	216 ACE	217 D
218 D	219 D	220 A	221 D	222 BD	223 D	224 B	225 A	226 D
227 A	228 B							

HAZARD AWARENESS – SECTION 5

229 D	230 CD	231 B	232 C	233 A	234 D	235 ACE	236 D	237 C
238 A	239 C	240 C	241 D	242 B	243 B	244 A	245 A	246 A
247 C	248 C	249 CD	250 A	251 B	252 A	253 C	254 BF	255 B
256 AE	257 A	258 D	259 D	260 C	261 B	262 B	263 C	264 A
265 B	266 B	267 CD	268 B	269 D	270 B	271 A	272 A	273 D
274 A	275 B	276 AE	277 C	278 B	279 BC	280 D	281 B	282 B
283 C	284 D	285 C	286 CD	287 AC	288 AB	289 A	290 A	291 B
292 A	293 ABC	294 C	295 C	296 C	297 ABE	298 C	299 D	300 D
301 C	302 C	303 D	304 ABD	305 ABC	306 D	307 C	308 AB	309 B
310 B	311 CD	312 D	313 ACE	314 ABE	315 A	316 A	317 D	318 D
319 A	320 D	321 A	322 B					

VULNERABLE ROAD USERS – SECTION 6

323 D	324 D	325 C	326 C	327 B	328 D	329 D	330 AD	331 B
332 C	333 D	334 A	335 D	336 D	337 B	338 D	339 B	340 D
341 D	342 C	343 AC	344 C	345 C	346 A	347 D	348 C	349 D
350 ABC	351 C	352 B	353 B	354 AC	355 ABD	356 B	357 D	358 A
359 D	360 A	361 D	362 D	363 A	364 A	365 C	366 C	367 C
368 D	369 ACE	370 D	371 B	372 A	373 C	374 D	375 C	376 C
377 A	378 D	379 D	380 A	381 A	382 B	383 B	384 D	385 C
386 C	387 B	388 C	389 AE	390 D	391 C	392 C	393 B	394 B
395 D	396 D	397 A	398 C	399 C	400 D	401 D	402 B	403 D
404 D	405 B	406 B	407 C					

OTHER TYPES OF VEHICLE – SECTION 7

408 B	409 A	410 A	411 B	412 B	413 D	414 B	415 A	416 BC
417 B	418 D	419 A	420 A	421 A	422 C	423 B	424 B	425 D
426 D	427 D	428 B	429 B	430 B	431 B	432 AC	433 BD	434 B
435 B	436 D							

VEHICLE HANDLING – SECTION 8

437 C	438 ACE	439 A	440 CD	441 D	442 A	443 BDF	444 C	445 D
446 C	447 DE	448 D	449 B	450 C	451 D	452 C	453 D	454 D
455 C	456 C	457 BD	458 BD	459 D	460 B	461 C	462 CE	463 C
464 D	465 A	466 A	467 C	468 B	469 ABDF	470 A	471 D	472 B
473 B	474 AB	475 BD	476 A	477 ACD	478 B	479 A	480 C	481 B
482 A	483 A	484 C	485 C	486 A	487 B	488 C	489 D	490 B
491 D	492 ABD	493 D	494 C	495 C	496 C	497 D	498 D	499 A

Section 15 – **Answers to Questions**

MOTORWAY RULES – SECTION 9

500 ADEF	501 ADEF	502 D	503 D	504 D	505 D	506 A	507 B	508 C
509 BE	510 C	511 A	512 C	513 A	514 D	515 A	516 C	517 C
518 C	519 C	520 C	521 C	522 B	523 C	524 B	525 B	526 A
527 B	528 B	529 D	530 CDF	531 C	532 D	533 C	534 D	535 A
536 B	537 B	538 D	539 C	540 A	541 B	542 D	543 A	544 D
545 D	546 A	547 C	548 B	549 B	550 C			

RULES OF THE ROAD – SECTION 10

551 C	552 B	553 D	554 B	555 A	556 C	557 D	558 ADF	559 BDEF
560 AD	561 A	562 B	563 A	564 B	565 A	566 D	567 A	568 D
569 D	570 C	571 A	572 ACE	573 B	574 C	575 D	576 BD	577 B
578 A	579 D	580 C	581 A	582 B	583 CDE	584 B	585 AE	586 B
587 A	588 ABD	589 A	590 B	591 B	592 A	593 D	594 A	595 D
596 C	597 D	598 D	599 BEF	600 D	601 D	602 D	603 C	604 C
605 D	606 A	607 A	608 A	609 C	610 B	611 A	612 D	613 AB
614 A	615 D	616 D	617 A	618 D	619 B	620 ABC	621 D	622 A
623 D	624 A	625 A						

ROAD AND TRAFFIC SIGNS – SECTION 11

626 D	627 D	628 A	629 A	630 B	631 A	632 D	633 B	634 D
635 D	636 D	637 A	638 C	639 B	640 D	641 C	642 B	643 A
644 B	645 B	646 C	647 C	648 A	649 C	650 B	651 C	652 B
653 D	654 D	655 C	656 D	657 C	658 B	659 C	660 D	661 A
662 D	663 B	664 D	665 B	666 A	667 A	668 A	669 A	670 B
671 B	672 A	673 D	674 ACEF	675 C	676 A	677 A	678 C	679 D
680 B	681 C	682 B	683 B	684 B	685 B	686 D	687 A	688 C
689 A	690 C	691 D	692 A	693 C	694 B	695 D	696 A	697 B
698 B	699 C	700 C	701 A	702 A	703 C	704 B	705 C	706 D
707 C	708 ACD	709 B	710 A	711 C	712 D	713 C	714 B	715 A
716 A	717 C	718 BDF	719 A	720 C	721 C	722 B	723 B	724 A
725 C	726 A	727 B	728 A	729 B	730 D	731 D	732 B	733 A
734 A	735 D	736 C	737 D	738 C	739 B	740 C	741 C	742 A
743 B	744 D	745 B	746 B	747 A	748 D	749 A	750 B	751 B
752 D	753 C	754 B	755 A	756 B	757 A	758 C	759 A	760 B
761 A	762 A	763 C	764 C	765 A	766 B	767 C	768 B	769 A
770 C	771 ACE	772 A	773 A	774 C	775 C	776 B	777 B	778 B
779 B	780 B	781 A						

DOCUMENTS – SECTION 12

782 C	783 B	784 B	785 BE	786 C	787 C	788 B	789 D	790 AB
791 D	792 D	793 D	794 C	795 CDE	796 CD	797 B	798 B	799 C
800 ABF	801 BCE	802 ABE	803 BD	804 D	805 A	806 C	807 ABD	808 D
809 B	810 C							

ACCIDENTS – SECTION 13

811 A	812 BCDE	813 B	814 ABE	815 A	816 ACF	817 A	818 ABD	819 ACE
820 DEF	821 ABE	822 ACF	823 AE	824 ACDE	825 C	826 BC	827 CDE	828 A
829 B	830 B	831 BDE	832 B	833 C	834 D	835 CD	836 D	837 C
838 C	839 B	840 D	841 B	842 BDE	843 C	844 A	845 B	846 AB
847 A	848 A	849 B	850 B	851 D	852 C	853 C	854 B	855 D
856 C	857 ABD	858 A	859 CD	860 CE	861 C	862 DEF	863 B	864 C
865 A	866 A	867 BE	868 ABCE	869 ADE	870 A	871 D	872 B	873 C
874 D	875 A	876 D	877 B	878 A	879 BE			

VEHICLE LOADING – SECTION 14

880 AD	881 A	882 D	883 A	884 D	885 BD	886 D	887 B	888 A
889 D	890 BC	891 A	892 A	893 C				